About this Book

D0453898

In Search of the Primordial Tradition and the Cosmic Christ is a must for those interested in the Western Esoteric Tradition and its relevance to understanding the contemporary crisis in religion, science, and human culture.

Its author, Fr. John Rossner, a visionary priest and professor of comparative religion at Concordia University in Montreal, argues convincingly that there is indeed a "Primordial Tradition" and a "Lost Esoteric Christianity" waiting to be re-discovered by those who are prepared to receive it.

In these pages you will find evidence for the following hypotheses:

• Throughout history "primal experiences" (i.e. visions, apparitions, out-of-the-body journeys, prophecies, divination, telepathy, distant-viewing, and healings) have played a certain role in the birth of great religions and civilizations of the world, including Christianity.

• Modern Western secular culture has lost contact with such psychic roots of ancient wisdom, and regarded them as little more than "pre-scientific superstition."

• Today, ancient spiritual insights and modern scientific discoveries have begun to surface and converge, in a process which will eventually bring us to a "second Copernican Revolution."

The author shares a new world of very ancient meaning waiting to be re-discovered within the major salvation myths, symbols and rituals of the religions of the ancient world.

" . . . John Rossner is one of those rare Christians who understands that words and concepts are mere pointers to a reality they can never capture. He invites his readers to journey beyond truths into truth, beyond tribal and sectarian gods into God. He recognizes the idolatry of biblical, ecclesiastical and scientific fundamentalism and sketches for us images that resonate with a universal mysticism. He will scare the religiously insecure, but for the honest pilgrim, he can be a Christopher Columbus discovering a new world."

—Rt. Rev. John Spong, D.D.
Bishop of Newark, Episcopal Church, U.S.A.

About the Author

Fr. John Rossner is an Anglican/Episcopal priest and a professor in the Department of Religion at Concordia University in Montreal where—since 1962—he has taught and done research in comparative religion and culture. He is a graduate of Trinity College, Hartford (1952), and holds subsequent degrees in Classics & Ancient History, Theology, Psychology & Religion, and the History and Philosophy of Religion.

Since 1972 he has been a pioneer in the applications of the findings of consciousness studies and psychical research to the scientific study of human religious experience. He was the first scholar in Canada to introduce such subjects into an academic curriculum for both graduate and undergraduate studies in the history and philosophy of religion. For several periods during the past ten years he has traveled extensively throughout India and Nepal, visiting ashrams and carrying on spiritual dialogues with Hindu, Jain, and Buddhist monks and religious teachers. In 1976, with the help of his wife and colleague, Dr Marilyn Zwaig Rossner, and a number of prominent scholars and scientists, he founded the International Institute of Integral Human Sciences. Today the IIIHS is established as the nucleus of a network of outstanding professional persons involved in mind-body research directed toward providing new paradigms for the reconciliation of science and spirituality.

To Write to the Author

We cannot guarantee that every letter written to the author can be answered, but all will be forwarded. Both the author and the publisher appreciate hearing from readers, learning of your enjoyment and benefit from this book. Llewellyn also publishes a bi-monthly news magazine with news and reviews of practical esoteric studies and articles helpful to the student, and some readers' questions and comments to the author may be answered through this magazine's columns if permission to do so is included in the original letter. The author sometimes participates in seminars and workshops, and dates and places are announced in *The Llewellyn New Times*. To write to the author, or to ask a question, write to:

Fr. John Rossner
c/o THE LLEWELLYN NEW TIMES
P.O. Box 64383-685, St. Paul, MN 55164-0383, U.S.A.

Please enclose a self-addressed, stamped envelope for reply, or $1.00 to cover costs.

About Llewellyn's Spiritual Sciences Series

SIMPLE, PRACTICAL, EFFECTIVE, COMPREHENSIVE, AUTHORITATIVE, INDIGENOUS TO OUR CULTURE

In a world and time that is becoming more complex, challenging and stressful, filled with "over choice" and "cognitive confusion," we are making available to you a unique series of books for self-exploration and growth that have the following distinctive features:

They are designed to be simple, cutting through abstraction, complexities and nuances that confuse and diffuse rather than enlighten, and focus your understanding of your life's purpose.

They are practical; theory always leading to practice to be crowned by devotion when followed through by you as the experimenter. You are the ultimate "laboratory" and "judge."

They are effective, for if you do the work, you will obtain results of psychospiritual transformation and expansion of consciousness.

They are comprehensive because they integrate the exoteric with the esoteric, the sacred traditions of the past with the best insights of modern science.

They are authoritative because they are all written by persons who have actually lived and experienced what they tell you about.

They are part of our Western Culture and philosophical and Mystery Traditions, which must be understood if the synthesis of the Eastern and Western spiritual traditions and Universal Brotherhood is to be realized.

This series will reconcile the fragmented aspirations of ourselves, and synthesize religion and science to bring about that psychosynthesis which is the greatest need of our age and its highest aspiration.

Other books by Father John Rossner:

From Ancient Magic to Future Technology
From Ancient Religion to Future Science

Llewellyn's Spiritual Sciences Series

In Search Of
The Primordial Tradition
&
The Cosmic Christ

Uniting World Religious Experience
with
A Lost Esoteric Christianity

by
Father John Rossner
Ph.D.

1989
Llewellyn Publications
St. Paul, MN 55164-0383, U.S.A.

International Standard Book Number: 0-87542-685-9
Library of Congress Catalog Number: 89-8107

First Edition, 1989
First Printing, 1989

Library of Congress Cataloging-in-Publication Data
Rossner, John.
    In search of the primordial tradition and the cosmic Christ/by John Rossner.
        p. cm. — (Llewellyn spiritual science series)
        Bibliography: p.
        ISBN 0-87542-685-9
        1. Psychical research. 2. Rossner, John. I. Title. II. Series.
    BF1031.R685 1989   89-8107
    133.8—dc20   CIP

Cover Art: Arthur Douet
"Overlighting Angels"

Produced by Llewellyn Publications
Typography and Art property of Chester-Kent, Inc.

Published by
LLEWELLYN PUBLICATIONS
A Division of Chester-Kent, Inc.
P.O. Box 64383
St. Paul, MN 55164-0383, U.S.A.

Printed in the United States of America

Dedication

To my dear Marilyn who through the love and childlike joy of a little saint, and through her daily inspirations from the heaven world, has shared with me over the past 15 years the cosmic vision and the wisdom required to undertake this quest of the Primordial Tradition and the Cosmic Christ.

And to all of those great souls whom I have met on earth and in heaven: Hindu yogis and rishis, Buddhist lamas and Jain monks, modern Hassidic rabbis, Sufi Islamic mystics, native shamans, Silva Mind Control instructors, Modern Spiritualist Mediums and their spirit guides and masters, Theosophists, exemplary Christians of East and West, including priests and bishops of the numerically small but great liberal Catholic Church in Britain, India, the U.S.A., Australia, and Europe, scientists who often at great personal cost have dared to be pioneers in the new fields of parapsychology, paraphysics, life energies research and consciousness studies, and to Saints and Sages of all the venerable traditions of Primal Wisdom on earth who have kept the Eternal Flame alive on this planet in their witness to the existence of the Primordial Tradition and the Cosmic Christ.

Table of Contents

Foreword

Father John Rossner has written a most remarkable work on the nature of religion as seen from an authentic but decidedly "esoteric" perspective, in the versatile tradition of classical Christian humanism of Pico della Mirandola and the "Renaissance Magi." He has produced what is perhaps the most authoritative contemporary work on the "Primordial Tradition"—or "ancient spiritual philosophy"—in existence. A modern Golden Bough, this book itself should help to stimulate that "New Copernican Revolution in Religion and Science" once called for by Professor J. B. Rhine and British science writer Arthur Koestler. This book is one of a series of works by Fr. Rossner on the central theme of the "Primordial Tradition," representing a prodigious output of encyclopedic learning.

The author has drawn from his own wide experience as a scholar, priest, and "traveler" of the outer and inner worlds, and especially from an ongoing dialogue with the many distinguished scientists, scholars, and world religious leaders, East and West, who are fellows of the International Institute of Integral Human Sciences, which he founded in Canada in 1976, in the United States in 1977, and in India in 1979.

Ultimately Rossner's work will certainly contribute to a realization of the "grand aim" of the French Encyclopedists of reconciling once again, as integrated human endeavors, the presently divided pursuits of religion, science, and philosophy.

In more immediate terms, this book is a treasury of important insights which should be extremely useful to all of those on a spiritual quest—to teachers, therapists, physicians, and priests as well as to ordinary men and women seeking to be informed about the Western Spiritual Tradition in order to lead more conscious and creative lives. It is a "must" for the serious student of the mysteries, of human nature, and all of the sacred arts.

Peter Roche de Coppens, Ph.D.
Prof. of Sociology and
Anthropology
East Stroudsburg University, PA

Father John Rossner . . . as Celebrant of the Alumni Eucharist, Trinity College, Hartford, CN., (Trinity Sunday, June 21, 1987) at the 35th reunion of his graduating class.

Preface

*I*n this book, and in others to follow in this series, I shall present a case for the existence—throughout the ancient world— of a widespread belief in a Primordial Tradition of primal wisdom derived from higher forms of human mystical and psychical experience, and for beliefs in the cult of a universal "God-Man" or pre-existent "Cosmic Christ," based upon visionary experiences which stimulated the very birth of Christianity as a world-religion.

The Primordial Tradition has left its precious fragments of transcendental intuition throughout the higher religions and philosophies of the ancient and modern worlds, both Eastern and Western. But its timeless source has not been fully embodied anywhere on this planet. For the Primordial Tradition about which I speak is not a static body of perfected religious faith or scientific knowledge capable of being fully captured, processed, or owned by an imagined, privileged few, a selected nation, or by any single world religion as such.

Its eternal source is, rather, to be *found*—by those who are awakened deep within the psyche in the "collective unconscious" of humanity, in the magical land of primordial archetypes or eternal "models." When touched and activated by what has been called—for lack of better language—the "spirit of God" (*pneuma*—Greek; *ruah*—Hebrew; *purusha* and *shakti*—Sanskrit), this source has emptied its contents onto the plane of human vision and thus historicized or incarnated its eternal archetypes, ideas or forms on the Earth plane in the lives and works of great men and women. The result has been all of the authentic gems that natural or human endeavor has ever known, in the beauties of nature, in the history of all art and science, religion and culture, and in the best moral and spiritual achievements of our race.

Thus, the Primordial Tradition is like the "Sanatana Dharma" of the Hindus, the "living Torah" of the mystical Jews, the "Tao" of the Chinese, the "Path" of the Sufis, or the "Way, Truth, and Life" of Jesus in the Christian gospels. It is to be found in every religion as its authentic core or source, and can be owned exclusively by none. It has left its traces as "sparks among the stubble" in varied forms and in various degrees of luminosity in all human cultures. Its scattered fragments of primal insight and intuitive wisdom may be found by those who have eyes to see and ears to hear.

At the beginning of the Western spiritual tradition, its "heavenly fragments" made their entry onto the plane of history, from the ancient pagan cultures of Egypt, Mesopotamia, India, Persia, Greece and Rome, to the Israelite patriarchs and prophets and their mystically oriented successors the Essenes in Qumram, from Palestine and Damascus, and from Leonopolis in Egypt, to Jesus and his followers, including St. Paul.

But the story does not end there. There is some very subtle evidence which we shall examine that a now-lost esoteric Christianity, complete with belief in a pre-existent, archetypical "god-man" or "Cosmic Christ," was once understood by its founder (Jesus) and earliest fashioner (Paul) as a particular synthesis of the larger Primordial Tradition, which had already long entered the mainstream of sectarian Jewish mystical consciousness. Jesus might thus be legitimately viewed as an heir of the mystery traditions of Egypt, Persia, and Greece, and of the wisdom traditions of India, as well as an heir of the "Law and the Prophets" of Israel.

In any event, the argument, whether for a Primordial Tradition or a lost esoteric Christianity, cannot rest on history alone, whether or not available historical documents can now be reasonably interpreted to support such a hypothesis. The main force of any spiritual hypothesis must rest upon the rediscovery by the enquirer of the same kinds of living psychic and mystical experience which the founders of a tradition had, experience which may have given birth to the tradition's original statements of faith and practice. It is for that reason that my own quest in search of the Primordial Tradition and a lost esoteric Christianity has led me into an incredible journey to recover our culture's lost insights in the human psyche and spirit.

The personal study of such disciplines as parapsychology, paraphysics, psychical research and consciousness studies is integrally related to the exciting discovery that there *is* a *real* Christian religion and for that matter a *real* Judaism, and a *real* Hinduism, Buddhism, Islam—with their origins and meaning in personal experience rather than in bureaucratic institutions and textual authority.

Many would ask, "How can we rediscover an authentic approach to religion?" There *are* esoteric alternatives to religious institutionalism and scriptural fundamentalism in all religions; and there are also esoteric alternatives to scientific reductionism and to the kinds of modern theology which would strip human spirituality of its magic and mystery. The esoteric alternatives depend upon personal experience and an understanding of the relationship between the code-language of myth and symbol, in which all scriptures are written, on the one hand, and familiarity with the types of primary mystical and psychical experience which the founders of religious traditions have had on the other. How does one gain such experience and understanding?

There are authentic, positive, and indeed universal forms of psychic and mystical experience which ordinary, sane people in many traditions can and do have today. Whenever the various objective and subjective factors and other surrounding conditions required for their operation are present, they may occur. If they are not suppressed, denied, or misinterpreted, they can and do provide the required esoteric insight into the experience and intentions of the founders of the world's religions, including one's own. It is in experiences such as these, and in the transformations of personal consciousness that they effect, that the Primordial Tradition can be rediscovered.

Both in the history of religions and in contemporary circumstances, transformative mystical experiences frequently involve one or more of the following elements of psychism: telepathy, clairvoyance, clairaudience, precognition, "out-ot-the-body" experiences, near-death experiences, visions, apparitions, prophecies, mediumship, channelling, and/or spontaneous "spirit" and "space" phenomena of various types.

Recent trans-cultural surveys show that the most common types of psychic and mystical phenomena transcend the doctrinal barriers of religion and culture all over the globe. And whatever they may be in contemporary, limited, "scientific" terms, psychic and mystical experiences involving so-called "paranormal" phenomena are not produced solely by hallucination or cultural conditioning. Such experiences have characteristically led to change in the world-views and cultural values of the persons who have had them, as well as change in the organization of their societies.

It is from such primal and universal psychic and/or mystical experiences that the "cosmogenic" and "soteriological" myths and legends embodying tales of healing, immortality, resurrection, ascension and apotheosis of gods and heroes, or other forms of transcendence of bodily death or transformation of consciousness, have arisen in ancient religions, among them Christianity, and cultures. The Primordial Tradition is thus not merely an ancient system of belief and practice to be found in its entirety in any one or several historical cultures. It is, rather, a whole set of archetypical realities waiting to be discovered, at the highest reaches of the human consciousness, by all people. Similarly the lost esoteric Christianity, which often seems to elude ordinary modern practitioners of organized, "exoteric" forms of the Christian religion, is to be found—like Jesus' description of the Kingdom of God itself—deep within the psyche (soul) of the seeker. The historical Church, and all religious organizations, are supposed to serve and bear witness to this reality, and to mid-wife the birth of the "new being" in humanity by awakening and sustaining the dynamic process by which it enters into human consciousness and action in the world. The process may be described, as Teilhard de Chardin described it, as the "Christification" of humanity.

Hindus in the Yoga and Vedanta traditions of India have called this process "Self-realization," or "God-realization." Buddhists have called it "becoming a bodhisattva." Sufis have called it "finding the inner way" and "becoming an adept or master on the Path." Pagan neoplatonists and Greek fathers of the early Church have called it the "divinization of humanity." However described, this common, singular, and most vital process of personal transformation by apprehension of a supreme transcendant and immanent reality is known to mystics of all traditions, and should be taken seriously for its proven effects within the consciousness and behavior of men and women.

The personal study of transformative forms of psychic and mystical experience, and of the myths and religious teachings to which they have given birth in all cultures, could provide Westerners with new perspectives and more universal approaches to issues of religion and culture. This could be of strategic importance for the creation of mutual respect among responsive leaders and peoples in all of the world's religions, and hence for the establishment of peace in the global village.

The blind leap of faith from particular myths or cultic doctrines is no longer adequate in the interpretation of humanity's thirst for transcedence. Today we need to examine universal forms of spiritual and psychic experience for their historical impact upon societies as well as for their scientific and their religious implications. For this we must use a new, non-sectarian philosophical language capable of being understood universally, and we require new, unbiased methods. By using such approaches in the study of human religious experience we can create more suitable conditions for a truly substantive dialogue among the world's religions and secular ideologies, including atheism and modern science.

Human beings in all places and times have discovered, through psychic and mystical experiences, the reality of open doorways between Heaven and Earth, between mundane realities and the higher forms of consciousness. The personal quest for a doorway to the archetypical font of "divine humanity"—of which the great myths and legends have spoken—is open to any who are ready to undertake it.

I will now attempt to share—as much as I can on printed page—my own quest, and my search for re-discovery of the new, but in fact very old, open secret of that doorway with you.

Fr. John Rossner, Ph.D.
Department of Religion
Concordia University
Montreal

"Mystics, Saints & Scientists"

Scenes from I.I.I.H.S. Tours of India, (1979-1984) and encounters with holy men and other leaders of modern India.

1

2

3

4

5

6   7

1. Garlanding Satya Sai Baba at Puttaparthi, S. India (1979)
2. A dialogue with Pandit Gopi Krishna in New Delhi (1979)
3. Welcoming H.H. the Dalai Lama to I.I.I.H.S. HQ in Montreal (1980)
4. Paying respects to the shrine of Mahatma Gandhi in New Delhi
5. With Dr. R.R. Diwakar, 96 year old chairman of the Gandhi Peace Foundation of India, an original disciple of Gandhi, and Hon. Chancellor of the I.I.I.H.S., and Sri M.V. Krishna Murthy, Secretary-General for Asia of the I.I.I.H.S., in Bangalore (1984)
6. With Indian Prime Minister Morarji Desai . . .
7. . . . in the garden of his home in New Delhi (1977)

Scenes from the "Land of Prester John"

All-India Tour of 1977: When a Priest, a Swami, a Psychic, and an Astronaut proclaim a message of "Yoga & Psychic Discoveries" (See Introduction)

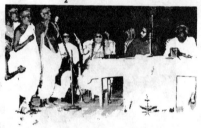

1. Reception Committee at Bombay Airport
2. With the Governor of Karnataka in Bangalore
3. Vedic priests chant a welcome to India
4. Apollo XIV Astronaut Edgar Mitchell addresses crowd of 10,000 in Bangalore park; Swami Vishnu Devananda (organizer of the tour) and Sri Dattabal, a mystic-yogi of modern India, listen attentively (R)
5. Steps to the Sivananda Ashram at Rishikesh, N. India (R)
6. Meditating with the monks of the Sivananda Order (L)

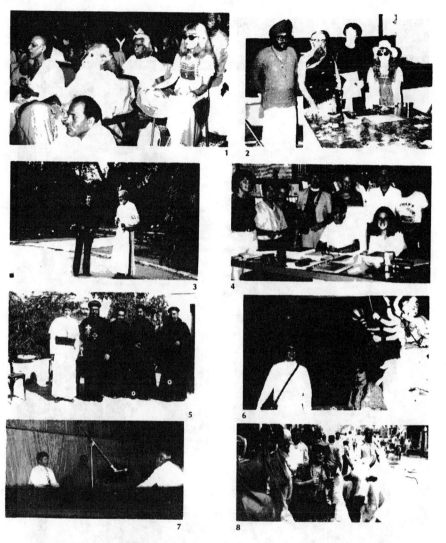

Exploring the Soul of India & the East

1. With Swami Chitananda, head of the Divine Life Society, Rishikesh, Swami Vishnu Devananda, and Swami Satchidananda... three of the leading disciples of Swami Sivananda, "the Saint Francis of modern India"... Marilyn on a visit to the Indian community in Kuala Lumpur (L)
2. Maharishi Jittabindu, "mystic-scientist of Vedic physics" in Bangalore, with a swami of Sivananda order (R)
3. With Fr. James, of the (Anglican) Order of the Ascended Christ, in New Delhi, where the original library of "Swami Abiksithananda" – a Roman Catholic priest who lived as a sunnyasin in Tamil Nadhu and contributed to the Hindu-Christian dialogue – is now housed
4. With the director of education at the Sri Aurobindo Society in Pondicherry (R)
5. With Bishop Hedra of the Coptic Church of Egypt, at Aswan, traditional entrance to Ethiopia from Egypt
6. Visiting Sivananda's private house, now a shrine within his Rishikesh Ashram in the Himalayas (R)
7. Meditating with Hindu monks
8. Visiting the ancient city of Hardwar, gathering place of sadhu's and a pilgrimage centre of Northern India at the headwaters of the Ganges

Exploring the Soul of India & the West

1. Swami Vishnu Devananda's re-furnished double-decker London bus, which had gone overland from Europe through Turkey, Iran, & Pakistan to India in 1984, on an All India "Yoga for Peace" lecture tour . . . in Bombay (L)
2. The author, Fr. John Rossner, with his wife, Dr. Marilyn Rossner, in Bombay.
3. Participating in Yogi Fire-Walking Ceremonies, organized in '83 & '84 by Swami Vishnu, in Spain, West Berlin & Amritsar . . . to demonstrate the theme that "higher consciousness can overcome that which would ordinarily destroy you, including man-made ideological barriers which might otherwise produce holocaust." (in Scene 6, right, the Berlin Wall, and Herman Goering's old Luftwaffe HQ building are in the immediate background).

Visits to Mother Theresa's
Orphanage in Calcutta, 1982

Introduction:
recovering cosmic vision

i. India 1977: the message of a priest, a swami, a psychic, and an astronaut

*I*n April and May of 1977, I traveled throughout India with a Hindu swami, Swami Vishnu Devananda, a psychic (my wife Marilyn), and Apollo XIV astronaut Captain Edgar Mitchell. We were lecturing on the topic "Yoga and Psychic Discoveries," and our message was this:

> *"Up to this point in the history of the West, we have developed rational sciences and material technologies. And we have been busy exporting them to the peoples of India and the Third World. Now we are here to ask you by all means to continue to take our technologies and our sciences as you have been doing.*
>
> *"But please do not take along with them our reductionistic Western philosophical assumptions. For these unnecessarily limit human psychic and spiritual potential, and ultimately will lead science into a cul-de-sac.*
>
> *"In an otherwise good and necessary race for modernization, do not abandon Mother India's ancient grasp of the reality of our 'subtle faculties' of psychic and spiritual perception. India's ancient yogic insights could one day be used by individuals in both East and West in building new psi-cognizant sciences. With such future sciences mankind could one day rediscover transcendent worlds of 'inner-space,' or 'hyper-space.' Humanity's quest for the Eternal requires us all to regain ancient sciences of the psyche and spirit. These are essential to the re-discovery of a multi-dimensional cosmos."*

Our traveling companion, Edgar Mitchell, was an astronaut who had gone into outer space, visited the moon, contacted the earth in a celebrated ESP experiment, and had what he described as a classical "mystical experience" in his lunar capsule. Ancient India's yogis may not have been astronauts, but they were indeed "psychenauts." For millenia such holy men and women claimed to explore and visit the various "astral" or "celestial" loca of the cosmos through human "inner-spaces," and to communicate data from such psychic and spiritual journeys back to our ordinary consciousness in the "outer-world" of the earth-plane.

India's psychenauts had indeed been very important to humanity's ageless quest for the Eternal. It was the experience of such great "inner-space explorations" that had first given rise to the so-called "yogic model of reality," and to the perennial human conviction that something inexpressible exists at the core of our mortal being, which is indeed quite immortal.

Saints, mystics, and the founders of the world's religions have often testified to the existence of just such an "immortal reality," based on extraordinary personal, spiritual and psychic experience. This experience has given birth to the faith of multitudes of others in the reality of a transcendent order behind and beyond the range of our ordinary physical and/or logical perceptions.

In order to testify to the possibility of the knowledge of an invisible transcendent order through the use of the subtle faculties of psychic and spiritual perception, Swami Vishnu Devananda, the organizer of our lecture tour, had asked Marilyn to demonstrate the gifts of clair-voyance, clairaudience, psychometry, precognition, and spirit-com-munication before large audiences of people throughout India.

As Marilyn presented a clairvoyant demonstration and we spoke about the significance of such subtle human faculties of perception, I became conscious of the fact that our odd group of pilgrims, which included a swami, a priest, a psychic and an astronaut, represented a dramatic convergence not only of science and religion, but also of the great spiritual traditions of East and West and of mankind's most ancient and most modern "technologies" of spirit and space.

Wherever we went we declared before large Indian audiences that the "yogic" spiritual and psychic skills required to explore the inner spaces of human consciousness are real, and that they are begin-ning to be understood again in the West through scientific studies. We also said that these skills need to be recultivated in their highest forms from the ancient religious traditions of India and from the native soil of our own Western psychic and mystical traditions.

Exposure to the great "yogic" traditions of India and Asia had opened up—for me and for many others in the West since the 1960s—new vistas for fresh, creative insights into the hidden areas of the human psyche and its latent powers. I was in India to humbly learn and to share what I had found of ancient insights and modern discoveries.

Through subsequent trips to India in 1979, 1981-82, 1984 and 1987, and through personal familiarity with both Christian monasteries and Hindu ashrams both there and in the West, I have been convinced that the psychic and mystical roots of the Western Judeo-Christian religious tradition contain insights and intuitions that deeply resemble the esoteric psychic and mystical conceptions of Eastern sages and Hindu, Buddhist and Sufi saints. I know that it is not "in vogue" for Western clergy, particularly for theologians, to say very much about this. But since studying the sacred traditions of India and the East, and the world-views of yogis, I have become aware of the nearly lost, "arcane" psychic and spiritual roots of the Western religious tradition, and of their unique role in human psychospiritual evolution.

Over the years since our first trip to India, as Marilyn and I have frequently met with holy men and women of India and Tibet—including Pandit Gopi Krishna, Satya Sai Baba, the Dalai Lama, the monks of the Sivananda ashram at Rishikesh in the Himalayas, and many others—I have been acutely conscious that with such persons I am in spirit closer to the ethos or world-view of ancient shamans, Persian magi, neoplatonic theurgists, the Israelite prophets, "astral-traveling" Merkebah mystics of Hellenistic Judaism, and of Jesus and his apostles than I could be in most modern theological colleges or cathedrals of the West. There seems to be something that the polished organizational men of the modern Western religious "establishment" have forgotten, missed, or perhaps never learned.

ii. *the personal background of the quest*

At the time of writing I have been an Anglican priest and a university professor in Canada for over a quarter of a century. A personal excursion into the realms of psychic and mystical experience, which began for me in 1972, has led me into a quest for the rediscovery of primal spiritual realities required for understanding the "Cosmic Christ" and "cosmic religion." These lie buried deep within the human psyche and spirit, and constitute the mythical roots of the world's religious and cultural traditions. Through an excursion into the "magical land" of "primal consciousness" I have found treasures which I could not have found through a million years of academic searching.

When I first considered the strange worlds of psyche, spirit and human "inner spaces" it became obvious to me that if any of the major claims of psychic research are true, then the "ground models" of the still-dominant 19th-century physics and of conventional varieties of philosophy and psychology would have to shift significantly. They would have to accommodate a psychically and spiritually informed view of human nature which is more compatible with classical religious and metaphysical cosmologies. I have now discovered—for myself at least—that the positive claims from over a century of scientific psychical research for the reality of ESP, PK, and the varieties of alleged "spirit communication" are of paramount importance for the historical study of the world's religions.

I have reviewed much of the cumulative evidence in contemporary areas of psiology and consciousness research which deal with human mystical and psychical experience. This has led me to a better understanding of the whole psychic and spiritual side of human life and its relevance to science and society. The history of the ageless quest for transformation and transcendence is inseparable from the history of primal forms of psychic and spiritual experience.

Over the years I have researched the scientific literature on dreams, visions, and apparitions, on claims to "spirit communication," and on what we know today about "altered-states consciousness," so-called ESP or "extrasensory perception," PK, or "psychokinesis," "OBEs" or "out-of-the-body-experiences," "NDEs" or "near-death experiences," psychic healings, and mediumistic communications. In addition, I have personally explored a number of these phenomena, including dreams, clairvoyance, precognition, psychometry, spontaneous "spirit phenomena" and mediumistic communications. I have then attempted to relate these to a formal study of the psychic and mythic roots of the world's religions, to the Judeo-Christian tradition in particular, and to issues in modern science and contemporary culture. I have studied data on several promising frontier areas of consciousness research which could relate to the next step in the development of such disciplines as the new physics, transpersonal psychology, comparative religious studies, a new integral medicine, and new rehumanized social sciences. This data—for myself as well as for a number of other pioneer thinkers today—is suggestive of revolutionary new paradigms of man and nature.

I have endeavored to show how such new paradigms and innovative lines of exploration could lead to the development of more adequate multi-dimensional cosmologies and intuitive psychologies. Such new models of reality in the sciences and in human culture could provide us with a way out of the present materialistic and reductionistic impasse between science and religion that is prevalent all over the globe. They could provide us at last with new "cosmic alternatives" to fundamentalist varieties of religion and science.

I have concluded that we urgently require a new physics of consciousness and bold new explorations of psyche and spirit which would make human religious claims to immortality, resurrection, and transformation more comprehensible and relevant to persons reared in modern secular societies. New, expanded sciences of consciousness and sciences of energy must be developed for dealing with a universal human psychic and spiritual potential. For the most part, the more limited empirical sciences of today are still largely based upon a collage of already outmoded rationalistic-materialistic *a prioris* and perspectives which are unable to cope with such vital human issues.

In a number of lectures, articles and books, published since I became involved in the study of the psychical and mystical phenomena in the world's religions, I have described what I have perceived as a " . . . recent re-convergence of images of man and of the cosmos from ancient religious and metaphysical philosophies with insights from the emerging future sciences of parapsychology, paraphysics, and consciousness studies." When rightly understood, these new sciences should enable us one day to interpret the subtle faculties of human perception in the new ways which are required for the eventual reconciliation of the sciences with the varied forms of human spirituality in quite universal terms.

iii. *my own awakening to multi-dimensional mind*

My own personal awareness of the psychic link between science and human spirituality began not in India but in the West. A new understanding of the inner worlds of psyche and spirit had opened up for me long after my years of theological studies and graduate work in comparative religion had passed. Through taking a popular, secularized course in psychic development in the West, and from another Christian priest, I discovered the Primordial Tradition—just where it has always been—hidden deep within the human psyche.

Early in December of 1971, a friend who was an Eastern Orthodox priest telephoned and invited me to join him for a new course in "Silva Mind Control," which he said he was planning to teach in a rented boathouse in Cranston, Rhode Island, during the Christmas holidays. Although skeptical at first of his somewhat exuberant claim to have a method by which he could "train ordinary people to develop ESP," I went to Rhode Island to investigate his new activities. The priest said that his father, who had been a colonel in the U.S. Strategic Air Command, had originally taken the same program in Texas. Now he, a bomber pilot's son and a priest in one of the most traditional of Christian churches, was teaching it.

I found approximately forty people from various conventional walks of life—a number of housewives, a couple of doctors, several businessmen, some clergy, a few military personnel, and several university students. Together in a boathouse for four-and-a-half days, we took a course taught by an Eastern Orthodox priest which would, it was said, "make us like Edgar Cayce," and "help us to develop our own natural, God-given psychic potential."

A. *An experience of clairvoyance, distant-viewing and psychometry.* The Silva course was amazing. It worked, and practically everyone who had enrolled in it, discovered for themselves that human psychic faculties are real. I found that I could do distant-viewing exercises, or "see" into distant places and describe what was there. In addition, I could do "psychometry," or hold objects which had belonged to persons unknown to me, and describe those persons, or specific circumstances related to the origins of the object itself. Occasionally, I could even trigger an accurate, pre-cognitive vision in a dream or waking-state, which could then be written down and verified later when the event occurred.

None of this was hokum; none of it was delusionary. It was all too accurate, verifiable, and real!

The impact of such an experience upon me was profound and was almost akin to a classical "conversion experience." I was morally obligated to investigate the whole field of psi research. I felt that I had discovered what ancient peoples were talking about when they claimed to be able to use "natural human psychic faculties" for communication with "higher dimensions of spirit, space, and time."

B. *An excursion into the uses of psi for "vertical communication" between dimensions.* After taking the Silva Mind Control course in psychic development in 1971, I subsequently studied contemporary forms of shamanism and had occasion to observe some of the positive and faith-building phenomena of mediumship and spirit communication in the Modern Spiritualist Movement. Suddenly the whole riddle of ancient religion, with its many so-called "miraculous" or "supernatural" claims, came alive for me. I witnessed and experienced for myself both the psychological and spiritual results not only of such strange, ancient powers as clairvoyance, psychometry, and precognition, but also varied forms of spirit phenomena and mediumistic occurrences. My own exposure to an ever-widening circle of modern shamans, mediums and mystics illuminated the "magical" roots of ancient religion far beyond the point that my academic studies ever could have carried me. Vertical communication between dimensions, as well as horizontal communication across space and time, became real to me.

I also began to research the history of so-called "occult ideas" and "esoteric traditions," both in the religions of the ancient world and in the Renaissance. These esoteric traditions—reflecting primal psychic and mystical experience—were revived in the 18th century by Franz Anton Mesmer and Emmanuel Swedenborg, in the 19th century by the Modern Spiritualist Movement and by Theosophy, and in the 20th century by various "new religions" and contemporary spiritual movements. But the relevance of these traditions has been either ignored, denied, or minimalized by established forms of religion and science in the West since the so-called Age of Reason.

It was at this juncture—in the summer of 1972—that I first met my wife, Marilyn, who in addition to being an outstanding children's therapist, special educator and a professor of special care counseling at Vanier College in Montreal, has been from birth an extraordinary "sensitive." Today she is widely known as one of Canada's most gifted, having appeared daily on the nationwide CBC-TV show *Beyond Reason* for a three-year period in the late '70s.

I was now convinced that the widespread belief, found in most of the religions of the ancient world, that human beings can—in rare or "peak" experiences—gain some authentic insight into transcendent realms of mind and spirit was indeed based upon real and not imaginary experience. That experience, to be sure, was not of an "ordinary" or "profane" variety. It was a form of experience that was at once extraordinary, psychical, mystical, and sacred.

I understood that it is, in fact, impossible in actual experience to separate so-called "psychic" from "mystical" or "spiritual" phenomena. The former is often the vehicle of the latter, since the psyche itself is the vessel through which the formless "spirit" must manifest. Consequently, I felt that it was my duty as a historian of religions to study first-hand the phenomenology of psychic phenomena, mediumship, out-of-the-body experiences, visions, apparitions, case histories involving so-called reincarnational memories, and the kinds of near-death experiences reported by Drs. Elizabeth Kubler-Ross, Raymond Moody and others.

For the next several years I tried to examine some of the now nearly lost varieties of shamanistic experience and arcane magical ideas which are buried deep within the psyche of persons in all of the world's religious and cultural traditions. I was convinced that the recovery of such forgotten "occult" themes could help us to better understand the foundational experiences and central myths of the world's religions, including Judaism and Christianity.

My own personal awareness of the "psychic linkage" between science and human spirituality had begun. A new understanding of the inner worlds of psyche and spirit had opened up for me, long after my years of theological studies and graduate work in comparative religion had passed. Through taking a popular, secularized course in psychic development in the West, and from another Christian priest, I rediscovered in myself the Primordial Tradition and a lost esoteric Christianity of the Cosmic Christ just where it has always been, hidden deep within the human psyche.

I have learned since that such studies are indeed very important to the history of religions. When combined with insights from comparative mythology, mysticism, and the history of occult ideas, psychical research can shed light on the origins of ancient belief-systems which have affirmed immortality. The various models of a multidimensional universe and of transcendent reality implicit in many ancient myths and creeds, including those of Judaism and Christianity, often become relevant for the first time to persons today when they experience or witness "live" psychic and spirit phenomena.

iv.   j. b. rhine's call for a "parapsychology of religion"

In 1972, I heard the late Dr. J. P. Rhine call for a "new discipline," which he said might be called "the parapsychology of religion." His idea was that research in parapsychology might serve to "ground" some of the so-called "miraculous" claims found in the history of religions in " . . . those kinds of psychic and mystical experiences that could be studied today with a scientific methodology."

In the mid-1960s, several years before my own experiences in psychic development, I had completed a historical study in religion at McGill University on "Psychic Extensions of Personality in the Ancient Near East and the Bible." I had reviewed the literature documenting the existence of various primitive "psychic solidarity concepts" throughout the ancient world. I noted that these ideas were simply assumed in the Hebrew Bible and lay behind many of the symbolic or creedal affirmations of the Greek New Testament.

I realized that many of the subsequent early Catholic Christian teachings concerning the nature of the Church and sacraments were also indebted to primitive psychic and mythic conceptions. In doing my research I reviewed the historical literature documenting the link between primitive and ancient-sacral psychic conceptions and the Christian religion. Such practices as the invocation of saints, veneration of relics, prayers for the dead, the common belief in apparitions, visions of angelic beings and deceased heroes and saints, demonic encounters, exorcisms, miraculous healings, "soul-trips" into celestial worlds and the like are found in most of the religions of the ancient world, as well as in early forms of Judaism and Christianity.

Still I could find no parallels in the data of the modern social sciences, in psychology, in sociology, or in modern philosophical or religious systems by which to make sense out of such ancient beliefs. I realized that the numerous accounts of "miracles" in the Jewish and Christian Bibles, and much of the historic teaching of Judaism or Christianity which is built upon these accounts would have to be put aside by sensible people, if the world is indeed made in such a materialistic way that no "real" psychic or spirit phenomena are possible. And yet such a negative conclusion is implicitly what the entire edifice of the modern scientific establishment has declared, and much of modern Christian and Jewish religious thought would accept.

After my own experiences in psychic development and spirit communication, I knew that I had found the missing key to unlock, for myself at least, the door to the origins of many of the so-called "miracle traditions" in the history of religions.

v. discovering the psychic area as the missing link between the sacred and the profane in modern western civilization

In spite of my wider interest in comparative mysticism and "spirit-phenomena," and the difficulties posed by the whole question of the experiential study of immortality which Rhine said he himself had temporarily "put on the shelf for later attention," I took up his challenge to try to develop a workable parapsychology of religion. His call for the establishment of a functional relationship between para-psychology and religious studies made good sense to me for a number of reasons.

I have subsequently found that there is massive evidence to suggest that very important value-systems, and even the spiritual foundations of entire civilizations, have been built upon psychic and mystical experiences. These are later expressed and codified in myths, in symbols and in various sacred scriptures. Such foundational spiritual and psychic experiences have included shamanistic and prophetic experiences, apparitions, visions, dreams, near-death experiences, healings, post-mortem contacts with the dead, and other "revelatory" phenomena, which often have served as the instruments causing conversion-experiences of one kind or another in most of the world religions.

The spiritual truths learned through such experiences by the founders of the world's religious traditions have subsequently been expressed in the code language of great cosmic salvation myths and mystery rites. We find them in ancient pagan religions of East and West, as well as in Oriental and Hellenistic Judaism and in primitive Christianity. In modern times we find many of these phenomena claimed as part of the so-called "new religions."

Several sociological and psychological studies conducted within the past decade in the United States and in a number of other countries are also relevant. They suggest that many persons are still being converted from profane world-views to classical, sacred ones—and to the concomitant ethical values of various religions—through having such psi experiences. Little-publicized, personal, inner psychic and spiritual experiences have often resulted in constructive changes in the perspectives, world-views, and values of countless ordinary persons in diverse cultures all over the globe.

It was his appreciation of this fact that led J. B. Rhine to call for the the inauguration of two new disciplines: the "parapsychology of religion" and the "parapsychology of medicine." He suggested that in the one, we should work for " . . . the systematic application of psi knowledge to the study of religions, and in the other, for the systematic application of psi knowledge to medical research." He said that this would " . . . greatly advance our scientific understanding of the nature of man."

It was in answer to Rhine's call for a "parapsychology of religion" that in 1972 I began a systematic examination of the entire field of psychical research and consciousness studies, in an attempt to apply whatever insights might be obtained to academic studies in the history of religions and in the comparative philosophies of religion and science. I observed at that time that "The psychic area is . . . the 'missing link between the sacred and the profane' " in modern Western culture. I perceived it as a missing mid-ground between science and religion in contemporary secular scientific thought.

I inaugurated a series of new graduate and undergraduate courses in religion and psychical research, and in myth, magic and ritual in the religions of the ancient world, in the fall of 1972, in the Department of Religion at Concordia University in Montreal. These courses were taught by myself and dealt with the psi-factor in the history of religions. In these courses I attempted to relate the history of religions to insights from psiology, consciousness studies, and comparative mysticism. To my knowledge, this was the first time this was done in a university anywhere.

Then, in 1975, I founded an institute to coordinate an international network of distinguished scholars, scientists, and religious leaders from a number of nations who were involved in exploring the interface between science and spirituality. This was the International Institute of Integral Human Sciences. Its basic purpose was to study psiology, consciousness research and the new sciences for their possible contributions to the interface between science, spirituality, and human values in today's emerging global village culture.

Among the earliest fellows of the Institute were J. B. Rhine, Marshall McLuhan, Arthur Koestler, Hans Selye, and many other well-known pioneers in a number of fields from around the world. A series of international conferences on psiology, science, and spirituality were held in Canada, the Bahamas, and India. Regular, ongoing seminars and workshops have been made available to IIIHS members in a network of chapters and study groups established in Canada and in the USA over the past ten years.

I soon learned that the predominantly "left-brain" orientation of most scientists and traditional religionists alike renders many persons not yet ready to listen to facts about the reality and relevance of psi to the various academic disciplines. All psychic and spirit phenomena have been banished from academic consideration by the so-called "Age of Reason" and the "Enlightenment" as pre-scientific superstition.

vi. recognizing the central problem of modern western civilization: the "left-hemisphere" dominance of scientific rationalism

The left hemisphere of the brain has been described by Roger Sperry, Robert Ornstein and others as the locus of our rational, logical, linear, verbal activities. It is because of the extensive use, they would say, of the left hemisphere of the brain that we have developed the physical sciences and technologies that have given us so many of the material blessings of modern civilization.

But many humanistic and transpersonal thinkers today have also warned us not to ignore or underdevlop our right hemisphere, or intuitive-creative functions. For the most part, rationalistic materialists do not even suspect that a wide range of psychic or mystical experiences themselves constitute a *possibly valid methodological approach* available to us for answering the greatest questions of life and death. Such persons, often dominated by "logical" left-hemisphere thinking, do not suspect that there are viable alternative paradigms for the reintegration of science (albeit a new kind of "science") with human spirituality, in truly universal or non-sectarian terms.

It is the intuitive, right-brain activity that humanity's greatest masters, sages, and saints have developed which has given birth to belief in immortality in the world's religions. This belief has been expressed in the great myths, symbols, and mystery rites of East and West. Saints and mystics have often claimed (1) to have experienced revelatory contacts with higher-than-human orders of being, as well as with the human dead; (2) to *know* that "man is immortal" through "near-death experiences," "out-of-the-body experiences" of their own, or through other forms of spirit contacts with the dead, and (3) to experience a wide range of mediumistic and shamanistic phenomena as perfectly natural and very often divinely guided occurrences.

I would suggest that it is a result of such right-hemisphere, or intuitive experience of mystics, saints and sages, that the rest of (less psychically developed) mankind has, in fact, learned—through faith in their testimonies—to affirm the reality behind such concepts as heaven worlds, human "immortality," and "life after death." This has led to the formulation of various creeds and cults dealing with such esoteric mysteries of the spirit in age after age. Christianity itself is based upon a collage of claims to such primary psychic and spiritual experiences by its founders.

Thus the greatest psychic and spiritual impressions concerning immortality, resurrection, and a new life in the spirit, including those of Christianity, have not been affirmed in what we today would call "scientific terms," but in the symbolic code-language of religion, myth, ritual, poetry, literature, music and folk-culture. But such finite impressions of immortality are, nevertheless, quite real indicators of an actual human potential to experience transcendent dimensions of this life and beyond. And I would suggest that you and I—and countless others from age to age—can experience the reality of such intuitions of immortality provided we do not close the doors of our minds in advance.

It may be of vital importance for us, and for countless others, to experience such transcendent realities for the sake of attaining inner harmony and world peace in our planetary human family in the years ahead.

vii. *resolving the challenge of psi: psychic warfare? or a humane hope for healing and immortality*

We read in the popular press today rumors that both Russian and American defense agencies are involved in a "psi-warfare race." *Time* magazine recently carried an article reporting that there are indications that the use of psychic techniques for warfare is actually being explored by the governments both of the USSR and the United States. Senator Claiborne Pell of Rhode Island is reported to have read in the U.S. Congressional Record the story of his visit to psi-research laboratories in Russia, and discussed the real potential of the use of psi powers in business, government, education, and the sciences, as well as for defense. Martin Ebon has discussed what he perceives to be the potential value of these powers for warfare and espionage in his *Psychic Warfare: Threat or Illusion?* He claims that the US government has been exploring psi for these possibilities. If we can affect one another's behavior by our thoughts, that indeed would be a tremendous weapon.

We all know that this idea is an old one. It was called "sorcery" or "black magic" in the ancient world and in the Middle Ages. Aside from the charge of an uncritical superstition, which old-guard rationalist-materialists might raise, this is perhaps one of the reasons why many scientists, scholars, and politicians instinctively have wanted to stay away from being publicly associated with those who are known to be doing this kind of psi research.

My own interest in all of this—in addition to the natural interest of an historian of ideas—is of a spiritual nature, and admittedly has something to do with a consciousness of my own self-identity as a Christian priest. While I am not comforted, of course, by the thought of the possible use of psi for warfare, I am nevertheless a realist. And I am enthusiastic about the possible uses of psi for what Eliade has called "breaking down the profane sensibilities," as well as for developing "personal psycho-spiritual quotas." We must learn how to build a higher consciousness in human beings of all persuasions. We must strive to render our species more open to the existence of higher worlds in spirit and space, and gradually to increase mankind's potential on this planet for finding "inner" as well as "outer" peace.

viii. *psi experiences as an existential basis*
for developing a personal ethic and
making the "immortality affirmation"

With my own involvement in psychic and spiritual awareness programs and the study of mediumistic experiences, I became convinced that developing one's own psychic and spiritual sensitivity can be an important element both in developing a personal ethic and in making the "immortality affirmation." Granted, not all psychics are moral persons. But I would argue that developing psychic sensitivity can be contributory to the development of ethical sensitivity.

People can learn to experience for themselves the underlying psychic unity of all life forms and also to sense the reality of the evidence for human immortality, or the survival of bodily death in a conscious, "transpersonal identity" through certain meditation techniques, prayer, and worship, as well as through such psi experiences as visions, dreams, out-of-the-body experiences and witnessing convincing forms of mediumistic communications. All of these forms of experience of an alternate reality can increase one's awareness of and sensitivity towards the needs of others.

If I can increase the sensitivity of my "soul," i.e. "psyche," so that I can really feel what you feel, and know what you know because of some mysterious psi faculty in me, then that psi faculty will become one of the real bases of my ethics, or of my concern for you. I am not as likely to hurt you *if* I really feel you to be *part of myself*. This experience of psychic sensitivity, in fact, seems to be behind the great doctrine of "ahimsa" found in Hindu, Jain, and Buddhist traditions.

No amount of law and order that a society sets up in its statutes can prevent its own people from harming one another or hurting peoples of other groups. We can never attain to an ethical society unless each person can learn to empathize, or feel that he or she, and all other living persons, are internally related to one another somehow, and connected to the very source of the universe itself. All living beings must be "sensed" by each individual to be part of a single tether of life. If one is ultimately to respect another's right to life, and attain the freedom required to develop one's divinely appointed potential, some degree of sensitivity of psyche or soul is required.

ix. establishing a starting credo for this book

We must, as a species, come to perceive that we live together in a living, psycho-dynamic universe. Typical reports of many of those who have had the near-death experience include such statements as: "I felt that I now know that there is no more important thing to do, while still alive on this earth, than to cultivate 'loving and creative relationships' with all living beings." There are those who are witnesses to the reality of such experiences of psyche and spirit who would agree with Elizabeth Kubler-Ross that "Now I not only believe in life after death and a higher world, a Higher Power, but I know these to exist," because "I've been there (to the land of the dead) and back," or "because so-and-so has been there and he or she has appeared to me" in an apparition or vision.

But it is precisely this kind of "right-brain" activity, or real psychic-spiritual perceptual function, that the more worldly persons who have created the dominant reductionistic versions of science and religion have characteristically disdained to cultivate in modern Western civilization. And there *is* a measurable loss in a society's "ethical" awareness-level whenever such a "hardening" or psychic desensitization process occurs on a wide enough scale.

I know that, in spite of the possible perils of misuse involved, there are very real ways that under God's guidance and grace we can use natural human psi faculties for increasing our creative potential, personal healing, spiritual growth, and human social betterment. Through both the scientific and spiritual pursuit of new modes of corporate human behavior we might learn to work effectively one day for the development of a higher consciousness in the whole human race.

I have reviewed some of the ways that this might be possible both in the present book and in others to follow. It is a thoroughly rational proposition that such a "higher consciousness"—gained through awareness both of the psi factor and of the spirit—could conceivably help us to build a new world-order. But first (with God's help and with that of the "angels, saints, righteous spirits" and other "higher intelligences") we must learn to solve and overcome the various man-made projections of egotism and tribal ferociousness into war, disease, hatred, and poverty of mind, body, and spirit that have so far proliferated all over this planet.

I realize that this is a gigantic hope, and will appear to many persons to be an excessively idealistic or visionary one. But is it? Could not learning an inner self-awareness and a higher level of divine self-control over our human psychic and spiritual dimensions affect ethics and morals, our collective motivation to do right by one another as members of one human family? I think so. This is, after all, essentially what, in various terms, the founders of most of the world's higher religions—including Moses, Buddha, and Christ—have taught us that it *is* indeed possible to do.

Closed minds on psi phenomena may result today from two

mutually opposed positions: *either* religious "Fundamentalism" *or* rigorous, reductionistic varieties of secular, rationalistic and materialistic "Scientism." Both have been equally inhospitable to the idea of an "open-ended universe" and to cultivation of the God-given subtle faculties of perception of the human spirit.

The primary assumption of this book is that rather than merely retreating to various brands of religious traditionalism or scientific reductionism, persons of intelligence and goodwill must begin to study human religious experience, including psychic and spirit phenomena, with *both* the left brain *and* the right brain. Well-balanced, universal, intuitive perspectives must be cultivated. New scientific methodologies which include a recognition of the reality and nature of the psychic and spirit dimensions will be required in order to understand, cultivate, and use this kind of experience constructively.

Higher, invisible dimensions of reality in the cosmos were manifested in the lives of the founders of the world's religions. It may be essential for us all to reach a cosmic awareness and experience such higher dimensions personally if we are ever to understand science and religion in ways which do not continue to divide the head from the heart, or reason from morality. The consequences of our individual and collective decisions either for or against the pursuit of such a "cosmic consciousness" will be determinative of our planetary future.

The Cosmic Christ and the World Religions.
From the painting by Arthur Douët.

Chapter 1

Ancient Insights and Modern Discoveries:
new paradigms for science and spirituality

i. primordial disclosures of immortality

Various psychic and mystical experiences, suggestive of human immortality in a multi-dimensional universe, have been claimed throughout history. They are found in the sacred literature of the East and West, in both ancient and modern times. They are virtually inseparable from many of mankind's most profound and historically significant religious and cultural commitments. Countless anecdotal tales of the wondrous psychic and spiritual powers and feats witnessed in the life of the shaman, the saint, the holy man or woman, the guru, the master, the god-man, the prophet, the adept, the magus or the seer run like a common thread of theurgic fiber throughout most of the great religious and cultural traditions of the world.

There are marvelous accounts testifying to special "disclosure situations" in the lives of the founders of religions:

- Visions and soul trips into heaven-worlds, higher spheres, astral planes and other dimensions of (what is perceived as) an essentially multi-dimensional universe of spirit and space;

- Visitations to the earth plane of various higher beings, gods, angels and devas, as messengers of divine revelation, in either physical, paraphysical or spiritual form;

- Resurrections and various forms of post-mortem appearances of ascended masters, saints and spirits encountering the living, offering guidance, healing, or giving encouragement or assistance in the fulfillment of a divine mission;

- Ascensions or translations into higher spiritual worlds of special holy persons or agents of a divine plan;

- Mystical experiences of the divine light, theophanies of divine

1

presence often accompanied by an illumination, a descent of divine wisdom, or higher understanding; and,

- A soul-empowerment by contact with the highest reality, or an endowment by divine spirit, with a new (cosmic) consciousness in order to carry the message of a new order and a new being to the human race.

Intimations, suggestive of immortality, of "other worlds," of a "higher life," here or hereafter, and of the various kinds of psycho-spiritual transformations that we might have to go through to attain them, have come to human beings through the primary vehicle of living, personal psychic and mystical experiences. These kinds of psychic and mystical experiences, whether they occur in Egypt, Greece, Persia or India, or in modern America, generally give birth in those who have them to a belief in immortality. This conviction on the part of charismatic founders of spiritual movements subsequently gets translated into various codified and institutionalized religious doctrines and philosophical conceptions of immortality and an afterlife.

ii. out-of-the-body experiences

E. R. Dodds, formerly a professor of Classics at Oxford, and at one time a president of the British Society for Psychical Research, observed that even Plato's well-known doctrine of the "separable self," or the "immortality of the soul," was not an idea which was simply thought up as a philosophical abstraction, but rather something Plato had learned through personal psychic and spiritual experiences with the shamans of northwest Greece and/or with the Pythagoreans, who practiced a form of induction of "astral projection," or what would today be called "out of the body experience."[1] This is a form of a psychic and spiritual experience which leaves those individuals who have it convinced that they have somehow left the physical body in a duplicate "energy body," or "body of light," and traveled about, either on the earth plane or in other higher "dimensions of reality," and thereafter returned to ordinary physical consciousness.

iii.   *the near-death experience and modern forms of spirit communication*

Today we know, from studies in the near-death experience which have been pioneered by Elizabeth Kubler-Ross, Raymond Moody, Michael Sablom, Kenneth Ring and others, that these kinds of experiences generally leave those who have had them convinced of human immortality and of the conscious survival of the individual personality after death. Such experiences seem to remain constant across religious and cultural traditions, and on many occasions appear to happen contrary to the tenets of the belief-systems and the expectations of the individuals who have had them.[2]

Writing in the January-February 1978 issue of the Parapsychology Foundation's *Parapsychology Review*, psychical researcher D. Scott Rogo makes the following assessment of the contemporary scientific research on the near-death experience and on death-bed phenomena in general:

> *"In short, collectively death-bed phenomena do indicate survival, but only when this entire body of literature is analyzed as a gestalt."*[3]

He then goes on to make an observation which should be obvious to those who are familiar with the earlier history of psychical research, in which the survival question and studies on mediumship were more common than they are today:

> *"Finally, I cannot help being impressed by how closely the findings of everyone from Osis to Moody match what Spiritualists of the Victorian age taught about death and the process of dying. This view may not be popular with some parapsychologists, but I fail to see that any of the "discoveries" by Osis, Crookall, Moody, or other researchers differ from what was really discovered and taught by the dedicated Spiritualists all those long years ago."*[4]

Thus, we do find reasonable argument to the effect that the Modern Spiritualist Movement has made—and continues to make—a significant contribution to the understanding of common human psychic faculties and experiences.

Contemporary experience of genuine psychic faculties and of spirit phenomena could also contribute to a personal rediscovery by Christians and persons of other faiths of the phenomenological origins of their own traditions of belief.

A comprehensive statement of the rationale and contemporary relevance of the modern Spiritualist movement was written by Dr. Marilyn Zwaig Rossner, Canadian special-educator and founder-president of the Spiritual Science Fellowship of Canada. It is a concise expression of the conviction of many Spiritualists today that the phenomenon known as "spirit communication" is not only (1) compatible with the major world religions, including Christianity, but also (2) essential to an understanding of their foundations:

> *"God regularly guides man, if he will listen, through his higher faculties of intuition and reason. Communication through our natural human psychic and spiritual faculties with other living human beings, with animals, and even with the plant kingdom is not only possible, but even demonstrable today in the laboratory.*
>
> *"Likewise, communication with our beloved "dead" through those same human psychic faculties which God has given to everyone to some degree is, and has always been, possible. It is possible simply because the so-called "dead" are not really "dead" but quite alive in another higher dimension of life to which we will all one day go.*
>
> *"Almost all of the great religions of the world have agreed in the affirmation of this truth, i.e. of the priority of the spiritual dimension over the mind and body and of its survival after the change called death.*
>
> *"Catholic Christians pray to the saints, i.e. to holy and worthy human beings living within the Spirit of God on the other side of life, in other words, the so-called "dead." Hasidic Jews have believed in the same reality of the possibility of spirit communication (see Martin Buber's "Tales of the Hasidim"). Hindus believe that ascended masters and deceased gurus often appear to their living disciples in meditation, in visions, and in apparitions, to guide and help them. This is really no different from the Spiritualist belief.*
>
> *"Spiritualism has been maligned in the modern world because it is a new religion (19th century), because it is small and, unfortunately, because there have been many dishonest mediums, as well as many true and dedicated ones. In fact, Spiritualism is not saying anything that has not been said before in Catholic Christianity, in Judaism, in Hinduism, in Mahayana Buddhism and among the Sufis of Islam. All of these religions assert, in one form or another, the real and not imaginary survival of the individual soul after death, and the rightfulness of communication with such souls when it fulfills God's will and purposes.*
>
> *"The Spiritual Science Fellowship believes that until the forces of Atheistic, Rationalistic Materialism in our society loose their grip on the mind and forms of consciousness of modern man, there can be no real place for vital or authentic religion in the modern world. And we believe . . .*

and know . . . that only tangible demonstrations of the reality of the human psychic faculties: ESP, PK, spiritual healing, and communication with the beloved departed in and through the Spirit of God, will ever break down the false Materialistic models of reality that some modern scientists and philosophers have erected. That is why so many persons today oppose the exploration of psychic phenomena with a blind rage and denials without honest, open-minded exploration. Psychic and Spirit phenomena are the Waterloo of all Atheistic Materialism and secular Rationalism.

"For, when you have communicated objectively by telepathy and have facts to prove it, when you have precognitive vision of a future event which cannot be denied, when you see auras and know accurately what is wrong with a person's body because of this heightened vision, when you have heard and seen in psychic vision the so-called dead and been given accurate verifiable information by them that you did not know, then no man will ever be able to convince you that we are merely material creatures who cease to exist at death.

Today, the great work of psychiatrists Dr. Elizabeth Kubler-Ross, Dr. Raymond A. Moody Jr., psychologist Dr. Karlis Osis, and others have shown us that such visions of the dead to the living, as well as "out-of-the-body" experiences of those who have been clinically "dead" and later revived . . . corroborate what we of the Spiritual Science Fellowship have always proclaimed in that man is an eternal spiritual being."[5]

iv. paranormal experiences in contemporary North America

Since the Age of Reason and the Enlightenment, Western culture has discouraged serious consideration of spiritistic beliefs and practices with an impressive ideological arsenal of assumptions, conceptions, operational methodologies and educational media in the arts, sciences, and conventional theologies of the major Western religious groups: Catholic, Protestant and Jewish. Schools, colleges and universities, churches, synagogues and nearly every major social institution present in the lives of Western people have inculcated Enlightenment principles, either overtly or subliminally. For the most part they have discouraged belief in such things as ESP and ghosts as either pure superstition or, at best, the unverifiable and irrelevant illusions of uneducated or mentally unstable persons. Children in our schools are still generally taught to ignore the scientific or cultural significance of the psi factor, and the standard curricula of studies everywhere ignores its role in the history of mankind in religion, and in the arts and sciences.

It is therefore highly significant that in spite of centuries of educational, cultural and scientific efforts to lay such things as ghosts and telepathy to rest, many of the common people who have passed through the establishment system would seem to be, on this subject at least, just where they were before all these efforts began. The startling results of a two-year poll conducted by the University of Chicago's National Opinion Research Center, concluded in February 1974, announced that 63 million Americans claimed to have had one or more psychic experiences (as in ESP) and/or supernatural experiences. A *supernatural experience* was described as one in which the persons felt "close to a powerful force that seemed to lift them out of themselves." An even greater number reported having had other kinds of mystical experiences. Sixty-one percent of these reported experiences of *deja vu*. Thirty-four percent reported "having contact with the dead." None of the persons indicated that their paranormal psychic or mystical experiences were drug-induced. Other recent polls and surveys also show that surprisingly high numbers of persons in the U.S. have had or think they have had paranormal experiences involving the dead.

Perhaps the most significant of all the recent sociological studies on belief in the paranormal was conducted under grant MH 20822 of the US National Institute of Mental Health at the Center for Studies in Suicide Prevention, Los Angeles. This study reveals that 44 percent of those queried in a sample survey in the greater Los Angeles area were convinced that they had had several experiences of post-mortem contact with the dead. Twenty-five percent of these persons indicated that the dead person actually visited or was seen at a seance, while over 60 percent of the incidents involved a dream.

The survey was conducted under the supervision of Richard Kalish and David K. Reynolds of the School of Public Health, UCLA, and the Scientific Analysis Corporation, San Francisco. Kalish and Reynolds have made several points in interpreting this material which are worthy of note and relevant to our present study:

> "Individual realities of persons claiming to have had encounters
> with others known to be dead often mark the experiencing individual as
> pathological. Nonetheless, a survey of the available literature shows that
> the experience is common both in preliterate communities and among the
> recently bereaved; some authors have indicated that it is more common
> among contemporary Americans than is normally presumed. The present

study queried 434 respondents in greater Los Angeles, divided approx-
imately equally among black, Japanese, Mexican and European origins,
whether they had experienced such an encounter. Approximately 44 per-
cent responded positively, with over 25 percent of these persons indicating
that the dead person actually visited or was seen at a seance, while over
60 percent of the incidents involved a dream. A sufficiently large propor-
tion of all population categories have experienced the presence of a dead
person to make this phenomenon worthy of further investigation as being
subjectively important.

"Personal encounters with individuals who are known to be dead
are rarely mentioned in behavioral or medical scientific literature, and
when they are mentioned they are treated in terms of the pathology of the
individual describing the encounter. Yet, in a very real sense, these
experiences have philosophical and psychological meaning both to the
person having the experience and to others in his social milieu. Except for
anthropologists studying primarily preliterate communities and for a
handful of others, serious research into such meaning has been virtually
unreported in the literature (outside of those journals devoted to psy-
chic phenomena)."[6]

Catholic sociologist Fr. Andrew Greeley, who conducted the
NORC poll at the University of Chicago which we have cited earlier,
has seen significance in the fact that so many persons in modern culture
are still having experiences of "post-mortem contact with the dead,"
in spite of centuries of rationalistic and materialistic conditioning to
the contrary.

"What does it mean to say that more than half the people in the
North Atlantic community believe in life after death, and that one-quarter
of the people in the United States report having had actual contact with
the dead? . . . post-mortem contact experiences have remained at such
a high level despite the attacks of the various secularizing forces to which
so much of the literature of sociology of religion is devoted."[7]

In 1985, Greeley did his survey again, and found that the per-
centage of Americans who had experienced "post-mortem contacts
with the dead" had increased to 42 percent. More specifically, 66
percent of the widows in America claimed that they have had "post-
mortem contacts" with their deceased husbands. All of this has
prompted *Omni* magazine to comment that "mysticism has gone
mainstream."

The rather obvious point is that such experiences appear to be so deeply ingrained in the nature of the human species that no amount of rationalizaton and/or materialistic conditioning can prevent them, even though most contemporary psychologists and sociologists have generally considered the whole subject unworthy of their consideration.

We might interpret the implications of all this as follows:

(1) The impression that one has had a "post-mortem contact" with a deceased person is not the unusual, bizarre, or even insane thing that modern, post-Enlightenment attitudes would condition us to assume. It is a quite "natural" phenomenon, and

(2) The unwillingness and/or inability to deal fairly or meaningfully with such subjects in the past by most psychologists and sociologists is itself quite a commentary on the power of modern *a priori* postulates which, unfortunately, still regulate our social sciences.

The recent research on "near-death experiences" by psychiatrists Elizabeth Kubler-Ross and Raymond Moody, psychologist Kenneth Ring, and others would indicate the relative "normalcy" of the conviction of being encountered by deceased loved ones or friends in so-called "out-of-the-body" states near their moment of death, and at times even after being pronounced clinically dead.

Belief in the "transcendent" or the "supernatural" is indeed not really dead in our culture. Contrary to academic rumor, it is alive, and now found in the guise of natural psychic phenomena apparently with every bit as much "divine power" as it has always had. Mind-to-mind communication, prayer, psychic and spiritual healing miracles, veridical apparitions of the dead and dying to the living, out-of-the-body experience, "astral trips" or consciousness projection into other dimensions, "other worlds," and to other places on the earth plane, spirit communication, materializations, teleportations, levitations, and many other impossible wonders are still claimed in the lives of many persons today, usually quite outside of the context of traditional religious groups. And these are not necessarily signs of emotional instability or drug-induced experiences, contrary to the prevalent attitudes still expressed in most "scientific" literature on this subject.

v. *images of man and the cosmos from ancient religions and philosophies*

Today a new breed of scientist has begun to make quite unconventional claims. Although still a small group in all, these men and women suggest that great universal, psychic, spiritual, and mystical insights from the most ancient religious and metaphysical traditions are related to the future of science and human culture. The ancient metaphysical insights about which they speak have not generally been appreciated by academic philosophers or by traditionalist theologians. But they have, remarkably, reappeared as models or paradigms at the frontiers of human knowledge in the new physics, in new transpersonal psychologies, and in the challenging "future sciences" of consciousness studies, parapsychology, paraphysics, and life-energies research.

Established research scientists in medicine, in psychiatry and in psychology have rediscovered the reality of some kinds of psychosomatic effects, i.e., the extent to which we can control our bodies by the way we think and feel, whether we think and feel positively or not about ourselves and about life in general. But allopathic medicine has in fact only begun to scratch the surface of psychosomatics.

It is only in the quite unconventional areas of oriental medicine, and in various new disciplines that some have begun to catch the fantastic vision that all manner of objects at their base level are fields of energy which are "alive" and "intelligently organized."

Thus a few seminal thinkers are already suggesting that what I have described as "new images of man and the cosmos" have made a strange but significant pilgrimage from ancient religion to future science. A number of leading thinkers—physicists Costa de Beauregard and Nobel Prize laureate Brian Josephson, and biologist Rupert Sheldrake—have also been convinced by their own investigations that an understanding of psi phenomena and human psychic experiences could be extremely important to the future of science, religion and human culture.[8]

Some have examined frontier areas of research in "life energies," as well as in "psychic energies," and putative "psi fields" (or "psychotronic fields," as the latter are called by Russian and Eastern European researchers). Models suggested by many scientists in these areas have arisen from the hard data of their observations of psychic phenomena in the laboratory.[9]

Some contemporary researchers are convinced that we are composed of an interlocking series of bioenergetic fields in a multi-dimensional universe. They say that we are capable of developing unsuspected powers of consciousness through the extension of these fields into space. A few pioneer scientists (Burr, Penfield, Eccles, Sheldrake, et. al.) have even conjectured that "consciousness" itself may reside primarily in such "energy fields." Burr has suggested that a blueprint or hologram of each life-form may reside in intelligently organized fields-of-life prior to the formation of material particles around the physical organism. Others have suggested that such an "energy blueprint"—called the "astral body" (*soma astra*) in ancient Greek metaphysical writings—may in fact be the intermediary agency linking the mind functions to the physiological brain (Tiller, et. al.). Burr himself postulated after much observation that consciousness and design, which appeared in the energy-forms or field-blueprints of embryonic salamanders before and during the formation of their material organism, might quite logically be expected to survive the disintegration of their physical bodies.[10] With this very new but in fact very ancient kind of scientific paradigm, we may have come around to a rational ground model for that ageless human aspiration: the existence of the soul and its survival of bodily death.

Researchers in the fields of parapsychology, paraphysics, and consciousness studies have filled in the data suggestive of such a rational ground model. Some have done the basic work in ESP and PK research suggesting that man's mind or spirit can indeed view objects, read thoughts, see into the future, and even affect the properties of physical matter without the use either of the five outer organs of sense or of muscular intervention (Rhine, Targ and Puthoff, et. al.).

Others have done research on out-of-the-body projection which suggests what ancient religionists and occultists have always claimed to know, e.g. that the consciousness or "soul" may at times leave the physical body in a bioenergetic, mobile center of consciousness and "travel abroad" on the earth, or in other dimensions or planes, and return with verifiable information (Osis, Tart, et. al.).

Finally, still others have researched the phenomena of death and dying and reported evidence suggestive of the ancient conception known to the primitive shaman, and to hierophants of the mysteries of Egypt and Greece, India and Tibet, that spiritual guides and loved ones return to assist the souls of the dying in the transition from this world to the next (Kubler-Ross, Moody, Osis, Ring, et. al.).

Historians of religion and anthropologists have for many years suggested that such psychic and mystical experiences are phenomenologically inseparable from mankind's earliest claims to immortality and survival of bodily death.

vi. contemporary psi claims

It is appropriate at this point that we summarize exactly what has been claimed for psi phenomena by those who have conducted psychic research. We shall review the research behind many of these claims at a later point within the course of this study.[11]

It should be noted that some of the more conservative laboratory "paraspsychologists" might themselves want to deny the validity or conclusiveness of some of the research which has been conducted by other, more adventurous psychical researchers. Following the lead of J. B. Rhine, they have often excluded certain areas from their own research on grounds that it is incapable of rigorous scientific verification at this point. They would not accept the survival question as presently proven or provable through research into psychic or mediumistic phenomena.

Nevertheless, in order to report accurately upon the entire field of psychic research as it exists today, I shall list here various propositions representing all areas of research, both those admitted by the conservatives and those not admitted by them.

The names of some of the principal parapsychologists or psychical researchers and other scientists who have conducted the research in each area and whose evaluations of that research are reported in this study will follow in parentheses after each proposition. The major claims being made by various psychic researchers today include the following:

(1) That human ESP faculties, telepathy, clairvoyance, clairsentience, precognition, etc. may upon occasion be used to receive or communicate information accurately in various altered states of consciousness in dreams and in waking states (J. B. Rhine, William Roll, Montague Ullman, Stanley Krippner, et. al.).

(2) That persons in primitive and non-Western cultures today experience various altered states of consciousness more naturally

than rationalistically and technologically oriented Westerners. In such states, often induced in cultic rites and in socially provided circumstances, primitive peoples and others in Asia, Africa and the Third World have produced significantly higher ESP scores for telepathy, clairvoyance and precognition than Westerners. Psychic phenomena, with the world-views that accommodate them, are consequently more common in such cultures. And these are the same cultures in which folklore and traditions have claimed elements of real magic in religious rites and daily life (Robert Van de Castle, Ronald Rose, A. Elkin, A. Foster, E. Bruce Lamb, S. Krippner, et. al.).

But many anthropologists, historians and sociologists have ignored questions of the possibility of psi phenomena in such magical elements and regarded them as superstition, or treated them only for their psychological and sociological functions. This has been done because such scholars have approached the subject of magic in religion and culture with negative assumptions about psi, without being familiar with contemporary parapsychological research.

(3) That spiritually significant, mystical experiences can be self-induced by new laboratory techniques (Masters and Houston, et. al.), and that by the use of these one may increase creative potential, inspiration, motivation, etc., and overcome various mood-blocks and personal problems.

In addition, problem-solving capacities in general may be enhanced by the control over brain-wave function gained by meditative or auto-hypnotic-type conditionings without the use of mental imagery during such altered mind states, much as in ancient Raja yogic or Western ritual-magic techniques. Part of the success of such problem-solving enhancement techniques involves gaining control over increased intuitive or ESP faculties, which are developed and tested in the course of mind-training programs (the Silva method, Milan Ryzl, etc.).

It is said that ordinary persons may be taught such techniques to increase general human potential as a part of ordinary public education or in private self-enhancement courses (George De Sau, et. al.). It is also claimed that ordinary persons might be given inner experiences of the kinds of higher states of consciousness known to saints and mystics by various methods (Masters and Houston, Walter Houston Clark, et. al.) or experience the oneness of all human minds and spirits in psychic development programs involving both ESP readings and projections of corrective images to ill persons. Such actions are said to be mental and spiritual processes by which prayer works (Jose Silva, Norris Clark, et. al.).

(4) That conditions favorable to ESP may be self-induced and/or induced in others through auto-hypnosis, hypnosis, yoga, belief-expectancy-and-desire, meditation, biofeedback training, ASCID equipment, laboratory techniques and various psychic development programs; and that to varying degrees one can train oneself in the controlled use of intuition or ESP for enhancement of information-gathering, problem-solving or creative functions (Montague Ullman, Stanley Krippner, Milan Ryzl, Jose Silva, et. al.).

(5) That hypnotic-type suggestions can under some circumstances be projected and transmitted to others by telepathic means and influence their behavior (Herbert Mayo, Leonic Vasiliev, et. al.).

(6) That one can potentially learn to control the alteration of one's own states of consciousness (by the use of autohypnotic and/or yogic and yogic-like meditational methods) and attain various degrees of conscious control over the autonomic body system, eliminate pain sensations, control bleeding, alter metabolic functions, and accelerate natural healing processes of the body (Elmer Green, Joseph Kamiaia, Barbara Brown, et. al.).

(7) That psychic healing (in which various forms of ESP suggestions or PK energies may be involved) is possible, and that one may be trained to it by proper mind techniques and subjective attitudes, and that such healing may involve a measurable energy transfer or transmission between healer and subject (Lawrence Le Shan, Thelma Moss, Dolores Krieger, et. al.).

(8) That various psychic healers have been significantly able to affect the rate of growth of plants and the rate of wound healing in mice under rigidly controlled laboratory conditions as well as to affect enzyme action in artificial cultures and the ionization content in water (Bernard Grad, Justa Smith, et. al.).

(9) That certain individuals seem to possess the psychokinetic ability to move objects and/or to change the properties and constituents of matter by the power of thought alone. Some individuals (Uri Geller, Mathew Manning, Nelya Sergeyevna, alias Mikhailova) have been able, it is said, to bend and break metals or move objects made of organic materials without touching them under sound

laboratory test conditions, in various institutes in the USSR, in the Stanford Research Institute in California, and other places (George Owen, Russell Targ, Harold Puthoff, et. al.).

(*10*) That various invisible energy fields exist around and in all animate and inanimate objects in nature, from rocks and plants to animals and human beings, and that these fields (in the case of living objects called *Life Energy Fields* or *L-fields*) would appear to guide, shape and govern the growth, organization and functioning of the physical body. Such L-fields (called the *soul-mold* by H. Burr, L. Ravitz, et. al.) may be measured with voltmeters, and photographed by the Kirlian process. Through their observation one may detect physical defects in the body in advance of their materialization.

(*11*) That such life-organizing L-fields are, as they extend beyond the skin, the *auras* researched by earlier scientists (Kilner) and by the Kirlian photographic process (T. Moss, K. Johnson, D. Dean, et. al.).

(*12*) That life energy fields (L-fields) are the secret of acupuncture, which stimulates an objective but invisible energy network in an energy-body (H. S. Burr, L. Ravitz, J. Pierakkos, et. al.).

(*13*) That such an invisible L-field or *soul-mold* inspired ancient religious, metaphysical or occult conceptions of an *etheric-pranic duplicate body* and a higher *astral body* composed of psychic or spiritual substance (T. Moss, Wm. Tiller, I. Bentov, et. al.).

(*14*) That other, unknown forms of energy outside of the known electromagnetic spectrum, i.e. psi energies or fields, may exist and be involved in the operation of ESP-PK phenomena. Organized in *fields*, these energy forms leave objective traces in the empirically known and measurable levels of energy or matter. But while such fields cannot as yet be measured, it appears that they can be detected by *psychometry* and, as in some instances of psi, are controllable. Various *paraphysicists* have also called such energy-fields "T", or *thought-fields*, because they would appear to act with more of the mysterious properties of consciousness rather than with the well-known physical properties of matter. It is said that, like gravitational fields, they cannot be blocked or shielded and they appear to travel outside of the known time-space-matter continuum (Leonid Vasiliev, B. Hoffman, Pascal Jordon, et. al.).

(*15*) That through such T-fields, physical objects and places can be impregnated with a record of the thoughts, images, emotions, and intentions of persons and events, and can be later read or reconstituted, as we have said, in the art of *psychometry* or *object reading* by sensitives or psychics (Wm. Roll, E. Mitchell, et. al.).

(*16*) That this may explain the basis of ancient religious and magical conceptions of the blessings of objects for various purposes, i.e. that physical things can be impregnated with thoughts and intentions to influence the auric fields and/or subconscious minds of other persons (W. E. Butler, I. Regardie, et. al.).

(*17*) That plants have a *primary perception* akin to ESP and can communicate with one another, and with man, registering something akin to an emotional response (Cleve Backster) and that their rate of growth can be affected by psychic energies projected to them by healers (T. Moss, B. Grad, Justa Smith, et. al.).

(*18*) That animals have ESP and can precognate when motivated to do so (J. B. Rhine, et. al.).

(*19*) That matter, which is energy at its sub-atomic level, may interrelate with mind through the interlocking of "T" and "L" types of energy-fields which permeate all things. For mind would reside in T-fields, which in turn would direct L-fields. Thus matter, or more properly speaking sub-atomic energies which comprise matter, would be open to influences initiated by the intelligence or mind-stuff residing within its own sub-atomic, sub-molecular, sub-cellular levels in T-fields. These in turn would be open to impulses from other individuated minds or points-of-intelligence in the universe. Intelligence is—according to this model—an integral part of all Nature, "steering it from within." This model might explain how psychokinesis works: by operating through ESP transmissions in T-fields in order to stimulate in turn particular responses from the particular intelligence within the L-fields which govern all material objects (Edward Russell).

(*20*) That individuals may upon occasion have out-of-the-body experiences in which personal consciousness somehow projects or extends itself or travels from the physical body either in sleep or other altered states into other physical places to retrieve verifiable information, or to affect physical objects in those places by psychokinetic means, and that in such out-of-the-body experiences it might be possible to measure objective physiological and informational correlates. This might suggest that personal consciousness may be sustained in some king of mobile center outside of the physical body, such as an energy-field, either during out-of-the-body experiences with living subjects, or after the death of the physical body (Karlis Osis, Wm. Roll, Charles Tart, et. al.). This research might provide some contemporary parallels with ancient Egyptian, Greek, and Indian shamanistic beliefs that an astral body or spirit-duplicate of the body could leave it in sleep or trance state, or finally at death. Hindu mystical and Raja yogic literatures, as well as that of some newer religious cults in the West today, are filled with accounts of such experiences. St. Paul and St. John of Patmos would seem to have claimed similar experiences.

This research will, in Osis' opinion, be useful in the scientific exploration of the survival hypothesis, because it uses living subjects. His argument is that if it can be proved that a living person's consciousness can be separated from his or her own material body and reside for a time in some extended form of field, then we would be only one step away from proving the possibility of the survival of death by an individual conscious human personality. This model for survival research has been pursued at the American Society of Psychical Research, and elsewhere.

All of the above statements are propositions for which some scientific parapsychologists and paraphysicists would claim existing experimental evidence. There are also a number of important propositions representing the various psi phenomena of Spiritualism which have been investigated since the beginnings of modern psychical research in the nineteenth century, for which a few—but again, not all—psychic researchers would say that varying degrees of possible evidence already exists. These propositions are:

(1) That the evidence from studies on some of the more gifted and authentic of mediums and sensitives contains, at the very least, clear indications of extraordinary forms of ESP and/or PK phenomena, and at best could quite possibly be indications of intelligent communication between living human beings and discarnate intelligences of deceased persons who have survived bodily death (F. W. H. Myers, St. Oliver Lodge, et. al.).

(2) That evidence from some carefully investigated seance-room phenomena of modern Spiritualism would indicate that certain individuals gifted with psychokinetic powers of mediumship are able somehow to cause various psychic phenomena, including levitation

(i.e., either the suspension and/or overcoming of the laws of gravity with regard to physical objects), are able to teleport physical objects from one place to another without passing through physical space, and to materialize and subsequently dematerialize various animated spirit forms. These forms are said to be made visible through their engagement with a form of bioplasmic energy mixed with a biochemical secretion called ectoplasm. It has been claimed that these forms possess measurable solid-state qualities, which have been measured on scales and with various medical instruments (Charles Richet, Baron Schrenk-Nolzing, Sir William Barrett, Sir William Crookes, et. al.).

The evidence would suggest both to Spiritualists, Theosophists, Rosicrucians, Occultists, and at least some scientific researchers a multi-dimensional model of parallel universes, varying frequency bands of energy and matter within this universe, and various discarnate beings, including the human dead, which live in another (i.e. astral) or higher energy state. In such astral spaces, called *loca* in Hinduism, various objects, including the human form, are said to exist in an energy state without the outer denser physical layers or sheaths with which they are normally clothed (Ernst Mach, Stuart Edward White).

(3) That (a) sensitive film can under certain conditions pick up spirit extras or the projected images of deceased, discarnate human beings. This occurs, it is claimed, where living persons who possess sufficient psychokinetic and/or ectoplasmic properties and other mediumistic gifts are present to provide the psychokinetic power required to pick up the projection from the discarnate mind to allow its impression on the film (Eisenbud, et. al.), and that (b) sensitive tape-recording machines have, in similar fashion, picked up the actual voices on tape of various deceased persons now still alive in the astral world, or in the parallel astral energy levels of the universe all around us (Raudive, Welch, et. al.).

(4) There is, again, some evidence from another area of contemporary psychical research for the proposition that the human soul or spirit not only survives bodily death in a mental and astral state, but also that it can reincarnate in a succession of different historical lifetimes, and in a series of new mind-body housings or psychophysical mechanisms, and develop new personalities in each lifetime that are suitable for learning various karmic lessons throughout a long evolution of the soul (Ian Stevenson, R. Bannerjee, Harmon Bro, Gina Cerminara, et. al.).

This belief has come primarily either from (1) the spon taneous memories of past-life situations of various persons in the world, in the East and West, which, when checked out, are found to contain accurate details impossible for the subject to have known by any normal means (Ian Stevenson), or (2) through hypnotic age-regression of the subject to pre-natal stages and beyond (H. Wambach, M. Netherton, et. al.), or (3) through various life-readings by psychics or mediums claiming to be able to read the Akashic record, or collective unconscious (Edgar Cayce, et. al.).

Of course, each of these psi experiences of alleged reincarnation could conceivably lend themselves to alternative explanations. It is possible, for example, that (a) some are fantasies with symbolic meaning in the subject's present life situation, assembled subconsciously, or that (b) accurate psychic memories of other people's lives or history are being "read" from the Akashic record, or that (c) people are really being influenced by discarnate entities with memories of the discarnates' lives.

(5) There has also been the suggestion from various scholars and even scientists involved in UFO research that the claims of present-day UFO contactee groups and movements resemble the myths and legends of antiquity in postulating the visitation to earth of representatives of celestial civilizations. Such beings, like the "gods" and "angels" or "demons" of classical mythology, would exhibit paraphysical control of mind over matter, telepathy, teleportation, etc., and often seem to exhibit as well the characteristics of archetypes and symbols deep within the human psyche (C. G. Jung, A. Hynck, et. al.).

Thus there have been recent studies in human consciousness which have suggested the revival of some of the most ancient conceptions of man. Biofeedback, auto-hypnosis, research in the laboratory with Zen meditators and yogis and in parapsychology, studies in "paraphysics," or the effects of mind over matter, the interrelationship between energy fields and physical, solid-state matter and quantum physics, have all contributed to the convergence of such images of man from religions of the past with the paradigms of possible "sciences of the future."

Whatever it may mean in hard "scientific" terms, cumulatively this research suggests—on the level of the images and ideas that it evokes—new (but in fact very ancient) insights into human nature, into the kinds of "phenomena" people report in various states and forms of consciousness, into the functions of the mind, and into the interrelationship of consciousness, the physical body, and the rest of nature. Such insights have begun to put back onto the map—for a few contemporary scientists at least—some of the Primordial "spiritual intuitions" of the Yoga and Vedanta traditions, of the Pythagorean and Platonic systems of Greece, and of ancient Egyptian, Persian, Hellenistic-Jewish, Gnostic, and primitive Christian beliefs concerning the various "levels" of mind in man—mind, body, and spirit.

The more adventurous and most interesting of contemporary psychical research also suggests the possibility of a model of parallel universes, and a hierarchy of spiritual and paraphysical beings in a multidimensional universe of spirit and space.

vii. *parallel universes, astral planes, and celestial worlds of spirit and space*

The late physicist Ernst Mach postulated "parallel universes," or "paraphysical hyperspaces," which would overlay and penetrate one another much as radio waves inhabit our physical space but remain undetected by the unaided human ear. These putative "parallel universes" would—hypothetically, at least—be detectable and reachable only through adjustments in the normal functioning of the human consciousness and its attendant mind-brain mechanisms.

Human beings are thought by those who have accepted such hypotheses to be capable of developing psychic and spiritual powers, or "subtle faculties of perception," and a higher consciousness through which they can communicate with one another and even affect the properties of their mental, physical, and social environments. A few would even claim that the previously mentioned "parallel universes," composed of higher-frequencied fields of energies, coexist with our own "earth-plane" and may, upon occasion, be "tuned-into" by sensitive individuals through the higher modes of consciousness operating within them. Such other worlds of spirit and space in which the human dead might live have, in fact, been claimed throughout the ages by ancient seers, mystics and mediums, as well as by prophets, masters and gurus. These have claimed that higher worlds of spirit and space are more real than our own mundane world.

Such parallel universes, if indeed they exist in consciousness or in hyperspace, would perhaps account for the countless visions into so-called "heaven worlds" and "astral planes" that are described by mystics, saints and other psychic persons after visions and out-of-the-body experiences. Tales of such things as apparitions of dead saints and spirits, revelatory visions, teleportations, so-called materializations of persons and objects from other dimensions, some of the more paraphysical and psiological types of UFO encounters, so-called "spirit photography" and the so-called "electronic-voices-on-tape" phenomena—whatever they may be in themselves, in scientific terms—nevertheless often implicitly carry with them the essentially religious claim that such other worlds really do exist.

viii. twentieth-century paradigms for immortality and resurrection

What paradigms could we construct in the twentieth century to reconcile our beliefs with the kind of mystical language, which seems to lie at the roots of a now-partially lost, Western Christian spiritual tradition? Whatever our answer to this question may be, one thing is sure: without personal psychic and spiritual experience, no paradigms, old or new, will make sense to "left-brained" persons of a rationalistic and materialistic mentality.

Christian gnosis is almost entirely lost because we have created a "cargo cult" out of popular versions of institutional Christianity. The term "cargo cult" is taken from an incident after World War II, when primitive peoples who were accustomed to American aviators landing on their island would come out and do a dance around the landed aircraft, thereupon receiving some "cargo," food, curios, etc. When the planes stopped coming after World War II, the native inhabitants of the island went out and made straw airplanes and danced around them, hoping to stimulate distribution of provisions from the "gods," or at least the same feelings they had when the real aircraft would land and distribute their cargo.

Like all people, "civilized" or not, we often worship the words or forms with the rites of our religious traditions. We tend to dance around them idolatrously and bandy about words, jargon, and formulae without understanding the inner psychospiritual events and processes to which they refer. These events and processes were originally experienced by the founders of great historical traditions, but we are not usually doing so. We do not sufficiently grasp the great universal maps of spiritual and psychical experience which our ancient scriptures are describing.

We modern Westerners have been extraordinarily limited in our whole approach to religion. We have been so conditioned by Enlightenment *a prioris* to fear "pre-scientific superstition," that we have refused to learn from so-called "pre-scientific" peoples. Until recently we have thought that non-Western peoples, and those from other great religious traditions of the world, have nothing to teach us. If we study them at all, we impose our own rationalistic, materialistic and reductionistic categories on them. But now, at last, we must learn to study the great esoteric, mystical traditions of the ancient world, which lie behind both the Christian tradition and non-Western religions, with open, unbiased minds. And we must be informed by the study of contemporary forms of psychic and mystical experiences if we are to understand them and rediscover an authentic Christian "gnosis" again. The study of psiology, consciousness studies, and human psychic and spiritual transformations will be, eventually, integrated into such new forms of religious studies for the future.

A valid approach to the relationship between psi phenomena and authentic mystical experience in religion may be developed through parapsychology and consciousness studies. But first, each researcher's own consciousness itself must be developed—or in ancient metaphor, "reborn" or "awakened"—into new and "higher forms" of perception, cognition, communication and operation, if that person is to understand either the religious experience of mankind or our own Judeo-Christian heritage. This "esoteric" idea is, in fact, present in the earliest Christian literature. It is found in the New Testament itself, wherever the idea of "metanoia" is present.

Metanoia translates rather badly into English as "repent." When John the Baptist says "Repent and enter the Kingdom of God," in New Testament Greek the word used is the verbal form of the noun. ("Metanoize," or "get beyond the mind," thus means "become a New Being," and "enter the Kingdom.") In Greek, *metanoia* literally means "beyond" (*meta*), and *nous*, the "mind." We must get "beyond the mind" to the Spirit, be ruled by the Spirit, or Transcendent "Higher Self," rather than be dominated by ordinary, lower, emotional, ratiocinative, logical physical and worldly concerns alone.

The whole issue of our own states and levels of consciousness is therefore very central to our understanding of the myths, symbols, and ritual experiences of the Christian tradition, as well as to an understanding of Asian religions or of the earlier mystery traditions of the Egyptians, Persians, and Hellenistic Greeks and Jews. It is inseparable from any scholarly or popular consideration of the ideas of immortality, resurrection, redemption, transformation, or salvation. To understand consciousness involves the necessity of "awakening" and "purification" or "cleansing of conscience," and in traditional mystical parlance, is said to lead—only then—to the opening of subtle faculties of psychic and spiritual perception.

It is precisely these "subtle faculties" that must be opened in scholars and scientists; and only then will they attain new perspectives and methodologies in psychical research, consciousness studies, and comparative mythology. This is a prerequisite to any adequate understanding of our own Western spiritual heritage, and its great archetypical symbols and myths which hold out assurances of "immortality" and "resurrection" to those who have eyes to see and ears to hear. Others—functioning only from left-brain consciousness—" . . . seeing, will not see; and hearing, will not hear."

ix. *conclusion: psi, mysticism and science in the recovery of the primordial tradition*

Twentieth-century discoveries in parapsychology, paraphysics, consciousness research, and life-energies have been claimed which some think could lead to what pioneer parapsychologist J. B. Rhine and British science writer Arthur Koestler have called a "Second Copernican Revolution" in the arts, sciences, and human culture on this planet. On the other hand, we must also note that present-day, established forms of science have been very resistant to such new data, characteristically either denying its verifiability out of hand without serious examination, or at worst attacking the credibility or honesty of the researchers.

I have suggested that it will not be the addition of more hard data by parapsychologists, paraphysicists, or consciousness researchers that will be required to convince the skeptical. It is, rather, a matter of the consciousness, and the perspectives of individual members of the scientific community itself, which are the issue. It is really a matter of the *a priori* philosophical assumptions of 18th century and 19th century "science" which have led to rationalistic, materialistic, reductionistic perspectives.

These perspectives have precluded the very possibility of psi phenomena and psi faculties. Personal experience in the psi area has often been suppressed in advance by inappropriate mental attitudes and various "left-brain" modes of functioning of the consciousness. These have proven themselves quite inimical to the operation of human psychic faculties or of psi events in the laboratory.

Nevertheless, in view of the cumulative evidence for the existence of real, and not imaginary, subtle faculties of psychic and spiritual perception and action in the human species, historians of religion and science today might reasonably want to take the contemporary claims of parapsychology, paraphysics, and consciousness studies with them into their investigations of the psycho-spiritual roots of ancient, and modern, religious and metaphysical traditions. In these, so-called "paranormal" events have been intertwined with the elements of mythology and symbolism which have become deeply imbedded in the Western psyche.

In the emerging future sciences of parapsychology, paraphysics, and consciousness research, the student of religion is confronted with claims to discoveries which could give him new perspectives on what I have called the "Primordial Tradition," or mankind's heritage of spiritual and psychic knowledge from ancient religions and cultures.

An understanding by the entire modern Western scientific community of the reality of the psi factor could thus be tantamount to the rediscovery of the "missing link between the sacred and the profane" in Western civilization. For this would inevitably arise from, and lead to, the further development of models of reality for the emerging "global village" of tomorrow which do not pit reason against intuition, or science and technology against human spirituality and the inner life of the human psyche.

Since we are witnessing all over the world a resurgence of the crude, 19th century warfare between fundamentalist versions of religion and reductionist versions of science, this issue is indeed quite vital. Men and women of intelligence and goodwill are surely looking for better alternatives than our radical polarization of science and religion have presented.

The new, but in fact very old, perspective revealed in the quest for "recovery of a Primordial Tradition" of intuition and insight could provide such a better alternative. In this quest a number of frontier scientists have already claimed to have discovered models for the reconciliation of science and spirituality and for the reconciliation of the processes of modernization and technology with the pre-scientific insights and intuitions of Third World and non-Western cultures today. In the present book I will share with you the hope that philosophers, scientists, and religious thinkers from all traditions might come together in the search to recover mankind's "first tradition" of intuition and insight, through contemporary, open-minded, scientific historical and cultural research.

There is an urgent need today to render the dehumanizing *a priori* assumptions of the 18th-19th-century materialistic-rationalistic philosophy of science less dogmatic. Our motive should not in the least be to harm science, or loosen its foundations of much-vaunted "rationality." To the contrary, our present need is to re-establish science on a surer foundation with more adequate, integrative perspectives, perspectives which do justice to the mind and spirit as well as to the body. We require perspectives which will allow for a "multi-dimensional man" who possesses subtle psychospiritual as well as physical faculties, and for life in a multidimensional universe of spirit and space.

It is the obvious inadequacy of present-day science to answer this need that has led many to a concern for new models and new paradigms for reconciling and reintegrating science with universal forms of human spirituality. We require a holistic vision for a better world. Both a new science and transcendental insights will be required for the discovery and right use of the root secrets of life, of mind, and of matter itself.

It is the psychic area that is the "missing link" today between the sacred and the profane, between spirit on the one hand, and observable effects of mind and the physical body on the other. Until both scientists in the major disciplines and theologians of the major faiths come to understand the area of psychic phenomena and the unconscious (including the pre-conscious, subconscious, conscious, and super-conscious) levels of transcendent reality with their interactions in life and mythic symbols, there can be no fruitful dialogue between science and religion.

In fact, I have come to the conclusion that the truncated versions of science that we now know, and religion as it is now organized and systemized, may never be able to interface successfully with one another. It will only be those new "psi-cognizant" and "mythopoeic" versions of science and religion in the future which will do so. And this will come about after the present-day "temple-priesthoods" of reductionist scientific thought and "fundamentalist" and/or "liberal" religious conceptualization have crumbled of their own weight.

Personal psychic experiences, such as those of yogis and mystics, have generally served to "break down the profane sensibilities," as Eliade has pointed out, or the so-called "common-sense" world-view of 18th-19th-century physics and psychology, as A. Koestler and J. B. Rhine have indicated. Such personal psychic and spiritual experiences can be used in the right context to open the doors to more creative living (Masters and Houston, et. al.) This should eventually lead to new conceptions of man in a multidimensional universe of spirit and space. These new conceptions are needed to break down the present schism between matter and consciousness, science and spirituality, the sacred and the profane that is present in Western civilization.

The ancient yogic and esoteric sciences of body, mind, and spirit—which a priest, a swami, a psychic and an astronaut proclaimed to the people of India in 1977—also render possible the human navigation of "inner" as well as "outer" spaces in the years to come. From this beginning there might follow the development of those new, higher, integrative myths and paradigms for science and spirituality which are urgently required for peace, justice and harmony.

Today in Western secular societies we have nearly lost sight of the concept that there could be sciences and skills for perfecting consciousness in the body-mind mechanism so that such transcendent spiritual, mythically expressed realities might be real to us and effect our transformation into new beings, from beasts into angels, from men into gods. This is the very message that the most primitive versions of the world's religions, including the earliest cosmic Christianity, once proclaimed with many "signs and wonders."

At the very least, as serious scholars, religionists must be prepared to concede that psiology is a fascinating area of research which could ultimately revolutionize our whole view of human nature, physical reality, immortality and human purpose in the universe. As the former Bishop of Southwark in the Church of England, Dr. Mervin Stockwood, once pointed out, we might think for example of the cultural impact, which could occur if subtle psychic and spiritual faculties—by which we might perceive the reality of human "immortality"—were *understood* before we started with our individual belief sytems.

If what I have called the "new sciences" of consciousness and spirit, and a new psycho-dynamic, multi-dimensional view of the universe were taught in the textbooks of our schools and universities, the implications would obviously be tremendous for religion, culture, and mankind's understanding of itself and its destiny. The late British science writer Arthur Koestler thought that the psychic sciences could bring us to what he called a "Second Copernican Revolution" greater than the first. And for this reason, when he died, he left the bulk of his estate—nearly a half-million dollars—to establish a chair of parapsychology at a university in the U.K. It is hoped that the field of parapsychology itself can expand its presently limited perspectives, horizons, and methodologies sufficiently in order to rise to the tremendous challenge which lies before it.

And for the scientific community at large, I would heartily recommend the suggestion of Brazilian psychical researcher Pedro McGregor that:

> *"If science were to ply its enormous knowledge of electronics, biochemistry, and nuclear physics systematically to the discovery of the spiritual nature of man, it could well make a breakthrough in the understanding of our nature and our predicament equal to (or far greater than) the impact of the discovery of how to split the atom."*[12]

Pedro McGregor has also seen another central point that I have been trying to make to both scientists and religionists. Any new religious philosophies, and/or scientific paradigms or methodologies, that emerge as successful ones for dealing with what Marshall McLuhan has described as the coming "pluralistic global-village culture" of tomorrow, will have to be ones which unite the full scope of the imagination as expressed in myth, symbol, "real-magic" (psychic phenomena), liturgy, and poetry of all mankind's authentic ancient and modern religious and spiritual quests of East and West, combined with a vision of the global sciences of the future:

> *"Religions, to have any meaning today, must take into consideration such diversities as the energy of the quasars, the millions of billions of possible worlds in the Universe, and the whole complex range of scientific knowledge here on Earth, as well as the moral and spiritual values by which the intelligent principle works. In a future world inhabited by super-civilization, religion will have an expression and a form beyond our present understanding."*[13]

It is to the development of the required "higher consciousness," and of that expression and form of religion for a New Age beyond our present understanding, that we must now turn our attention, if we are each to save and to fulfill the best in our own religious traditons for a better world tomorrow.

We do have ample historical evidence to suggest that any tradition or form of religion which can do justice to the psychic and spiritual faculties of man, and to the universal reality of the inner "intimations of Immortality" which can be received through those faculties, should prosper in that New Age.[14] But both religion and science will require new paradigms and new methodologies for understanding the psi factor—the currently missing link between the sacred and the profane in Western civilization. For those who have "the eyes to see and the ears to hear," the process of the convergence of science and spirituality, East and West, has already begun.

"Milton and the Spirit of Plato" by William Blake.

Chapter 2

The Quest for the Primordial Tradition:
cosmic science and cosmic religion

i. *the case for a "primordial tradition"*
of intuition and insight

Is there a Primordial Tradition of intuition and insight, a higher wisdom, or "gnosis," concerning hidden powers of the mind and other dimensions of spirit and space? Are there universal metaphysical truths, expressed in "archetypes" discoverable only in "higher forms of consciousness," which cut across all man-made doctrinal and ideological barriers? Are these expressed in the great myths and symbols of the world's religions and cultures?

Carl Jung thought so. Eastern mystics—Hindu yogis and Buddhist monks—as well as the founders (including Plotinus, Plato and Pythagoras) of Western religious and philosophical traditions have also believed that there are. They based their beliefs about immortality and higher worlds on their own personal psychic and spiritual experiences of such archetypes. The various myth-and-mystery traditions of India and Asia, of Egypt, Persia and the archaic Greece of Hellenistic Jewish mystics, of Gnostics, primitive Christians, and several of the greatest of the pre-Nicean Church Fathers, and of the Sufis of Islam, witnessed to the reality of what they would describe as universal metaphysical truths available to those who had achieved higher states of consciousness, in which a heightened form of perception is possible.

There has been frequent testimony in "esoteric" or "occult" circles within the major religions of the world of the existence of such archetypes and universal metaphysical truths, and of the possibility of attainment of the "higher states of consciousness" required to perceive their significance. And there has been a historically documentable "alternative-reality tradition" from earliest times to the present in the East and the West. This "alternative" tradition provides repeated testimony of the effectiveness of various arcane "technologies" of the human mind and spirit for achieving such higher forms of intuitive perception. Through such higher faculties, it has been said that the pioneers of the human evolutionary process (masters, teachers, prophets, saints, sages, seers, yogis and rishis, gurus, adepts, avatars, magi, and god-men, et. al.) have received divine revelations, inner guidance and an "initiation" bearing insights into "higher worlds," into various astral and celestial planes, into "samadhic" and "nirvanic" consciousness, and into the ecstasy of the Godhead itself.

But this great heritage of arcane testimony . . . has been set aside and even scorned for the past two or more centuries by worshippers of a "scientific world-view" and by the institutional guardians of the exoteric religious establishments operating in the present modern, secular, Western context.

The very idea that there could be such a universal "first tradition," derived from higher "intuitive" forms of perception, is almost entirely missing from the modern secular, post-Enlightenment worldview. It is certainly nowhere entertained seriously in the conventional textbooks of natural or social sciences today. Nor is it considered an option in modern philosophical systems, or in the humanities.

This widespread negation of a universal sacred world-view is not surprising to those who would proclaim its existence. It has been said by psychics, mystics, and occultists in many arcane traditions that the verification of the existence of such a Primordial Tradition of spiritual intuition and metaphysical insight depends upon the existence and awakening of real, not imaginary, subtle faculties of psychic and spiritual perception. Such subtle psychic and spiritual faculties have not been recognized or cultivated in modern materialistic and rationalistic approaches to science.

Limited—and limiting—philosophical theories ("epistemologies"), concerning the ways that human beings can know objective or subjective realities, have made it all but impossible for so-called "empirical sciences" or "rational theologies" today to take seriously the reality of such subtle faculties of perception and communication. The ancient claim of a Primordial Tradition is thereby robbed of all possible forms of verification. Nevertheless, primary psychical and mystical experiences and the resulting belief in the existence of a Primordial Tradition have played an important role in the foundation of many of the higher spiritual traditions of mankind of both East and West. The idea of a "dharma," "mystical Torah," "Tao," or other universal, living and dynamic "natural laws" are found everywhere.

And it has only been since the so-called "Age of Reason" and "Enlightenment" in the modern West that we, alone in all the world, have created a dogmatic rationalistic and materialistic model which postulates only the reality of the physical world. This has eliminated the place of psychic and spiritual sciences, the yogas and religion, from consideration as practical aids to living. We have forgotten and suppressed, or denied, the idea that there could be universal, non-arbitrary, non-imaginary metaphysical realms, principles, and laws either in the human psyche or in Nature which could be studied and observed through rare, "subtle" psychic and spiritual faculties, transculturally and quite independently of sectarian doctrines and traditions.

Western civilization has also lost sight of the widespread, ancient conviction that such faculties of psychic perception, or of intuition and spiritual insight, were awakened in the pioneer examples of the human race (i.e., in the saints, masters, avatars, prophets and sages). It is they, after all, who have claimed the existence of such a Primordial Tradition and of the forms of higher intuition and insight which permit illumined souls to gain a real, not imaginary, perception in archetypal forms of transcendental, universal, higher metaphysical realities. What were the "facts" of the ancient sacral world-view which ancient metaphysical traditions—of East and West—once held in common?

ii. *primitive spiritual and psychic conceptions*

Contemporary writers familiar with the data from pioneering mystical and psychical research have claimed evidence from experimental and field studies which is highly supportive of the world-view of the Primordial Tradition, and of various ancient religious and/or metaphysical conceptions of man, his immortality, his faculties of perception and communication, and his relationships within the natural order of the universe. In an attempt to interpret their own scientific findings, a few of these scholars have constructed new paradigms for understanding man and nature which approximate models of reality which are found in some of mankind's most ancient religious and metaphysical cosmologies.

When used as guiding images for further research, some of the models and paradigms found in ancient, esoteric religious systems are yielding quite tangible, empirically testable data about a heretofore uncharted range of psychic faculties in ordinary human beings and animals, and possibly even a primitive form of perception in plant life. It is at this very point of convergence between the religions of the past and the sciences of the future that some scholars today explore the nature and potential of man.

Some of the particular ideas from ancient Oriental and/or Hellenistic religious traditions, paralleled by psi theories being suggested today by some of the more adventurous parapsychologists and paraphysicists, include the following: (1) the idea that Nature is directed from within by a higher intelligence or mind; (2) the belief that all minds in the universe are linked together by participation in one universal mind or source; (3) the conviction that all living things possess a potential ability to communicate among themselves panpsychically, in the case of man and animals by ESP, and even in the case of plant life by some sort of primary perception; (4) the belief that future events can under some circumstances be known in advance by precognition or prophecy; (5) the idea that various mental or physical rituals can sometimes effect what they symbolize, or set the proper conditions in motion for the desired events or result to occur, as in both modern techniques for inducing various altered states of consciousness which might be conducive to psi (sympathetic magic in primitive and ancient-sacral religious rites also involved this conception); (6) a view of the relationship between matter, mind, and spirit which would occasionally allow mental or spiritual forces to act directly upon matter either to change it or move it, as in both modern psychokinesis experiments and ancient alchemical texts; (7) the belief that prayers, thoughts and mental projection (and, hypothetically at least, various higher intelligences, i.e. God, gods, devas, jin, angels, saints, spirits, etc. in a hierarchically ordered spiritual cosmos) might directly heal sick and diseased persons through the release of powerful, life-giving energies; (8) the concept of a quasi-material astral body, or a body made of an energy-field which is an invisible duplicate form serving as a pattern or mold for the physical body in which the soul resides, and which may at times during sleep or trance states leave the physical body and go on astral trips into other places in this world or into other worlds; (9) the conception of other dimensions, astral worlds, or heaven worlds in a multidimensional universe in which the human dead, as well as other discarnate entities, whether higher or lower on the evolutionary scale than man, may dwell or come from other planes to encounter those still living on Earth; (10) the conviction that thought can produce quasi-physical forms, impulses, fields, or energies with an independent power of their own which, once initiated, can project themselves, travel abroad, or otherwise communicate, affecting other minds and bodies in this and other worlds and the purposes with which they have been imprinted; (11) the idea that physical objects can be impregnated with various magnetic vibrations which can be read by sensitive individuals through the process known as psychometry, and that these impressed vibrations can instrumentally accomplish blessings, healings or curses through such physical objects; and (12) the belief that the individual human personality and consciousness survives bodily death and maintains an interest in human affairs, occasionally communicating with the living by means of various methods of mental or physical psi phenomena or in other spontaneous manifestations such as apparitions, visions, materializations, etc.; (13) the Eastern religious belief that the spirit reincarnates in a series of personal existences, and that upon occasion an individual may have either spontaneous or hypnotically induced glimpses into a past life in which memories may be studied for their objectively verifiable content; (14) the possibility that higher intelligences from outer or inner space—whether in physical, paraphysical, or psychic form—have visited the earth in the past and continue to do so, causing ancient myths and legends of gods and angels and various widespread modern accounts of encounters with UFOs and their occupants.

iii. *ritual, prayer, meditation and psychic powers as effective "technologies of the mind"*

The Primordial Tradition of the ancient world pre-dated the emergence of the organized religions of the West. The latter, including Judaism, Christianity, and Islam, nevertheless rested, to varying degrees, upon the common earlier belief in such a Primordial Tradition. This included a view of man, for example, which made it completely logical to think of such things as prayer, meditation, rituals, out-of-the-body experiences ("ecstasy"), clairvoyant powers, visions and apparitions of the dead and of gods, angels, and saints, as real, and various psychic and spiritual powers as effective "technologies" of the mind and spirit. These were thought to be, within their own proper spheres of operation, just as effective as any of the physical technologies were within theirs. Thus such physical skills as engineering and the construction of tools, buildings, and cities were paralleled by spiritual and psychic skills in meditation, prayer, ritual, extra-sensory perception, psychokinesis, and spirit communication.

The basis of all belief in the instrumentality and effectiveness of psychic and spiritual powers was the actual experience of such powers, along with a psi-cognizant world-view and a conception of the nature of man which made that experience seem reasonable.

In most of the ancient "esoteric" spiritual traditions of both East and West there was a common world-view, a cosmology. There was a paradigm of the cosmos and of man, and of many various levels of mind and its functions of consciousness and psyche, "inner planes," "astral worlds," worlds of spirit and space, and the interaction of mind and matter. This "psi-cognizant" world-view, or model, cuts across many of the specific religious, ideological, and cultural barriers of both Eastern and Western traditions. The Primordial Tradition arose in the first place—it was claimed—out of primary, "clairvoyant" psychic and spiritual observations of the human mind in operation, and of the several "subtle bodies" of "energy vehicles" of man, both in life and after death. The ancient traditions themselves claim that direct knowledge of such things arose from spiritual and psychic experiences of the inner planes of consciousness, and of other worlds or spheres of existence and their living, non-physical denizens.

Such a Primordial Tradition or "perennial philosophy" postulated a higher "technology" of mind and of the spirit, from the various yogas of the Orient to the magic and alchemy of meditation, prayer, and sacraments in the higher religions of both East and West. These technologies were included in mystical forms of Judaism and in positive gnostic forms of the primitive "pre-orthodox" Christianity in the first two or three centuries, A.D.

In this Primordial Tradition there were said to be very real psychic-spiritual sciences available for the attainment of the transformation, sanctification, and divinization of human beings. Both in classical Greece and in the yogic traditions of India, the goal was to put it in contemporary terms—holistic health in body, mind and spirit. The complete integration of the body and mind with the spirit was postulated as the preliminary step towards the goal of human psychic and spiritual evolution. No kind of religious justification, redemption, or salvation, whether individual or collective, could be envisioned as occurring before a process of "consciousness awakening" (as well as of psychophysical development and holistic, spiritual self-integration) had begun in an individual.

The very idea that inner, subtle skills could be taught and learned in order to facilitate human psychophysical and psychospiritual transformations, and to assist the awakening and growth of persons into saints, sages, and god-men, rests upon an arcane psychology and physiology of humans found in the yogic traditions of India and Asia, and in Egypt, Persia, and Greece, that we have all but forgotten.

iv. the several "bodies" or "sheaths" of man

The rishis of India, the magi of Persia, and the priests of Egypt preceded the Greeks in teaching a multi-leveled view of man. This included the conception of three "energy bodies" or sheaths: (1) the physical body (in Greek, *soma sarkekos*, or "flesh body"), the outer "sheath" composed of solid-state matter; (2) the etheric body (*pranamayakosha*); Indian yogic physiology, or the *ka* of Egyptian hieroglyphs; (3) the astral body (*soma astra*, Greek; *manomayakosha*, Sanskrit; or *ba*, Egyptian) which was viewed as a "blueprint body," or the first "formal body" housing the soul ("psyche"). This soul-body or psychic-sheath was said to be able to leave the physical body during sleep or trance states, to travel abroad on the Earth plane, or go into astral worlds, and then to return to the physical body upon awakening. It was this astral body which, as a "mobile energy-housing" for the individual consciousness or psyche, was said to depart a bodily death.

Just as there were three basic levels of body, or three "bodies," so were there said to be three basic levels of mind, or three mental "sheaths." We find an ancient paradigm for understanding the three "minds" and three "bodies" of man in classical Greek metaphysical philosophies of Pythagorianism and neoplatonism, as well as in the ancient yoga psychologies of India, in Persian metaphysical traditions, and in Egyptian Hermetic traditions.

The three levels of mind, or types of mind-functions, were generally described as follows:

(1) The instinctive or subconscious mind, which man shares to varying degrees with the animal kingdom. This lower level of mind-function was known as the *manas* in Sanskrit yogic texts. It was said to provide the unconscious programming of the autonomic body system,

as well as the lower "cybernetic" or calculative functions of our more mechanistic types of subconscious logic.

(2) The ratiocinative, conscious mind, or the analytical consciousness which allows a human being to create abstract conceptions of things, including conceptions of himself. The abstract concept of the empirical self which a person creates and projects into being as an illusionary reality through which to operate in the daily world is called by yogis the "ego." In yogic and other Eastern philosophies, the "ego" is said to be a "false" or lower, limiting kind of non-reality which must be transcended, or else it becomes a block which must be removed before any discovery of the true self (*atman*) can occur. (Note that quite a different meaning is given to the word "ego" by many modern Western psychologists, who speak of "ego" as the center of authentic personhood.)

(3) The spiritual, or superconscious mind (the *buddhi* in Sanskrit, or *nous* in Greek) is the "modulous transformer" between the pure, formless Spirit, and the conscious mind. In yogic terms, the *buddhi* ("spiritual mind" or "super-conscious mind") is said to be the formative channel for all higher revelations, whether in the areas of art, science, or religion. It is this higher level of mind which is used by the true self or spirit (atman) to guide us to fulfillment in our scientific, religious, and cultural pursuits.

(4) Above all of these three levels of mind, and above all the three levels of the body, there is the "true Self," or the "pure formless spirit" (the *atman*, in Sanskrit; *pneuma* in Greek; *ruah* in Hebrew). This is, both for classical Indian and classical Greek philosophers, the true immortal Self, the spark of God in Everyman. In yoga, to discover this "true self" is to realize that one is " . . . not the body, not the mind, but Sat, Chit, Ananda." That is to say, one perceives in the highest states of consciousness that one is "pure existence, pure consciousness, and pure bliss." This is said to be the goal of all the yogas, and of all religious sciences and technologies.[2]

Out of such an "atmanic consciousness," yogic adepts were able to say "I am not the body; I am not the mind; I am pure existence, consciousness, and bliss." This is, in Indian religious terminology, tantamount to saying: "I am *in my highest self* (*atman*), divine, or one with divinity ("Atman and Brahman are One").

The *atman* which is "manifested God," or "spirit of God in universal Man" is in its individuated form, in a given person, the *jiv-atman*. But, in itself and in its universal and primal connotations, it is said to be One with Brahman or One with the Universal Divinity. In anthropomorphic terms, this could be expressed by ancient Indian rishis, as Jesus did in ancient Israel, with the phrase: "I and the Father are one."

Thus, great yogis and rishis were said to be able to proclaim "I and the Father are one" from personal experience of a higher mystical variety. "I am in Him, and He is in me." The "Son" was thought of as the universal atman—or God outside of Himself, "God manifest." The hidden "Father" was the Universal Brahman, or God in Himself, unmanifest.

Thus "No man can come to the Father (i.e., "Brahman") except through Me (i.e., the *atman*)." Such an affirmation, like that reportedly made by Jesus in the fourth Gospel, would have certainly been recognized by at least some learned souls in the ancient world. In the "yogas" of India they would have been—and are today—seen as words following "samadhi" and proceeding from the peak experience of highest consciousness by a great mystic, saint, sage or "god-man" who had succeeded in "realizing the Self," or "realizing God in the Self."

v. consciousness and the various levels of body, mind, and spirit

Ancient metaphysical writers generally did not postulate a radical conceptual gulf between religion, science and technology in the manner that we have done since the time of Descartes and the so-called Age of Reason. The pursuit of human knowledge in a systematic manner (*scientia*) and the mastery of human skills (*techne*) always included "religion" in its primordial sense.

It is interesting to note that the root meaning of the word "religion," which comes from the Latin *religio, religare,* is "to integrate," "to link," "to yoke," "to bind together" all of the levels of man—body, mind, and spirit—with the divine ground-of-being. The Sanskrit word *yoga* has essentially the same meaning as the Latin word *religio*. It comes from *yug* or "to yoke" or "to integrate" the levels of man with the divine. Thus the knowledge and skills which lead to the integration of the seven levels of man in the Indian yogic psychology were the consummate "spiritual sciences" or (in Sanskrit) "yogas." And in Latin, they were "religion" in the primordial sense.

Those "sciences" and "technologies" which had as their objective the transformation of the human body-mind-spirit complex into the "temple of the divine" were the "yogas" in the East and "religio" in the West. Such spiritual and psychic sciences have as their objective psychophysical integration and psychospiritual awareness. They were considered in every way as valid and essential as all other physical sciences and technologies.

To summarize, there were said to be three bodies or three levels of sheaths—the physical body, the etheric body, and the astral body; and three minds, or three levels or sheaths of mind: (1) the subconscious or instinctive mind; (2) the "conscious mind" or "rational mind" and (3) the "superconscious mind" or "spiritual-intuitive mind." Above both the body and the mind there was postulated (except in Theraveda Buddhism and in some other later traditions) a "true self" (*atman,* the formless "spirit," etc.). The *atman* was viewed as ever "one with its source," or with the "universal God" (Brahman). The same basic knowledge ("gnosis") was expressed in various languages and symbolic terminology in the ancient Egyptian, Greek, Indian, and Iranian traditions. Such esoteric knowledge about the levels of body, mind and spirit was said to be intuitively derived by Indian rishis and yogis, by the Egyptian priesthood, by Persian magi, or by other mystics from their own primary psychic and spiritual experience. It constituted a Primordial psychology and cosmology which, by Hellenistic times, had been synthesized into various esoteric "wisdom traditions."

In this arcane cosmology each person was not viewed as today, as a single, intellectually or physically isolated entity. Rather, each person was viewed, with respect to the mind and spirit at least, as intrinsically connected with one universal, divine source, and thereby united to all other living things in the cosmos. It was clearly against the background of such arcane teachings that Hellenistic Jewish mystics, Gnostics and primitive Christians alike developed various conceptions of the three-part nature of man. In Greek metaphysical psychologies, the seven levels of man are thus combined into three. All of the three bodies are one; all three minds are one; and the Spirit is one, making three.

Jewish mystics and early Christian Fathers—at least to the time of St. Athanasius, and beyond—knew of the commonly assumed existence of the "etheric" and "astral" bodies, and of the three levels of mind.

The Eastern religions, and to a certain extent the mystical traditions in Western religions (especially esoteric traditions within Judaism, Christianity, and Islam), have thus retained a mystically based, more holistic and integrated view of the world. This world-view is in some respects still very much like that of what I have called the Primordial Tradition in the ancient world. It still makes good sense to someone who is Sufi, a yogi, Christian mystic, or Qabalistic Jew, for example, to believe that through meditation one can "still the mind" and start the mind functioning in different higher states of consciousness.

There are said to be other, higher and lower functions of the human mind (just as today we say that some computers can be used to do higher functions of reasoning). By learning to control these levels of thought, the yogi can learn to control the emotions and to focus the mind. According to this perspective, the objective is to still the intellectual static, so that the "superconscious" or the "spiritual mind" can begin to bring in impressions that will guide him. There is also a realization in the yogic tradition, and in Western occultism, that the subconscious mind can tell us more about our own body and its needs, and the needs of the physical organisms around us, than our logical functions can by reasoning alone. It is said by both traditions that we can pick up sensations from other persons, animals, and plants by sympathetic psychic action in our own bodies and minds.

The superconscious (*buddhi*) and the subconscious mind (*manas*) are thus said to be able to provide us with reliable information quite apart from what we can logically compute or physically observe. However, following René Descartes, Francis Bacon, John Locke, and David Hume, modern Western sciences and psychologies have limited and reduced us to admitting the reality only of what we can (1) physically observe, and then (2) logically compute on the basis of what we have physically observed.

The Eastern traditions, and *mystical* traditions in Islam (Sufism), Christianity, and Judaism (Hasidism) have known better than this. For these traditions teach that a man can be guided by insights that come through his superconscious mind (*buddhi*) from the Spirit. This is the "higher self" (buddhic and atmanic consciousness). Indeed, this is a common belief shared by many classical religions, from shamanism through the ancient sacral traditions of Egypt, Mesopotamia, Iran, Greece, and Rome in the West, to the religions of India and Southeast Asia.

Spiritual insights are thought to come into the minds of human beings from a number of sources outside of the ordinary mundane intellect. It is said that through meditation, prayer, and other consciousness techniques, a person can be in touch with both the physical cosmos and the energy fields around him or her via the subconscious or lower mind (*manas*). One can also become aware of the thoughts and emotions of other people, living or dead, and the thoughts of one's own higher mind (*buddhi*) or "higher self" that might not otherwise be let onto the threshold of consciousness. The latter are intuitions and insights that might otherwise be cut off and suppressed.

Now this ancient model for understanding the levels of mind is one which spiritual people of most traditions have generally accepted in one form or another. Psychic or sensitive persons tend to assume such multidimensional and integrative models of reality. The spiritual person in most religious traditions usually likes to assume that what goes on in the psyche, what goes on in the spiritual side of life, is quite real and not imaginary or arbitrary, and can accomplish its effects directly in the physical and social world as well. As a matter of fact, that is precisely what "being religious" should mean. It is being able to use spiritual and psychic technologies effectively, to be free in a responsible sense from principles of blind, mechanistic stimulus and response, to feel that we are effective, that we count, that what we do in the world is not unimportant simply because we are only one statistic, or one number, among millions of people. In any spiritual world-view we are not helpless cogs in an impersonal, machine-like universe.

To be spiritual means that we think of ourselves (on the level of mind and spirit, at least) as equal participants in a "universal network." We must not feel impotent, i.e., we are not psychically and spiritually powerless, even though we seem to be politically, economically, or socially powerless in a particular society, government, state, community, or family. We will always have access, through spiritual and psychic means, to the unlimited power of God, to universal mind or Spirit, to higher powers, angelic beings, ascended saints (in Western tradition) or ascended-masters and "devas" (in Eastern tradition). Through sharing in the divine life—however differently conceptualized— we are said to have access to a universal level of higher intelligence which we can draw upon within ourselves. In universal spiritual terms we are therefore, potentially at least, effective by virtue of our very constitution as human beings who are, in mythical terms, made in the image of God. We may be spoken of as "gods in the making," or as "vessels filled with the Holy Spirit."

In the same language of ancient sacral, mystical traditions there were also said to be a number of common characteristics by which one could discern or recognize genuine higher types of mystical experience. Indian yogis, Persian magi and Zoroastrian sages, Greek philosophers and Hellenistic Jews, Gnostics and primitive Christians have described with many common words the uniform and universal characteristics of what they would call the "highest state of consciousness."

Some writers on mysticism, in both the medieval and modern periods in the West, have concurred with their judgment. This has led several contemporary scholars (including myself) to try to find evidence for a Primordial Tradition through the study of comparative mystical and psychic experience.

vi. mystical experience and human psychic faculties

The late Dr. Shoneberg Setzer, of the Academy of Religion and Psychical Research, has written a most insightful summary of fifteen apparently constant characteristics of mysticism. He has combined this with a description of the three identifiable, constant stages of mystical development. These universally basic, observable types of mystical experience often cut across both belief systems and ideological linguistic traditions. We include here Setzer's outline from his essay *Making the Mystics Make Sense*:

> "... a mystic is defined as 'one who strives for, and/or has attained, an immediate and unitary contact with things divine, rather than being satisfied with inferred or institutionally mediated knowledge about the divine.' Also 15 apparently constant characteristics of mysticism are noted, namely:
>
> 1. That the mystic believes in the existence of a super-sensory and super-rational ultimate reality,
> 2. Which can be known only by direct personal contact,
> 3. In a manner that constitutes union with that reality,
> 4. And that this union is no mere illusion.
>
> Further, the path toward union is:
> 5. Constituted of active and passive phases,
> 6. Requires a great love and longing for this ultimate reality, and
> 7. A disciplined program of self-purification.

The experience of union produces:
    8. *A view of the harmony of all things within the ultimate reality,*
    9. *A sense of sacredness,*
   10. *A transformation of values,*
   11. *A commitment to sacrificial service, and*
   12. *The release of new energies for living.*

The experience is:
   13. *Transient,*
   14. *Ineffable, and*
   15. *Can be related only in poetry, analogy and paradox.*

The three stages of mystical development were pointed out as well,
      that is:
    1. *Awakening,*
    2. *Purification,*
    3. *Illumination.*[4]

vii. mysticism suggestive of immortality

Dr. Setzer has pointed out that it is erroneous to assume, as both Christian or Jewish theologians and many Hindu, Buddhist and other Eastern religious thinkers in the modern period have done, that true mystical or spiritual experience has nothing to do with psychic phenomena. Setzer lists five basic typologies of mystical experience which have been accepted by the founders of many of the world's religious traditions as related to, or phenomenologically identical with, either their own or other's spiritual awakening to a transcendent and immortal reality upholding all existence. These are:

A. *Pure Consciousness Mysticism.* The experience of a pure, formless "existence, consciousness, and bliss," as in Samadhic or Nirvanic experiences, or in the formless "ecstasy of the Spirit" described by Jewish, Christian and Islamic mystics. (Unfortunately this is the only type of mysticism understood by many modern religious thinkers).

B. *Archetypal Mysticism.* The great symbolic, archetypal visions, apparitions, and dreams, of figures like Ezekiel, St. John on Patmos in the Book of Revelations, or the great myths of Hinduism and Buddhism. (These experiences are certainly not "formless," but they do convey mystical experience of awakening, and ineffable majesty, and can also lead to spiritual transformations.)

C. *Spiritistic Mysticism.* Mystic encounters with spirit entities, believed to be real and not merely symbolic. This includes the Biblical angels, Indian devas, Islamic jin, spirits of deceased Catholic saints, the ancestors in shamanistic cultures, spirit-guides in modern Spiritualist groups, and ascended-masters in mystical or esoteric traditions of Christianity, Hinduism, Buddhism, Judaism, Islam, etc. (In all of these cases a sense of the Divine Presence is mediated to the human subject through the ministry of such spiritual entities, who are believed to share in divinity or immortal qualities, to varying degrees, in a celestial existence).

D. *Clairvoyant Mysticism.* Psychic-mystical experiences, in general, including prophetic visions, apparitions, out-of-the-body experiences, distant-viewing, retrocognitive experiences, near-death experiences, healing miracles, etc., which lead one to a dramatic realization of the transcendent power of mind and spirit, to a higher order of consciousness and, ultimately, to a reality beyond that seen by physical senses or calculable by logic alone.

E. *Nature Mysticism.* Experiences in which contemplation of the natural beauty and wonder of the physical world, or stars, leads poets, artists, or scientists to an inner sense of awe, harmony, and peace, and thence to the conviction that there is an ultimate order of causal reality behind the phenomenal universe which mankind may discover in peak experiences of exalted consciousness.[5]

Of these, types B, C, and D are clearly recognizable as containing the ordinary markings of psychic phenomena. Even A and F, while not involving perhaps the form or characteristics of what we ordinarily call "psychic phenomena," nevertheless directly involve basic transformations of the psyche, and its customary modes of perception and evaluation of reality. In order that meaningful studies in religion and psychical research might take place—studies that are not arbitrarily limited or reductionist—certain unexamined *a prioris* in both Oriental and Occidental philosophical and religious traditions would have to be squarely faced and exposed to the light. The first of these is the tradition that psychic and spiritual experiences are radically distinct, appositive phenomena. This is the often-repeated non-truth that all psychic experience is somehow unimportant or, at worst, an impediment to true spiritual development.

A careful analysis will reveal that, in spite of warnings by Patanjali or

Buddha, and despite the so-called Deuteronomic prohibitions or the denigrations of psychic experiences by many modern religionists, Western mystics and Eastern gurus, "psychic" experience has been the cradle or vehicle out of which many of the central religious insights, revelations, myths, and even ethical reformations of mankind have emerged. Certainly this was so with the experiences of the Biblical patriarchs and prophets, with Abraham, Moses, Jesus, St. Paul, and St. John on Patmos. The human psyche or consciousness is the instrument through which psychospiritual transformations take shape and manifest in this world; therefore, in a very real sense psychic experience is integrally related to spiritual development. Consequently psychical research should be integrally related to the study of the history of religions.

Scholars should not forget that the word "psychic" comes from the Greek word for the "soul" (i.e., *psyche*). Thus there can be no spiritual development without "psychic" (or "soul") development. And one's soul development will certainly involve an inner understanding of the natural faculties of the soul, i.e., its "psychic powers."

The issue should be centered on the type of soul development, or psychic development undertaken; it has never been a real human option to avoid soul or psychic development on the way to spiritual self-realization (Hinduism), liberation (Buddhism), or salvation (Christianity).

The point is that psychic or soul development, including the natural discovery and use of intuitive and psychic powers, must be accompanied by, or the result of, real spiritual and ethical transformation of the whole person (evolved into higher states of being), where higher forms of consciousness, perception and interaction with the world(s) is a natural or appropriate response to humanity's participation in the cosmic evolutionary process.

In the West, we find this model of reality only in the occult literature of the Rosicrucian Manifestos of the 16th-17th centuries, in Mesmerist tradition, in the Modern Spiritualist Movement, in the Theosophy of the 19th century, in Anthroposophy, and in many of the new religions of the 20th century. In the East, however, it has been continuously extant in the teachings of Hindu yogis, Buddhist and Jain monks, and Sufi mystics from earliest times. Today we also encounter it, or traces of it, in the modern West in the speculations of some contemporary researchers in "New Sciences" of consciousness as they have attempted to make sense out of their own empirical findings.

This alternative model of reality presents a challenge to presently established "modern" (19th-century), Western, rationalistic and materialistic forms of science. The latter have all but written off any attempt to reconcile themselves with religion in the universal or generic sense as described earlier in this chapter.

viii.   conclusion: recovering an understanding

Today in Western civilization religion is considered to be quite separate from our technology and our science. We think about religion as something that we must treat subjectively, and that usually means to us that it's all inside of our heads. It is usually thought to be each individual person's own private domain. As a result of this, spiritual things or religious matters are thought by many to be purely arbitrary. Most people today would say that there isn't any objective way to measure the concerns of the psyche. On the other hand, we can pay objective attention, it is thought, to such "sciences" as biology, chemistry, physics, and geology, i.e., to the physical sciences. We think that we can map only quite observable behaviors in modern psychology. These alone are objective factors, many say. We have thus created a radical separation between our science and our religion. We have admitted the reality of natural sciences, life sciences, and social sciences, but unlike the ancient world we do not admit the objective, universal validity of the spiritual sciences, or sciences of the human consciousness and psyche.

The result is that many people approach religion only as an "impractical art" in the modern period. Because of the Primordial world-view which they held, people in the ancient world generally considered that whenever one prayed or when one meditated, or when one sent a thought to someone or something, one could actually somehow affect that person, place, or thing by the prayer or meditation. The ancients thought that one could actually change what would happen to a person by changing his or her "inner spaces." The ancients generally believed that one could operate on "outer space," the physical space around one, by internal psychic technologies. Religious persons still tend to believe this; but modern secular man does not think this way. He has separated his technology and his science from whatever goes on inside of his own mind, consciousness or spirit. And many of us are rather schizophrenically divided between being religious and secular personalities as a result.

It is understood that if one is a complete Materialist, or a complete Rationalist, one doesn't believe in any of the spiritual-psychic faculties. Such a person believes with the modern materialistic-rationalistic position that only what can be physically seen and logically computed is real and that everything else is not. *One cannot be a "religious" or "spiritual" person in the classical sense and at the same time deny the existence of subtle faculties of spiritual and psychic perception.*

In modern times, "technologies" are said to be executed only with physical means in order to accomplish something "objective" in the world, with the body. In the ancient world there were thought to be "technologies" not only of the body, but also of the psyche (of mind and spirit). It was natural for people in ancient traditions, for example, to take seriously the effects of meditation in the control and navigation of inner spaces, and to take seriously the objective effects of the psyche on other persons, places and things through prayer and psychic projections. Psychic communications between man and man, between animals and plants—intuitions, feelings, and energy-field projections and penetrations—were taken for granted as axiomatic.

At the same time, historical research has also begun to uncover these same themes in the primitive psychic and social solidarity conceptions of the ancient Near East and the Bible. Thus a convergence has begun between similar themes in ancient metaphysical traditions and modern scientific discoveries. Today, some pioneer scientists, discontented with the lack of answers to the great questions of life, death, and human existence, have begun to uncover new data in unorthodox areas of research in parapsychology, paraphysics, and consciousness etiologies which, they claim, resembles some of the major themes found in mankind's most ancient religious beliefs.

Is it possible, indeed, for us to say that a few modern scientists—in the guise of parapsychologists, paraphysicists, consciousness specialists, life-energies researchers, clinical psychiatrists, psychologists and others—have come up with new ideas as a result of their research, observations, and experiences which resemble the ancient conceptions of the Primordial Tradition.

A. Psychic experience is not irrelevant to true spiritual development.
The greatest challenge to the survival of human belief in a transcendent order behind, in or under the phenomenal world today is the

world-view shaped by three or more centuries of rationalistic, reductionistic materialism. Spiritually aware persons do have one, and perhaps only one, hope to turn back its otherwise inevitable tide. The hope is that some scientists and some religionists will once again turn their attention to the study and cultivation of those higher forms of consciousness and experience, including psychic-spiritual experiences, through which the whisperings of immortality and resurrection (and the existence of higher worlds of Spirit and space, and the goal of a "new heaven and a new earth") can be brought back into humanity's line of vision and hearing.

Unfortunately, neither the majority of scientists nor of theologians as yet see the relevance of the New Sciences to their views of man, nature, or reality. Many religionists have never known or have forgotten that mystical or spiritual experience takes many forms and shapes, all of which involve the psyche or soul, and hence the mediation of the natural psychic or soul powers and experiences.

There are at least the following five types of mysticism: (1) "pure consciousness" or "formless" mysticism; (2) "archetypal" or "symbolic" mysticism; (3) "clairvoyant" or "psychic" mysticism; (4) "spiritistic" mysticism; (5) "nature" mysticism, or "scientific" mysticism.

At least three of the above types of mystical experience ("archetypal," "spiritistic," and "clairvoyant") would presuppose the reality of, and involve the operation of, awakened human psychic faculties as the normative modes or instruments of revelation.

It is obvious that, in fact, the normative modes of revelation in the world's major religious traditions—from shamanism to the Bible, the Koran and the Asian holy books—have included "archetypical," "spiritistic," and "clairvoyant" psychic experience at their roots. It has been a frequent academic error by Eastern and Western writers alike to assume that "pure consciousness" mysticism is the only variety of such experience worthy of the "higher" and more "advanced" religions. Many Eastern religionists, Hindu, Buddhist, et. al., and Western religionists—especially Roman Catholic scholars taking St. John of the Cross out of his late medieval reformist context, and various "dispensationalist" Protestants—have persistently done so. The fact is that "archetypical," "spiritistic," and "clairvoyant" types of psychic-mysticism constitute the largest part of the psychospiritual roots and classical religious imagery of Christian myth, symbol and history.

One form of the Primordial Tradition of psychic and mystical insight that has re-emerged in our century is the "perennial philosophy" of Aldous Huxley. Such a tradition had surfaced much earlier in the esoteric and occult traditions of the Middle Ages, the Renaissance, and the Enlightenment. "Ritual magic," "alchemy," occult metaphysical systems, and other alternative reality traditions found in the 18th-19th century and North America represented the fragments of a far greater, unified, occult theory of life and nature. This had embraced the meaning of God, gods, angels, devas, spirits, elementals, devils, man, and the animal and plant kingdoms on this planet, in the other planetary systems, in the stars and galaxies, and throughout the cosmos.

B. *Religious and scientific paradigms cognizant of psyche and spirit are a prerequisite to authentic religion and science and to peace.* The many and varied types of Eastern and Western religious traditions are themselves confused and radically divided over the role of psychical and mystical phenomena in human religious and cultural experience. Thus, it is not only modern scientists who dispute the reality of these faculties from their own rationalistic, reductionistic, and materialistic left-brain consciousness; it is also modern "exoteric" theologians and church administrators, priests, rabbis and ministers in the West, and Hindu swamis and Buddhist monks who are equally left-brained or rationalistic, and who have never known the psychic and mystical experiences of the founders and saints of their own traditions. They have consequently not understood the *original contexts* of their founders' various "warnings against" the pursuit of psychic powers (for egoic or selfish motivations), and have often issued blanket condemnations of all "psychic" powers as either evil or irrelevant obstacles to be avoided by their disciples.

Nevertheless, for my own part, I would like to suggest that the psychology of human perception as understood in the ancient *esoteric* systems of the Asian yogas, in Neoplatonism, and in other and Western occult systems of "high magic" or "theurgy" may in fact be the presently missing key to the future of para-psychology, to the future of religious studies, and to the future of science itself. These esoteric systems not only understood the psychic faculties but also prescribed the self-regulation of the observer-participants' human consciousness itself, as well as the learning of the skillful use of intuition.

Such esoteric psychic-and-spiritual traditions in both East and West may also be the key to the development of the new holistic sciences, and the new psychospiritual and psychophysical technologies of tomorrow. With this in mind, some contemporary scholars and scientists of East and West, beginning with Carl Jung and contemporary transpersonal psychologists, have taken an interest in the study of ancient esoteric systems and their understanding of the various sheaths or "energy bodies" of man, and of human psychic faculties in general. Some physicists and biologists have also become involved in this pursuit.

Through my own rather "psychospiritual-evolutionist" and Teilhardian or Aurobindian perspectives—and in light of contemporary insights from emerging future sciences of parapsychology, paraphysics, and consciousness studies—I have concluded that research in psychic phenomena, and in the forms of human psychospiritual awareness and psychophysical integration known in ancient esoteric religious systems, and in Oriental yogas, should be central to comparative religious studies as well as to the life-sciences of the future. The reconciliation of emerging new sciences with an understanding of the hidden potentials of the human psyche and higher human spirituality is essential to peace in the global village in the years ahead.

Chapter 3

A Crisis of Faith in the Modern Flock:
the primordial flame that went out

i. the crisis of faith in western civilization

There is at present a crisis of faith in Western civilization concerning the reality of the supernatural and those tenets of the traditional faith which rest upon it. An exposure to genuine experiences of psychic and spirit phenomena today—and the study of the laws by which they operate—could save theologians and laity alike from a loss of traditional faith in the "supernatural" or "supernormal" elements in their own traditions.

In 1980, a poll in Holland among Dutch Catholics revealed that over 60 percent of those registered on the census rolls as "faithful Roman Catholics" did not believe in, or were unsure about, the cardinal Christian affirmation and dogma of life after death. They questioned the personal survival of the individual human soul, or consciousness, after the physiological death of the body.[1] The interesting point in this study from our perspective is that many of these persons are still "practicing Catholics" in some sense, and would profess "belief in God." However, with regard to such "belief," many of them would be quite non-traditional in their understanding of what that commitment means in itself.

The report indicated, for example, that many of the Catholics polled did not conceive of God in personal terms at all, and usually had difficulty understanding what the "divinity of Christ" might mean. The basic obstacle to belief in or understanding of this central Christian affirmation could be attributed, it was said, to a failure of the general credibility of the "supernaturalistic conceptions" and the "miracle stories" upon which the traditional categories of the Christian faith rests.

Even more significant findings from the standpoint of our study

51

emerged from a nationwide poll in Canada conducted during the same year by a sociologist at the University of Lethbridge in Alberta.[2] This poll indicated that only 28 percent of Canada's nominal Christians are regular churchgoers and, more significantly, of this 28 percent only approximately 55 percent still believe in the "supernatural" dimensions of their faith in such traditional doctrines as the divinity of Christ, life after death, and other cardinal dogmas.

Yet, in spite of the decline in belief in the "supernatural" among traditionalist church men and women, belief in the supernatural is by no means dead in Canada. To the contrary, the Lethbridge survey when combined with other indicators suggest that such beliefs are moving outside of the traditional churches. Twenty-two percent of all Canadians are *sure* that ESP powers exist; and an additional 47 percent believe that they exist. Forty-four percent of the Canadians who would categorize themselves as "very religious" believe that communication with the dead is possible. But of those who categorize themselves as "somewhat religious," 42 percent say that they also believe that communication with the dead is possible, as do 36 percent of those who claim to be "not very religious." But most believe that "science" and not organized religion is the place to seek future answers to these mysteries.

This is doubly ironic, since most members of the "scientific establishment" in Canada and North America are at present either actively skeptical or otherwise disinterested in the relevance of parapsychology to their domain, or to any other domain, including religion. And most of the contemporary "religious establishment" is still theologically oblivious to the relevance of living psychic phenomena or of human psychic faculties to the experience of its own founders.

In view of the crisis of faith currently being confronted by Jews and Christians in Europe and the Americas, it is time that the mainline churches and synagogues, and the theologians of Judaism and Christianity, paid serious and open-minded attention to the scientific study of parapsychology, in transcultural terms, for its possible relevance to Jewish and Christian theology, liturgy, life, and experiences of prayer and meditation.

Reginald Bibby, the University of Lethbridge sociologist cited above, reported that 60 percent of Canadians spoke positively of the "primal experiences" (including psychic experiences) which they said they had. Bibby correctly commented that such statistics reveal a "pool of religiosity in contemporary secular society which is untapped by the established religions. But one might observe that this "pool of religiosity" *is* being tapped by many new religions and quasi-religious movements.

Since primary psychic experiences are among the chief catalysts for the "awakening" state of mystical or spiritual life in most of the world's religious traditions (see Setzer above), it would seem that the established Christian denominations today are depriving themselves of a major source of converts by ignoring this pool of contemporary psychic experience so widespread in Western societies today. Yet in order to recognize the significance of such primal experiences, it would be necessary for the modern Christian churches to have another look at their own religious history, and learn to identify the nature and role of similar experiences in the lives of the Founders, e.g. patriarchs, prophets, Christ, apostles, martyrs, and saints. And until the kind of non-reductionist or non-abstract theologies which can accomplish this task are adopted, there can be no recovery of the Primordial Tradition of intuition and insight which originally gave birth to the now-lost esoteric Christianity with which we are concerned.

"Revelations" (general and personal), "healings" (natural and/or supernatural), and all other manner of "miracles" may only happen if "the world is made that way." And if "the world *is* made that way," then both new forms of science, as well as ancient forms of philosophy, might legitimately study God, angels, spirits, and men.

Furthermore there is real evidence, intrinsic to the texts of both Old and New Testaments, that the foundations of Judaism and primitive Christianity were laid within the context of such an understanding. Unlike most modern Christians, Jewish Essenes, Hasidists, and Kabalists, as well as the writers and editors of the New Testament and the father of the pre-Nicean Church certainly were well aware of the need to keep their "scientific" and philosophical understanding of the metaphysical laws of the universe in line with their understanding of religious experience and of how the latter could verify the former.

To see this point, one need only consider the Christian Gospel, with all of its very "occult" and "esoteric" claims to a special "gnosis" concerning the *modus operandi* of the "Kingdom of God," in the midst of the physical, historical, and social world. Human experience of "heaven worlds," apparitions of angels, visions, special revelations, healing miracles, etc. were indeed possible because the real world was "made that way."

Unfortunately, many modern, traditionalist Christians in their naiveté would object to the suggestion that the study of these phenomena in a secular and/or non-Christian context could help the "case for God." But there surely is much more to authentic spirituality than the question of whether or not positive psychic and spiritual experiences are possible in non-Christian, or "unorthodox," contexts.

Findings from psychic research could help achieve a better understanding of the specific phenomena and language of the Bible and the roots of the Christian tradition. However, there is a hardening of attitudes among traditional Christian theologians which could prevent a clear view of the relevance of the psi factor to religion. Such issues must be addressed and clarified before the establishment of a "parapsychology of religion" in Christian theological circles is possible.

ii.   the modern church's attitude to psychic phenomena

In covering the story of the visit of Pope John Paul II to Africa in May of 1980, an article in *Time* magazine described what it called " . . . the deepest challenge to the future of Christianity in Africa" as "ritual backsliding into primitive tribal practices." The author of the article was concerned that the underlying African folk traditions of psychic and spirit experience were not being sufficiently excluded from Christian practice in the thousands of new African independent churches:

> "Along with wild and colorful services, they usually emphasize healings and personalized visions and prophecies . . . putting the merest Christian overlay upon witchcraft, sorcery, and ancestor worship."[4]

In Africa and throughout the Third World many individuals are converted to cults through their own primary experiences. S. G. Lee reports that before joining such cults among the Zulu in South Africa, for example, most individuals reported "numerous visual and auditory hallucinations, dreaming, and so on"; and many reported healings which they attributed to the Gods or medicine men, or to the magical techniques of the cult.[5] Although the primitive Christian church abounded with similar tales leading to conversion from paganism to Christ, modern established churches, including the Roman Catholic, have absolutely no ministry, or psi-cognizant theologies, which would allow them to compete with such cults today, whether in Africa, Europe, or America.

It is not only in Africa and the Third World that the Christian churches are confronting a challenge from paranormal phenomena and a widespread interest in psychic and spirit experience among the public. The so-called "Occult Revival" of the 1970s and the rise in the popularity of new religions and cults in North America have given ample witness to this fact.[6] Rather than lamenting this widespread sociological and cultural fact, Christians have good reason to rejoice over it. The lockstep of materialism and rationalism has created a despairing, pragmatic, de facto atheism all over the world.

Reversions to an earlier cosmology full of open-ended mystery would enshrine the belief that the individual is more than a helpless pawn in a vast, impersonal universe. Such cosmologies possess certain nearly forgotten elements of truth about the "energetic basis of matter," indeed of the psychoenergetic nature of the whole universe itself, and promote an intrinsic relationship which modern Western culture has forgotten between mind and body, spirit and nature, and the sacred and the profane. In modern parapsychology laboratories, there appears to be such a thing as "real magic" in the form of verifiable psychic technology—ESP, PK, healing, and spirit phenomena— as J. B. Rhine showed. This could go a long way toward helping us to understand the natural basis of the universal religious practices of prayer and sacrament in both ancient "religious" and contemporary "scientific" terms.

Yet today, in traditional "religious" and "scientific" contexts, even the so-called "faithful" are often conditioned by secular, rationalistic and materialistic thinking to assume that such things are simply impossible, and that the Christian faith must be "translated into a modern terminology" which allows only for the reality of cultural and socio-ethical factors in the Judeo-Christian tradition. This often does not allow for the survival of the primary psi experiences (or for any ontological and metaphysical conclusions to be derived from them, whether by "savages" or by Christianity's Founders).

The experience of authentic psychic and spirit phenomena today could demonstrate that many of the same kinds of "miracles" claimed by the patriarchs and prophets of Israel, by Jesus and the apostles, and by the greatest saints and mystics throughout the history of the Church still indeed occur.

iii. the implicit cosmology of psychic and mystical experience: its importance for maintaining a view of transcendence

Certain psychic and spirit phenomena, such as those found in ancient times in prophetic Judaism and in New Testament Christianity, could demonstrate once again the "transcendent" elements in religion. These might provide an explanation for the ancient belief in an active initiative from "heaven worlds," or in the daily interventions of God, angels, saints, ascended masters, devas, mahasiddahas, or bodhisattvas, and other guiding forces from higher dimensions of reality in the ordinary affairs of mankind.

Even most conceptions of psychic and spirit phenomena rest upon a cosmology or world-view which is implicitly different from that of modern Western science and the secular civilization that has been built upon it. The world-view represented by most contemporary psychic and spirit experience is, in fact, of a piece with the various primitive shamanistic, miraculous, and magical traditions of so-called "pre-scientific" cultures. Together, the insights claimed by persons of all times through psychic and spirit experience comprise a veritable Primordial Tradition of living intuition. It was, contrary to the claims of modern doctrinalists in both science and religion, such a Primordial Tradition of timeless spiritual and psychic intuition that formed the universally recognizable foundation, or "rock of ages," of authentic faith-and-knowledge ("gnosis") upon which both the Biblical experience and the primitive Christian Church were built.

It is for this reason that particular types of psychic and spirit experience have been selected for study and review. These materials have hopefully shed light on the origins of many of the ancient conceptions of the Christ as the fulfillment of both the mystical Jewish and ancient pagan archetypes of the god-man, and the origin of the church or universal company of all human beings "awakened" or "reborn" as the mystical, or psychic-and-spiritual "body of Christ," or the "New Israel."

The code-words "Christ" and "Church," or "Israel," were at first used by Gospel writers and by St. Paul to refer to universal spiritual realities that did not belong to any particular religious establishment. "He has broken down the middle-wall of partition separating Jew and Gentile," declared the convert Paul. The present series of books will hopefully shed new light on a primitive view of the Church and sacraments as psychic and spiritual extensions of what was perceived to be the pre-existent Christ's Presence among all of God's people in every age. It is my conviction, after much study, that both "Church" and "sacraments" originally incorporated Primordial technologies of the mind and spirit of humankind, much akin to the traditions of shamanism, theurgy and alchemy, or "high magick," for achieving psychic and spiritual solidarity with the archetypical God-Man, who represents the dormant "High-Self," or "Imago Dei," in "Everyman."

The study of such things could help to illuminate and revitalize such universal religious beliefs as the efficacy of prayer and spiritual healing, as well as such cardinal affirmations of both Christianity and other religions as the immortality of the human soul, the intercession of the saints, and/or the active intervention of the "spirits of the souls made righteous" from the "heavenly places," in the affairs of contemporary men and women.

A study of modern forms of psychic experience is available to intellectually honest scholars who seek it through popular psychic development programs and in psychic and mystical groups within Western esoteric traditions. An exposure to the genuine phenomena of the Modern Spiritualist Movement is possible as well. This could be employed in the revitalization of the classical doctrine of the survival of bodily death and even the theistic affirmation of the existence of real "supernatural dimensions," and of the "living Power of God." A general acceptance of such an affirmation would indeed effect urgently needed changes in the present forms of organization of our physical and social worlds. At the root of this acceptance lies recognition of Jesus' own yogic-like or Eastern mystical teaching concerning the possibility of the discovery and awakening of the "Kingdom of God" within the inner recesses of the consciousness of everyone—or at least everyone who is open to the process.

What emerges from this study is that the ancient religious worldview or cosmology, upon which primitive Christianity and the earliest pre-Constantinian "Catholic faith" rests, finds corroboration in the personal experience of genuine psychic and spirit phenomena in many religions, East and West, old and new, today. Such experience could serve as a powerful antidote to the corrosive and debilitating attacks of the secular "Enlightenment" philosophy which, after two hundred years, has all but destroyed the "inner faith" of the traditional Christian churches in Western Europe and in other parts of the modern world. A new exploration of the alternative forms of human consciousness known from contemporary psychic experience might assist in the rehabilitation of the adherents of Christianity and other world religions who have been undergoing a crisis of faith in their attempts to remain loyal to their ancient traditions after rediscovering the transcendent in the midst of our era of modernization and secularization.

It is my conclusion from these studies that Christian theologians must once again learn to grasp through personal experiences of psyche and spirit the presently "missing link" in Western culture: that psychic dimension to which much so-called God-talk refers. Until they and the clergy they train do so, the traditional churches and synagogues will not be able to enter once again into the full comprehension of the Biblical message.

In this volume the reader will find a new/old approach to the Christian archetype of the god-man, to the "Catholic" doctrine of the Church as the "mystical body," and to the sacraments as psychic and spiritual "extensions" or vehicles of the personality and life of the historical Jesus as Christ. This approach is really very ancient, but it is also new because it is conducted in the light of data from psychical research and contemporary studies in consciousness.

It is to the whole realm of psychic and spirit phenomena— "consciousness studies"—and to the exploration of parapsychology, paraphysics, and studies in psi-based mystical experience that theologians might now turn. It is essential for them to reground presentations of the Bible, of ancient Judaism, of the Christian Gospel, and of the authentic faith of the Church in universal, psychically and mystically based terms. Such terms must be meaningful and self-evident to contemporary persons, and at the same time do justice to the ageless wisdom in the often "unorthodox" or "pagan" forms which embody it in today's global village.

Many persons are, in fact, already on a psychic and spiritual quest for transcendence outside of the Judeo-Christian tradition or any other traditional religious framework. It is among such persons, and especially among newer religious and spiritual groups, that the rediscovery of the Primordial Tradition of psychic intuition and spiritual insight has already begun.

iv. the rationalist's argument

Yet many secular scholars, themselves strangers to psi phenomena, who are studying religion today would still say that all mystical experience is merely culturally conditioned behavior. Some think that it is simply due to expectations and perspectives that are unconsciously conditioned into an individual, who then produces, as delusions or projections, his or her own mystical experiences. Such scholars would often argue that mystical experiences or psi phenomena cannot possibly be the points of origin for the valid religious beliefs that mold civilizations.

But, if that is so, why do people in India who are raised as Hindus, people in New York who are raised as Catholics, Protestants, Jews or agnostics, people in the Middle East who are Moslems, people in Southeast Asia who are Buddhists, etc., all experience basically the same mystical and psychical phenomena without ever having read any of the literature on such things as "near-death experience," "out-of-the-body experience," or mediumship, and the like? And how are some places on this planet to which they have not been familiar to them, solely as a result of psi experiences such as "out-of-the-body" projections, "distant viewing," or "traveling clairvoyance"? How do healers in widely separated cultures all report essentially the same phenomena of healings?

v. historical evidence for immortality

There is ample evidence for those familiar with spontaneous psychic and spiritistic experiences that claims to extraordinary or "paranormal" psychic and spirit phenomena, which are encountered in various forms of mystical-cum-psychic "disclosure situations," have in fact formed the basis for those human belief-systems which have postulated mankind's noblest ideas of transcendence and immortality. Varieties of such mystical-cum-psychic disclosure situations are found in the religious literature of the East and West in both ancient and modern times. Of course, it is usually not even suspected by those scholars who are unfamiliar with psychic and spirit phenomena that such experiences could explain the origins of human belief in life-after-death or of traditional conceptions of after-death states.

Nevertheless, a historian of religions, Mircea Eliade of the University of Chicago, has taken note of the continuity and persistence of claims to all forms of the paranormal in human religious experience from ancient to modern times.[7] He has stated that there is no more important issue confronting his discipline today than the question of the "reality" of such phenomena. He has cited the Italian ethnologist Ernesto de Martino to suggest that there may indeed be a factual parapsychological or psi component in such claims which might now be investigated and discovered by those qualified to do so.[8]

Another religion scholar, Huston Smith, has more recently mapped the central place which belief in the psychic dimension played in the ancient Oriental cosmologies underlying most classical religious conceptions of the sacred.[9] But I myself am probably the first member of a university department of religious studies in North America or Europe to have attempted to reconstruct the role that primary psychic and spiritistic experiences appear to have played in the development of the Western religious tradition.[10]

vi.   academic problems in studying forms of mystical experience and conceptions of immortality

Most contemporary academics who are involved in religious studies, theology, philosophy, anthropology, psychology and/or other social sciences and humanities have not yet attempted to deal seriously with the paranormal element in human religious experience, from the vantage point which is available to them from consciousness studies and psychical research. This is certainly unfortunate. From a phenomenological point of view, the common thread of theurgic, mystical, and shamanistic fiber is woven so tightly into the fabric of our human spiritual traditions all over the globe that it is virtually impossible to realistically separate so-called mythic materials from their possible real psychic content, or from later interpretive philosophical or theological traditions concerning them. Transcendence, immortality, meaningful experiences suggestive of a life after death, and credible maps of an after-life are often lost in a confusing welter of mythological, philosophical, and theological interpretive traditions.

The imagery of such shamanistic or spiritistic, "real magic" or psychic, and archetypical mystical experiences, like the imagery of religious myths and of our dreams, is so bizarre by modern secular standards that it is difficult, if not impossible, for many people today (including scholars and theologians), conditioned as they are by contemporary investigative methods, to relate to them. The result is that we have found ourselves, at least since the Age of Reason and Enlightenment, astride a tremendous, ever-widening gulf between our religious and our scientific traditions concerning the basic issues of life and death, and the possibilities of an after-life. Such possibilities of an after-life are often embarrassing to our sciences, including our medical sciences, our social sciences and even our modern philosophies, because we do not have the imaginative paradigms or psi-cognizant methodologies required either to deal with such issues or with the study of human psychic and mystical experiences in general.

Modern scholars are most uncomfortable with precisely these kinds of experiences, while our main spiritual traditions have often, originally at least, been founded upon them. Our most ancient, sacred traditions have consistently formulated human hopes for transcendence and immortality by employing language whose psychic and/or spiritistic experiential referents are simply unknown to most academics, including both historians of religion and theologians.

vii.   a common phenomenology of mystical experience

Christians, Jews, Buddhists, Moslems, Hindus, agnostics, atheists and everyone else have "out-of-the-body experiences," "near-death experiences," unsolicited impressions of post-mortem contacts with the dead, precognitive dreams, ESP, PK experiences, visions, apparitions, etc. And all people react basically the same way to these common experiences, which are contrary to their previous belief systems. Their whole outlook on life, and their value systems, are often changed as a result of these universal experiences. Psi experiences are suggestive of a transcendent order, of man as a multidimensional being; and their potential as catalysts to "religious conversion" of one kind or another is a constant in all cultures.

It is only the saints and mystics of the world's religions, East and West, and those who have discovered an authentic spiritual path through personal psychic and spiritual awakening and awareness, who claim that there are indeed universal metaphysical, ethical, and spiritual truths and realities which remain constant across all ideological and intellectual or religious traditions, and that these truths and realities can be rediscovered through a higher mode of functioning of the human consciousness. They would say that it is only by a combination of hard work, self-purification, denial of the inauthentic claims of the ego, plus divine grace in one form or another that one can proceed to develop such a higher consciousness, regardless of one's sectarian labels, or the particular mythological or symbolic language of one's tradition. And the "fruits of the Spirit" remain the same for mystics and saints of all traditions: love, joy, peace, forgiveness, service, and a positive reliance on transcendent sources of strength with a corresponding sense of detachment from worldly criteria of worth or pride.

Thus there is one area in which we find a common phenomenology of meaningful subjective experiences with a more or less constant range of effects on the persons who have those experiences. This is the area of "mystical" experience. Contrary to the rationalist's opinion that mystical experience is merely conditioned by traditionally developed religious beliefs, there are certain constant characteristics of mysticism that unite persons in all religious traditions.

And like psychic experiences, mystical experiences characteristically occur in altered states of consciousness, suggest a transcendent order and/or the multidimensional nature of man, and leave people's perspectives, world views, and value orientations changed. Both psychic and mystical experiences and their effects suggest that there is a constant "higher order," a "substratum," "above," "in," or "under" the human psyche, and that universal principles and forms governing its operation exist which are beyond the conditioned cultural and linguistic traditions. This of course is exactly what most of the major religious traditions of the world have contended, precisely on the basis of such experiences on the part of their founders.

viii. *customary* a priori *assumptions in the modern scientific paradigm*

By contrast I do not need to remind you of the kind of assumption that, at its most reductionistic moments, the modern scientific paradigm has often been thought to contain since the Age of Reason and Enlightenment. Willis W. Harmon of Stanford University, in his *Incomplete Guide to the Future*, has listed ten of these common postulates of the modern scientific paradigm.[11] I need only paraphrase five of them in order to make my point. These are common beliefs that are often assumed as the basis for the world-view that we use, or have used, during the past two or three centuries, when studying the natural world.

A. Consciousness is nothing more than a by-product of physical and biochemical processes going on in the brain. Not all scientists have said that, but a basic, frequent assumption is that if something isn't physically based, it isn't real.

B. Man can acquire knowledge only through his physical senses, or perhaps through a kind of memory storage in the genes.

C. The concept of a free, inner person is a pre-scientific explanation for behavior which is really determined by external environmental forces and internal organic reactions.

D. Mental activity, as mere fluctuations in the brain, and as internal to the physical organism, cannot possibly affect the properties of matter in the external environment, or directly influence the outcome of events. (By contrast, for example, religious people usually believe that real changes can be brought about through hopes, attitudes and prayers.)

E. The individual cannot conceivably survive the bodily death of the biological organism, since the latter is the basis for all formal identity, consciousness, and thought activity.

Since the 19th century it has not only been the more narrowly defined frontier discipline of "parapsychology" which has been slighted and denigrated by those scientists and philosophers biased by these particular *a priori* assumptions. It has also been very difficult to obtain a fair and balanced study of the whole gamut of human spiritual, mystical and intuitive experiences within mankind's religious history. In spite of their strategic importance for the history of religions, we have had until very recently no serious, multi-disciplinary examinations of these human psychospiritual experiences which attempt to shed light upon any possible psi components in them, or upon their often important ethical and socio-political effects.

Willis Harmon observes:

"Research into consciousness and psychic phenomena is such a bitterly contested battleground because the data in these areas challenges all of the above premises. Yet it was on the basis of these above premises that

> the increasingly prestigious, scientific world-view has been able in the
> past to dismiss as of secondary consequence the entire religious, aesthetic,
> and intuitive experiences of mankind and hence to discredit the value sys-
> tems based upon these subjective experiences."[12]

ix. modern heresies in religion: (1) "dispensationalism," (2) "institutionalism," (3) "demythologism"

Just as many modern scientists have had difficulty accepting the reality, validity, and relevance of psi phenomena due to the prevalent, *a priori* assumptions of secular rationalism and reductionism, so have many modern theologians, affected by fundamentalist, institutionalist, or liberal *a priori* viewpoints, had difficulties of their own, stemming from many years of hardened attitudes. Three of the most commonly held positions which act as obstacles to understanding the role which parapsychology could play in the recovery of the shamanistic and theurgical roots of the Judeo-Christian tradition in Hellenistic Judaism, in the New Testament and in the primitive Church today are "Dispensationalism," "Institutionalism," and "Demythologism."

1. "Dispensationalism" is a particularly fundamentalist conception used in the 16th century by Calvin, Luther, and other reformers. They assumed—in their fight against the concepts of an ongoing, authoritative Catholic tradition—that the "miracles" of the Old Testament prophets and of Jesus and the apostles in the New Testament were once and for all unique occurrences, or special "dispensations," which stopped with the writing of the last book of the New Testament. Dispensationalism is also popular among orthodox Jewish rabbis, who often teach the same concept but would end "miracles" somewhat earlier, i.e., with the last book of the Old Testament, Malachi, at about 400 B.C.

A "rabbinic council," convened at Jamnia in Asia Minor during the last decade of the 1st century A.D. declared the process of divine revelation through the prophets to have terminated with Malachi, in the 4th century B.C. This was probably done in response to the attempts of Jesus' disciples to ground their claims for his divinity in such scripture as the apocryphal books of Enoch and Daniel, in which the "Son of Man" is portrayed as a god-man, and the mysterious archetype of the divinely restored human nature. History was to repeat itself when the Church Fathers were to "close" the canonical New Testament scriptures within three centuries or less after Jamnia.

In modern Jewish and Christian forms of "Dispensationalism" there are several underlying modern assumptions that were unknown in the ancient world, either to the patriarchs, prophets, or to Jesus, and to his original disciples. These assumptions are:

> (a) That "miracles" are contrary to a "natural law" which is fixed and immutable for all men, but that God had "dispensed" the chosen "people of God," and Jesus and His apostles, from these "natural laws" in order to put His stamp of divine approval on their teachings and deeds in front of selected witnesses. Such an idea of "natural law"—limited as it is to materialistic and rationalistic criteria—could, in fact, not have existed in its present form among Jews or Christians until after the humanist Renaissance and the Enlightenment. Therefore, I have called this a "modern heresy."

> (b) That there are no such things as "natural psychic" or "natural spiritual" powers for ordinary persons, and

> (c) That wherever "paranormal" phenomena of any kind occur outside of the Bible, we can immediately assume that "Satan," the "Devil," or other "supernatural forces" inimical to God are operating.

The fact is, however, that as any competent historical review will illustrate: (1) extraordinary natural psychic and spiritual phenomena have occurred throughout history among all peoples, in all religions and cultures, and (2) these phenomena are neither good nor bad, per se, unless and until they are used by men (or angels) for divine purposes, in the fulfillment of God's will, or conversely, for negative purposes.

2. The second heresy which has become widespread among many Roman Catholic, Eastern Orthodox, Anglican, and Protestant churchmen, who are often not Fundamentalists, is "Institutionalism" or "Churchianity." This conception is often used by churchmen who do accept that "miracles" occur or have occurred since the time of the New Testament and the primitive Church. But in order to avoid accepting the idea that God, or "nature," would initiate such "miracles" among people "outside of the Church," Institutionalists have invented

the idea that true miracles, or "God-given" ones, are only allowed by God in order to seal, reinforce, or instill belief in the teachings of the Church or in presently "Christian" groups. This usually means some form of so-called "Catholic" or "orthodox" Protestant dogma or doctrine in its commonly accepted form.

The heresy of Institutionalism assumes that God *is* a respecter of persons, as it were, who bends otherwise inflexible "natural laws" for the sake of the faithful only. Institutionalism, like Dispensationalism, thus also assumes that natural psychic faculties do not exist, or that if they do, they have nothing to to do with "Revelation," which is an exclusively "orthodox" affair.

Institutionalists will therefore sometimes concede that parapsychology might be a secular science, but that it has nothing to do with religion. For in true religion, which is some form of "orthodox" institutional Christianity only, God reveals Himself through selected, rare, paranormal occurrences for specific, (later-to-be) canonically approved purposes.

3. "Demythologism" is the third and perhaps most formidable obstacle standing in the way of an appreciation of the functions of the parapsychology of religion today among mainline churchmen in so-called liberal theological traditions. "Demythologization" may be quite legitimate and necessary as a method for dealing with those portions of scripture or tradition which were either (1) not written in the first place to be taken literally, or (2) written to be taken literally but also to contain a transcendent meaning, a divine truth, wrapped, as it were, in a historical event. But the modern heresy of Demythologism is something rather distinct from this legitimate use of demythologization. It is the use of demythologization techniques where they are inappropriate, i.e. in the removal of contemporary belief in the "real miracles" of natural, universally possible psychic and spirit phenomena, that rationalistic and materialistic scholars neither understand nor accept.

The heresy of "Demythologism" is peculiar to some modern liberal theologians who have accepted, either consciously or unconsciously, the whole secular, Enlightenment world-view in which "miracles," especially "nature miracles" like those in the Bible, simply do *not* occur, whether in ancient or modern times. Such theologians think that they are performing a valuable task by "rescuing" the kernel of philosophical or ethical truth from the Gospels by making it possible to reject the veridical content of such things as dreams, visions, apparitions of angels, saints, or spirits, miraculous healings, resurrections and reappearances of the dead to the living, supernormal powers of mind or of spirit over matter, etc., from the Biblical and ecclesiastical traditions.

Unfortunately, such rejections leave little hope for the Christian, who is then sealed in by the fixed, mechanistic universe of "modern science" once again. The omnipotence of God and His sovereignty within nature is forfeited. We are left with a new, heretical form of Christianity which has nothing much to do either with the Bible, the Primordial Tradition, or with those recent insights from the frontiers of scientific research in human consciousness, parapsychology, or paraphysics.

These three widespread modern heresies, Dispensationalism, Institutionalism, or Demythologism, differ sharply from the original form of primitive "Orthodox-Catholic" Christian Paradosis, which once rested upon a Primordial Tradition of natural spiritual intuition and psychic insight which was widespread throughout the ancient world. "Revelation" was, in this ancient perspective, not to be contrasted to "Nature," or to "natural vehicles" of human perception and communication, whether psychic or physical. *All* of the channels of human communication, i.e., ordinary sense perception *or* ESP and PK, could be used by God, angels, spirits, or men to reveal themselves to one another in a living psychodynamic universe.

In fairness, it must be observed (1) that not all Fundamentalists today are Dispensationalists in the pejorative sense described here, (2) not all ecclesiastically concerned Catholic or Protestant churchmen are Institutionalists, and (3), not all liberal Christians are guilty of what I have called the heresy of Demythologism. I have merely made the point that these three distorted positions are wide-spread today, and that they do prevent the admission of the relevance of psychic faculties and psi phenomena to religion in many theological quarters.

x.   earlier predecessors of modern fundamentalists or institutionalists: scribes, pharisees, and certain church fathers

From the standpoint of the phenomenology of religion, a persistent habit of Jewish and Christian polemicists, whether in the Rabbinic or Patristic traditions, has been to try to isolate Moses and the Israelite prophets, or Jesus, from the universal psychospiritual experience of mankind that I have referred to as the Primordial Tradition. In their zeal to show the superiority and uniqueness of Biblical figures, they have often resorted to condemnation of all holy men, prophets, magicians, god-men, etc., of other traditions as either frauds or diabolical imitations. Such a biased ethnocentricity fails to grasp the simple fact that universal spiritual, metaphysical, and psychic laws might exist, and that "holiness" and "divinity"—if they are real at all—must belong to the whole human evolutionary process.

The Biblical tradition itself incorporates the entire gamut of arcane psychic and spiritistic experience of the ancient world. Both the canonical Old Testament and New Testament are full of so-called "supernatural" events which in today's language would be called "psychic phenomena." These range from the officially sanctioned oracles of the Temple at Jerusalem (using the Urim and Thummim), and the utterances of canonical prophets (like Samuel and Nathan, who give psychic readings and precognitive warnings), to those claims of encounters with angelic beings (on the part of Abraham, Moses, Peter, et. al.) or deceased prophets and saints (i.e., the encounter between Elijah, Moses and Jesus at the "Transfiguration"), and to the stories of miraculous healings (Elisha, Jesus, etc.), the resuscitations from the dead, and various "nature miracles;" and to levitation, walking on water, and materialization (manna) and the teleportation of objects. And yet modern theologians have for the most part consistently rejected any systematic attempts to pursue modern psychical research, in which such phenomena may be studied.

"Psychic" experience is often feared by many traditional clergy and laity, as is the contemporary revival of interest in "occult" ideas and the "new religions" stemming from Eastern and/or Western esoteric religion and philosophy. The roots of this fear may be traced to certain unfortunate philosophical and theological assumptions longstanding in the Judeo-Christian tradition. These must be squarely faced before any progress can be made toward understanding the operation of universal, natural human psychic and spiritual faculties and their role in the development of the world's religious traditions.

Unfortunately these very judgmental, *a priori* dogmatic assumptions concerning psychic and spirit phenomena are widespread among Christians and others today. Such assumptions militate against an understanding of the universality and naturalness of human psychic faculties. Modern Fundamentalists, for example, have tended to condemn all psychic and spirit phenomena as "Devil-inspired." This generally stems from the misconception popularized by some of their writers that the natural human psyche is itself so utterly corrupted in most people that it is not to be trusted, and is virtually incapable of receiving messages from "good spirits." For these Fundamentalists it is deemed impossible to perform such natural human psychic feats as contacts with the departed under divine sanction. The psyche is also deemed to be utterly incapable of discernment.

This assumption has as its corollary in Fundamentalist circles today in the erroneous claim that the so-called "Deuteronomic prohibitions" of "divination" were directed against the kinds of "spirit communication" that modern Spiritualists practice with loved ones, guides, saints, and angelic beings. As we shall see in the present study, the claim is ill-founded. It will not hold up under the light of either informed Biblical scholarship or a careful examination of the many positive forms of contemporary psychic and spiritual experience of modern Spiritualists. Unfortunately, the zeal of such Fundamentalist writers widely exceeds their understanding of the realities involved.

Another assumption, frequently made by Fundamentalist and Liberal theologians alike, is the idea that the "resurrection of the body" in the New Testament is alien to, or even opposed to, the pre-Christian and primordial conception of the "immortality of the soul." As we have seen, this is an idea based upon a semi-literate historical scholarship which fails to perceive what either of these equally ancient and quite complementary concepts (i.e., "immortality" and "resurrection") really mean. In any event, when one uses the double-edged sword of good historical scholarship combined with contemporary spiritual discernment, it is possible to conclude that many of those modern religious "authorities" who would loudly condemn all psychic and spirit phenomena as Devil-inspired, or illusory, stand perilously close to being in a direct succession to those "scribes and Pharisees," or "Saducees," who condemned Jesus himself for healing and performing other "forbidden" miracles . . . "through the power of Bealzebub, the

Prince of Demons." In both cases there seems to be a common cause for the condemnation: spiritual blindness and the failure of discernment, harnessed to vested interests (i.e., to retain authority over non-physically awakened congregations), and just plain bad scholarship.

xi. the misreading of the so-called "Deuteronomic prohibitions"

Uninformed varieties of traditional Jewish and Christian scholarship have, for centuries, used the so-called Deuteronomic prohibitions of psychic and spirit phenomena to condemn all forms of psi which occur outside of a specifically Jewish or Christian cultic context. However, recent scholarship has shown that divination and psychic readings were performed by the Israelite prophets themselves, and by the official priesthood at Jerusalem. What was condemned by the Deuteronomic redactors seems to have been the particular form of divination and spirit phenomena of Canaanite seers employing the names of other gods. Furthermore, the form of communication-with-the-dead on the lower astral planes which seems to be condemned in Deuteronomy appears to bear no relationship with the benign mediumistic experience of the Modern Spiritualist Tradition. It was, rather, a form of black magic in which the corpse of a person was used in necromantic rites in an attempt to summon the soul of the deceased and compel it to serve the needs of the sorcerer.[13] No form of higher religion, ancient or modern, would sanction such a lower form of psychism.

xii. evidence for the earliest positive attitude of Jesus and the primitive church to psi experience

In the canonical New Testament we find evidence that Jesus himself sanctioned and performed something resembling what modern Spiritualists would call a "materialization" and/or "transfiguration seance," involving two "dead persons," by speaking with the deceased prophets Moses and Elijah on Mount Tabor in the presence of Peter, James, and John.[14] St. Paul enumerates other psychic gifts of the Spirit as including prophecy, miracle working, and healing.[15] Prophecy in the early Christian community clearly included what we would today call clairvoyance, clairaudience, precognition, and distant viewing; and miracle working included psychokinetic phenomena of various types as signs of the divine presence in the works of apostles and other Christian missionaries. Among the pre-Nicean Fathers, Ignatius of Antioch writes:

> *"Some in the churches must certainly have knowledge of things to come (prophecy). Some have visions, some give clairaudient messages and heal the sick by laying-on-of-hands, and others speak in tongues."*[16]

St. Paul had admonished his contemporaries " . . . not to forbid those called prophets to speak in the churches, else we be found to muzzle the Holy Spirit." In the early second century A.D., the canon laws of Hippolytus in Rome repeat this admonition of St. Paul to be sure to allow the prophets (those who had visions, as well as clairvoyant, clairaudient, and precognitive experiences) to speak in the churches. Other Patristic writers, including Tatian, Justin Martyr, Tertullian, Irenaeus, Origen, and Eusebius mention such psi experiences as commonplace in the Christian communities of the Empire prior to Constantine.

xiii. sealing the "psychic doors between heaven and earth"

But after the Church had become the "religious affairs department and salvation-machine" of the Roman state, "live" psychic and spirit communications, in the form of visions, apparitions, and gnostic dialogues with the ascended Savior and other saints, were gradually prohibited in the interests of religious uniformity, and conformity to state-sanctioned episcopal control in dissemination of the now canonically approved version of the New Testament scriptures. In the 4th century, St. Jerome, who had just translated the Koine Greek version of the canonical New Testament books into the Latin Vulgate, forwarded his translations to Pope Damasus in Rome with the advice that it would not be wise to " . . . permit those called prophets to speak openly in the churches as they please, lest they be found to contradict in some points the doctrines contained in these books."[17]

That advice was taken, and institutional Christianity thereafter— in spite of St. Paul and the Canons of Hippolytus—was generally to condemn rather than encourage live psychic and spiritual demonstrations by Christians, as well as by pagans and unorthodox heretics, such as the various Gnostic Christians were now to become. Bishops and emperors—such as St. Ambrose of Milan and the emperor Theodosius—were to join forces to issue edicts against churches employing persons who used spiritual gifts. This went so far as the active persecution and slaying of both pagans and Christians deemed to be heretical for engaging in psi practices. The Montanist heresy was wiped out by means of this method.

Since then, throughout Christian history a fair and reasonable approach to the study and/or practice and development of one's natural psychic and spiritual gifts—in the most orthodox Christian religious contexts—was to be blocked. It is no accident that the first persons in the 18th and 19th centuries to become interested in psychic and spirit phenomena were often secular "Free-Thinkers."

The custodians of the church of Jesus had attempted to seal the psychic doors between heaven and earth, and now the God of Abraham, Moses, Jesus, Peter and Paul would have to use Swedenborgians, Shakers, Mesmerists, Spiritualists, Theosophists, and Rosicrucians of various types to force it open as a counter-poise to the rationalistic and materialistic reductionism of the emerging 19th-century secular-humanist religion of "Scientism." It was at this juncture that the founders of the various societies for psychical research entered the scene in an attempt to suggest a missing link, or mid-ground between fundamentalist and institutionalist versions of religion, on the one hand, and equally dogmatic or fundamentalist and institutionalist versions of science, on the other.

xiv. the secular heresy of "scientism"

There is an equally widespread heresy of rationalistic, materialistic "Scientism" in some contemporary secular scientific circles which works to prevent the admission of the relevance of psychic faculties and psi phenomena to science. Like the three negative religious positions cited above, it rests on arbitrary, *a priori* philosophical assumptions, combined with deep-set prejudices and an insensitive, debunking methodology.

This has frequently manifested in the past few years in the public stance of the aggressive "professional skeptic" who in the name of "science" suddenly appears on the scene—often accompanied by a publicity-seeking stage-magician—to denounce and/or defame whenever a legitimate professional psychical researcher or parapsychologist is given any publicity or recognition for significant findings. The characteristic method is usually the same: first flatly deny the data, then punch holes in the methodology of the experiment with out-of-context objections and, if that does not convince the audience, use *ad hominem* arguments by accusing the researcher himself of sloppy scientific discipline or even outright fraud.

In the early days of the impeccable research of the late Dr. J. B. Rhine, similar comparatively low-key debunking methods were used against the then-new parapsychological findings. In the long run, however, each objection was carefully met by painstaking reduplication of basic psi experiments by over 200 professional researchers in over 27 nations during a 40-year period. Yet the harm was done by irresponsible detractors whose philosophical prejudices were threatened by valid parapsychological findings. One may read an accurate history of this effort in D. Scott Rogo's *Parapsychology: A Century of Inquiry*.

Now, after over 40 years of gathering evidence for the validity and reality of psi, we are still treated to the increased efforts of even larger numbers of naive scientists and threatened philosophers of 19th-century science who, often without any prior training in experimental parapsychology or real experience in the field of ESP or PK, have set themselves up as self-appointed committees for the investigation of so-called "paranormal" psychic phenomena.

Such groups are usually not composed of open-minded, careful scientists, trained in the field of parapsychological experimentation, who really desire to research and to find the truth—whatever it might be—in a given situation. Rather, they are often "professional skeptics" zealously representing the "religion of secular humanism," who, like over-credulous persons at the opposite end of the spectrum, are often the least qualified by emotion and motivation to have the patience or predispositions to discover or admit anything that they do not want to hear or see.

xv. the threat of philosophical reductionism and rationalistic materialism to transcendental faith

Today there is a far greater, far more persuasive and pervasive threat to the survival of Christ's real Gospel than even the most extravagant occult revival or collage of "new religions." "Science" and "technology" as we have understood them in the modern West have all but "quenched the Spirit." The impersonal, reductionistic and mechanistic world-view that has been spread everywhere through the instruments of Western culture, through our educational systems and media, all but made it illogical and impossible for many modern men and women to believe in the Gospel and in its implicit affirmation of supernatural elements, communication with higher worlds, the efficacy of spiritual powers, and the promise of life-after-death.

As many contemporary transpersonal psychologists have pointed out, the present "outlook of science" has all but destroyed the natural capacity of modern man to hope, to believe, to love.

> *"More and more of our patients complain of a sense of meaningless-ness in life. More and more often, the reason is the outlook of science. Or what has come through to them as the outlook of science. Sometimes it is called reductionism . . .*
>
> *"Thinking people tend to feel that science has cut Man down. It's explained away everything that matters in terms of smaller, meaner things that don't matter. Religion is nothing but wish-fulfilling fairy-tales. Love is nothing but body chemistry. Art is nothing but a surge of conditioned reflexes . . .*
>
> *"Science leaves Man shut-in, futile, doomed . . . It feeds on the work of its countless laboratories, to trap people in closed systems—chemical, biological, or physical systems—where all color has gone and all hope is lost.*
>
> *" . . . under these mental pressures many people have become seekers after transcendence, not rejecting science within its proper sphere, but reaching out in dissatisfaction to something beyond."*[18]

The British writer Geoffrey Ashe has commented that academics trained in the "scientific method" will always counter such insights with the objection that the "rebirth of magic . . . although an under-standable response to this feeling, is a mere escapism, a flight from reason." But Ashe would respond to this objection with an insight which this writer shares. He addresses the would-be "scientific skeptic" or debunker of psychic and spirit phenomena as follows:

"You claim to speak for scientific, progressive Humanism, and you equate it with reason. I'm telling you it hasn't worked. On the one hand we live in dread of technological horrors . . . On the other hand there's a powerlessness to do much about it. A failure of will—because of this feeling that a darkness of soul is closing in and death is the end and science has made everything hollow and pointless. Now if that's so (and I can give you evidence, clinical, scientific evidence, *that it is), then I wouldn't call it a flight from reason to look elsewhere for rescue. It's thoroughly rational. At least, it can be."*[19]

Again, this is clearly a crisis caused by the long acceptance in modern Western civilization of so-called "Enlightenment" postulates, the *a priori* materialistic and rationalistic, logical-positivistic categories of thought which have shaped the modern Western psyche. This has created, through two centuries of reductionistic educational conditioning and media, a whole secular *Weltanschauung*. In this worldview such conceptions as "heaven worlds," the intercession of deceased saints living in higher dimensions of reality, objectively real visions and apparitions of angels, post-mortem saints and spirits, magic or "real Power" exercised through various "technologies" of the mind and spirit of man (such as prayer, meditation, and the "alchemy" of the sacraments, miraculous healings, resurrections, ascensions, and the like) are looked upon as so much primitive mythology to be interpreted away by clever exegitists or revisionist-modernist scholars as pre-scientific foolishness, and a threat to the reasonableness of religion.

The resurgence of the search for transcendence in the world, and the search through psychic and spirit experience, reveals the natural operation of a very rational "safety-valve" built into human nature, both individually and collectively. Instead of siding with the secular, rationalistic and materialistic use of "reason" as a battering-ram to destroy alleged "superstition"—as they have been doing for the past three or four centuries—the modern mainline Christian churches might even now realize before it is too late that they have an obligation to study such psi phenomena impartially, and to see them for what they often are, i.e., natural expressions of the breaking into our world of transcendence. These phenomena do break into our world in primitive, paranormal forms; but they await the contribution that the Church could give to them by reshaping them into a God-centered, "natural theology of experience."

The widespread experience of the reality of the psi factor through eclectic forms of religion, psychological, and philosophical experience through folk religion and culture—in Africa and in the Third World, and in the West through the new religions and other quasi-psychological movements, may be God's *gift* to our mechanized and routinized "brave new world." And it *could* provide contemporary Christians with a viable alternative to increasing the reductionistic Orwellian scenario, and a natural resource to use in the deeper understanding of the truly "multidimensional" nature of man and of the universe.

xvi. *conclusion: the limitations and strengths of psychical and mystical experiences in pursuit of religious truths*

From the perspective of the Revelation contained in the Christian Gospels and in Church tradition, contemporary psychic and spiritual experiences are generally considered to be at best partial and private "natural revelations" of the Spirit.

Certainly no responsible scholar would presume to recommend that all control or regulation of "orthodoxy"—whether in belief or ritual practice—could easily be set aside either by the present-day Christian churches or by other established world religions. The proliferation of extravagant "prophecies" and/or the use of psychic powers for egoistic purposes could disrupt the central proclamation and communication of the major religions' tradition and their classical forms of transmission.

Therefore, in order to allay the legitimate fears of traditional religionists, it shoud be made clear that it is not the function of the academic "parapsychologist of religion" to prescribe substitution of ideas of contemporary psychic movements, or of various new religions, for those of any religious tradition, including those of classical Jewish or Christian orthodoxies.

But the competent and careful parapsychologist of religion could, nevertheless, greatly assist in the serious study of the natural human psychic and spiritual faculties and their primal role in the history of human religious experience. Such a study is essential today for all of those—Christian or otherwise—who would presume to study Judeo-Christian origins and the history of Western religious thought, which first arose within the context of an esoteric, psi-cognizant, ancient-sacral milieu.

And the fact is that there are many in all religious traditions who would consider themselves to be more awakened, and better, wiser, and more sensitive persons because of their exposure to genuine, positive varieties of psychic and spirit phenomena. Involvement in yoga, meditation, psychic development, and some systems of psychospiritual experience derived from Oriental religions have helped a number of individuals to rediscover for themselves the psychic and spiritual roots of their own Western religious tradition.

For this and other reasons, one can only hope that traditional religionists, Eastern and Western, will not impede the wide range of scientific and educational research beginning in the areas of comparative religion, consciousness studies, parapsychology, paraphysics, and life energies. Some traditionalist religionists of the West, whether fundamentalists, institutionalists, or liberals, have too frequently demonstrated that they have understood these areas little better or less than modern, secular rationalistic and materialistic skeptics.

Some Eastern religionists have understood psi issues little better. The higher religious meditational arts of the East often teach a complete withdrawal from, or negation of, all things in the world—including psychic phenomena—which might distract one from realization of the transcendent element within. This is valid advice for beginners in pursuit of ultimate spiritual objectives. But it is not sufficient advice for those who are naturally sensitive or psychic and who must learn to understand and control what may otherwise become uncontrolled psychism. And such advice was never intended to discourage "siddhas," or those like Jesus and other avatars, saints, and god-men with spiritual and psychic gifts whose pathway to God included the performance of "miracles," to bring others to God.

In addition, such "pure consciousness" mysticism represents only one form of mind-spirit technology. It is *one* effective route to the achievement of higher spiritual consciousness. But it is not the only path, and in any event it, too, automatically conveys to those who follow it a skilled psychospiritual development and gnosis for practical use.

The "form" of all religious revelation is itself symbolic and is processed through the human psyche. Thus "psychic" understanding and skill is necessary in order to deal with religious issues in a mature fashion.

Ordinary persons are confronted with the necessity of a here-and-now reprogramming of life's everyday situations from negative to positive habits, and to courses of positive thinking and action. For this there is, as various esoteric and occult traditions including the yogas of Indian and Asia have always implied, an additional, quite specific psychic technology which must be learned.

The mind must be trained and the intuition developed if the fullest human potential, including the natural psi faculties, are to be used efficiently for integrated living on all levels: physical, mental, and spiritual. Fundamentalist, institutionalist, and liberal Christians or Jews are not exempt from this, the requirement of Nature itself. And there is no necessary opposition between using both (1) the transcendental, spiritual-meditational arts, and (2) practical psychophysical and psychospiritual techniques, both for general self-improvement, health, and active help to others in the world, as well as for "spiritual development" and "sanctification."

As a matter of fact, these two types of inner technology, i.e., the higher spiritual *and* the psychic-pragmatic, are quite *inseparable and complementary* in spite of the negative language often used by many biased or uninformed religionists who do not understand the legitimate place and use of the soul or human psyche and its natural psychic faculties in religion and daily life.

There is, in fact, authentic [Christian, Jewish, Islamic, Hindu, Buddhist, et. al.] justification for teaching positive and beneficial forms of psychic development, just as there is theological and ethical justification for teaching modern Western medicine to Third World peoples, or for learning in turn the techniques of meditation, Oriental medicine, Ayuraveda, herbology, and various forms of psychic healing from them. All forms of natural faculties and powers, and all forms of human wisdom, belong today to all peoples.

For those whose perspectives are "religious" in a theistic sense, the intervention of the sanctified or divinized will of man into the natural and social order may be viewed as the fulfillment of the purposes of God in the creation. In theological terms, it will only be through a now-lost, holistic, sacramental use of spiritual, intellectual, psychic, and material "technologies" that a new civilization can be built which will begin to allow the kingdom of God—within every man, woman and child—to be built. It is only in this way that, ultimately, the Kingdom of God about which Jesus and the founders of other world religions have spoken can be realized, or materialized "on earth, as it is in heaven."

The primary act of faith required by Theists is to believe—because of trust in God's promise of the spiritual, psychic and physical transformation of the world—that this can and will eventually occur. If one thinks about it logically for a moment, this can only come about through the creative and redemptive activity of God and the free, intelligent, and disciplined cooperation of man.

Man must open himself in his inward parts to the process of psychic and spiritual transformation of his consciousness by the higher, Divine Presence. Man must first become sensitive to that Presence, then open himself to it for cleansing, repentence (*metanoia*—a "new mind"), and a "second birth" in the Spirit.

Man must then eventually relearn the now nearly lost meditational arts and psychic skills with which God and Nature has equipped him. These were clearly in the possession of Jesus and of the earliest Christians, and also belonged to the founders of many of the world's great religions. Modern man must rediscover these, along with the Kingdom of God deep within the most authentic levels of his own being, if he is to cooperate once again as a co-creator and co-worker with God "to till and to keep the Garden."

Even more than his material technologies, these will be essential to the fulfillment of his co-creative vocation. In a fascinating monograph on "Self-Training for Psychic Development," Dr. Hiroshi Motoyama of the Institute for Religious Psychology in Tokyo has written (1982):

(1) "Human beings have a far larger, deeper, and more multi-layered existence than present-day science understands.

(2) "Existence does not stop even after renunciation of our physical bodies.

(3) "Anyone can acquire the abilities of ESP, PK, and pre- and retro-cognition if they can release their mind from the confines of bodily limitation by means of such exercises as yoga.

"I have described: A method for breaking through the shell which confines the mind (and) . . . The abilities which can be acquired when such a breakthrough is achieved and the mind is free to evolve; and the higher world of spirits and divine beings which can be reached following acquisition of these supernatural powers. When people can realize such higher abilities and higher worlds, they will come to know how they should live in this world."[20]

The essential reason for personal psychic and spiritual development is—as Dr. Motoyama has so succinctly put it—"Not to acquire supernatural powers, but rather . . . in order to understand man in a holistic sense." It is such an understanding of man in a holistic sense, including his now-unsuspected "deep and multi-layered existence," that the modern West must now recover in order to reground religon in general and Christianity in specific upon the Primordial Tradition of esoteric gnosis, psychic intuition, and spiritual insight which the ancient world once knew but which—since the Age of Reason and Enlightenment—we have lost.

Our contemporary global human culture awaits the recovery of the lost Primordial Tradition of ancient gnosis and esoteric insight through frontier discoveries in the "future sciences" of parapsychology, paraphysics, and consciousness research. And it is fitting that Christian scholars should begin to prepare for such a recovery of ancient esoteric insights—by turning their attention to the recovery of those elements in their own tradition which played a central role in the lives of the founders of the Western religious tradition.

Chapter 4

Recovering a Lost Esoteric Christianity

*i. was an authentic "esoteric christianity" of the
    "Cosmic Christ" heir to the "primordial tradition"?*

*T*he claim frequently made by 19th- and 20th-century occult writers
that an original "esoteric Christianity" of the "Cosmic Christ" was
itself heir to a forgotten Primordial Tradition is as shocking to most
modern Christian traditionalists as it is foreign to most academicians in
the secular arts and sciences.

Yet this is precisely the claim which I shall take seriously enough
to examine in this book. Is there a nearly lost body of ancient esoteric
insight into the foundational "mysteries" of Christ, the Gospel, and
the Church? And is there, behind that, a forgotten Primordial Tradition of higher, intuitive knowledge or "wisdom" concerning the
metaphysical order of the universe?

I shall present the case for an affirmative answer to both of these
questions, and for my own hypothesis that both the Primordial Tradition and an "esoteric Christianity" originally were based upon now
largely unfamiliar varieties of shamanistic, psychical, and mystical
experience which yielded a body of symbolically and mythically
expressed "wisdom." This, it was claimed, transcended all man-made
religious and cultural barriers.

I will endeavor to translate an ancient argument for this assertion
into contemporary terms. And I will do so in the company of Hellenistic mystics, Jewish and early Christian gnostics, the authors of the
canonical New Testament, early Christian Hellenists, and a venerable
tradition of Fathers of the Church, from Lactantius and Justin Martyr
to Clement of Alexandria, Origen, and beyond.

For the sake of those of secular perspectives who may not be particularly impressed with the authority of such pre-Nicean Fathers of
the Church, I will also invoke the contemporary testimony of

a host of ordinary persons from many and/or no religious persuasions who have claimed to have had primary mystical and psychical experiences of the same types as those claimed by the founders of ancient religious traditions, including Christianity.

The latter are those countless persons from all walks of life and many backgrounds who have claimed conversion to a belief in immortality and in a transcendent order of reality behind the visible universe on the basis of having had personal psychic and mystical experiences of their own (i.e., telepathic or precognitive experiences, out-of-the-body experiences, near-death experiences, miraculous healings, post-mortem contacts with the dead, and all manner of contacts with higher worlds of "spirit and space").

I feel that the timing of this exercise is significant. Never before has it been as important to substantiate as relevant and significant such perennial claims to the reality of esoteric knowledge about the meaning of life, based upon what appear to be universal forms of psychic and spiritual experience.

Today we have created what the late Marshall McLuhan called a "global village," in which information can be exchanged within a matter of seconds all over the earth. Yet throughout the world, from Beirut to Belfast and beyond, "left-brain," tribal, religious and ideological strife, which is deaf to "other people's truth," is responsible each day for savage warfare and the various brutal phenomena of a fanatical terrorism.

The peoples of our global village urgently need to know, to be told, and then to discover for themselves that there are indeed universal forms of higher or intuitive human experience, which they can share with their brothers and sisters of all faiths. It is important for us to know if there really are transformative varieties of religious, psychic and spiritual experience which can traverse the man-made barriers of creed and caste, and which can change people's ethical standards, rehumanize their values, and point the way of access to a higher reality, a common vision of a higher order of being, and a universal membership in one human race.

Our world today is in a condition of religious and cultural ferment, of transition from the "old order" to something new which has not yet finally emerged. In this regard it has been said that we are witnessing a creative, culturally synthetic period of human history which bears many resemblances to the period from the conquests of Alexander the Great (333 B.C.) to the rise of Christianity and its triumph in the

Roman Empire. That was also a period when the world "shrank," as it were, and the many religions and philosophies of humankind were brought close together in the free marketplace of competition.

In those days, it was a new religion (i.e., Christianity) that emerged as the great synthesizing force, drawing together and fulfilling central strains and motifs of myth, ritual, and philosophical insight from systems as diverse as the "pagan" mystery cults of Egypt, Persia, and Hellas, and the philosophical schools of India and Greece, together with the early shamanistic Yahwist tradition and the later codified presentations of the "Law and the Prophets" of Israel.

And, in those days as in our own time, it was especially urgent to develop a system of universally relevant religious and philosophical belief and practice which would point the way to the affirmation of such a common higher reality, a higher order of being and purpose, in terms which were meaningful to persons of diverse backgrounds.

In those days it was the new religion, Christianity, which managed to do this and to defeat its competitors by skillfully using the code-language, metaphor, and great storehouse of mystical experiences of the previous religious traditions, both "of Jew and of Greek," for whom, as St. Paul said, Christ had " . . . broken down the middle wall of partition." This victory was—in cultural terms—largely a successful exercise in eclecticism, and in forging a new synthesis of the "ancient wisdom," or Primordial Tradition, that worked. The name of this new synthesis was the "Catholic Church."

Today, in the modern West, a number of individuals have claimed to have found authentic "transcendent experiences" entirely outside of this past synthesis represented by the institutional Church, through an exploration of Eastern philosophies, psychic experiences, meditational disciplines, New Religious Movements, and various quasi-religious, transpersonal psychologies. As a result of such experiences, some have determined to find a link and to fashion a bridge between the archetypes of their childhood religion, Christianity, and their new "experiences of the Sacred." A few of these persons have even undertaken to use their newly gained insights to contribute to the renewal of an all-too-often reluctant Church. Jacob Needleman has recently written about some aspects of this process in his book *Lost Christianity*. This process is an attempt to carry on a "living patristic tradition" of higher truths originally revealed by God to persons of other faiths. This is precisely what many of the greatest Fathers of the Church did in their own day.

No one except the most unimaginative church administrators and traditionalist clergy or laity should fail to see the strategic importance of this endeavor for the survival of Christianity and its continuing relevance to our changed and changing worlds.

If the ongoing "paradosis," or "living tradition" of encounter with the Holy in its Christian, Incarnationalist form is to continue to be relevant in our time and into the future, Christian scholars and lay-persons must be prepared to meet and accept, on its own terms, what I have called "the New Quest" for an "esoteric Christianity" and the Primordial Tradition.

For it is only by relating the experiences of the Holy claimed in the Gospels, in the lives of the saints, and in the sacramental experiences of the Church to the experiences of the Holy claimed by Hindus, Buddhists, Moslems, Jews, etc., and by New Religionists of various stripes, that the "saving link," or the "strategic bridge," can be built over which authentic forms of Christianity may pass to become once again a significant force in the global village.

It is now time—perhaps even our last chance—to recover an authentic tradition of Judeo-Christian "gnosis," or esoteric wisdom. We must bring to life and to light once again that fullness of the Gospel of which St. Paul spoke, and those hidden treasures of the Catholic faith about which St. Augustine wrote when he said:

> "What is now called the Christian religion has existed among the ancients, and was not absent from the beginning of the human race until Christ came in the flesh, from which time the religion which already existed began to be called Christian."

Both the Gospel of Christ and the Catholic Faith rest upon a Primordial Tradition of universal, esoteric intuition and insight. Unfortunately, most of our modern theologians, clergy, and church administrators appear to know or care little about such universal, esoteric intuitions and insights. This is so precisely at the time when an applicable working knowledge of such esoteric insights is most urgently needed to break down the defensive and oppressive distrust between the religions, ideologies, and peoples of the world.

It is my hope that this book will be useful in this task. Its purpose is to point the way to a new, non-sectarian, fully rational, and also "supra-rational" affirmation of the Transcendent. We must rediscover an accessible higher reality, a higher order of being, and the reality of a universal membership in one human race if we are to overcome the twin oppressions of cultic fanaticism on the one hand and bitter rationalistic skepticism on the other.

It is to participation in the emerging race of "new beings in the making," foreseen by saints and seers and prophets, that Krishna, Buddha, Moses, Christ, Mohammed and the masters of all generations and cultures have issued an invitation. That invitation is universal, for it is addressed to all who are capable and worthy of the high calling "to till and to keep the Garden," i.e., planet earth.

ii. new insights into esoteric christianity

In writing the article on "Christianity" in the 1974 edition of the *Encyclopaedia Britannica* (vol. 4, Macropaedia, p. 530ff. *passim*), Ernst Wilhelm Benz, professor of history at the Philipps University of Marburg, West Germany, has observed that (1) an esoteric and mystical tradition has existed in Christianity from the beginning, (2) that these esoteric elements, involving claims to an understanding of universal higher psychic and spiritual principles, were suppressed or pushed aside in the course of the development of Christianity into an institutionalized church, (3) that the revival of such esoteric elements has been important right up to the 20th century in various attempts, so far unsuccessful, to restore the lost "spiritual substance" of primitive Christianity to the Church, and (4) that the other world religions, new religions and "renewal movements" within the "younger churches" of the Third World have recognized and incorporated these much-needed esoteric elements.

Benz writes:

> *"A tradition of esoteric Christianity has long existed alongside institutional Christianity. It traces its roots to the New Testament and the early church, which adopted many pre-Christian elements of the arcane disciplines.*
>
> *"The esoteric form of teaching and its related form of community and liturgical practices represent an original form of religious experience, understanding and community life that has been present in Christianity from the beginning, that was able to find a connection with certain basic esoteric elements of Christian tradition and that had been suppressed or pushed aside in the course of the development of Christianity into an institutionalized church.*

"In the 20th century it faced the danger of losing its genuinely Christian substance when it opened up to non-Christian religions. On the other hand, many scholars are concerned that an esoteric Christianity in the 20th century is needed to fulfill a positive task as a counter-movement to a loss of spiritual substance of Christianity in a dogmatically, institutionally, and socially stale church organization.

"Besides the new religions, Christian renewal movements spring up all over the world as the result of a new transcendent experience.

"Significant in this respect is the great share that the so-called younger churches have had in this development, because they possess an inexhaustible life of piety and are frequently closer than their mother churches to the charismatic roots of the gospel. They contribute to (or alleviate) the (established churches' present) experience of a one-sided type of a theologized, intellectually diluted, demythologized Christianity, so that it is filled again with new expression of ancient spiritual contents."[1]

The discovery of the Dead Sea scrolls (1945) and the Nag Hammadi library (1946), together with subsequent scholarship on religious developments in Graeco-Roman Palestine in the centuries immediately preceding and following the advent of Christianity, have made possible important new insights concerning the nature, origins, and varieties of Gnosticism and its relationship to Christianity during the latter's formative years.

In the first place, we can observe with some assurance that many foundational gnostic conceptions arose from earlier traditions of esoteric knowledge which were widespread in the ancient world, and which—in their original contexts—were not always "world-denying" or negative in their appraisals of the worth of this world and the possibility of the earth's transformation by divine power into something better.

Secondly, it becomes obvious to those who are familiar with the varieties of human psychical and spiritual experience today that the earlier, more widespread traditions of esoteric knowledge (upon which the Gnosticism of the early Christian centuries was based) were themselves originally derived from primary forms of psychic and spirit experience, which were often either unknown to, or rejected by, the emerging orthodox party and other critics of Gnosticism.

And finally, it would appear that the kinds of psychic and spirit experiences that gnostics themselves claimed—direct visions and channelings from Christ, Mary, Phillip and other apostles, angels, etc.—performed a more central role in the formation of pre-Christian

Judaism and the pre-Nicean Christian Church than the more polemical passages in the Apostolic Fathers and Apologists had hitherto led us to believe. These contemporary insights could have a significant impact upon Christian theology in the decades ahead, and could eventually begin to soften and revise the generally negative attitudes toward the legitimate place of psychic and spirit experience in the life of the Christian and in organized Christianity.

Elaine Pagels, professor of religion at Columbia University, has produced a seminal study (*The Gnostic Gospels*, Random House, N.Y., 1980) of the implications of the early Christian gnostic documents discovered at Nag Hammadi in Egypt in 1945 and only recently made available in English translation by James M. Robinson (*The Nag Hammadi Texts*, New York, 1981.)[3]

It has generally been recognized that some of the more Hellenized of the early church Fathers, such as Clement of Alexandria and Origen, described what they believed to be a genuinely Christian "gnosis"—or tradition of esoteric wisdom—in the Gospels and in the primitive Church. Orthodox Fathers, such as Polycarp, Ignatius of Antioch and many others, wrote of the sublime "mysteries" of the Gospel and of the Church and sacraments in language apparently borrowed from the pagan mystery religions and from pre-Christian philosophical traditions. Most of these references made clear that there was a rich phenomenology of mystical experience in the earliest period of the Church involving both spiritistic encounters and various forms of psychical perception. But in modern times, only Theosophists, Spiritualists, Hindu and Buddhist scholars, yogis, and others outside the Christian establishment have taken these references seriously enough to postulate the existence of a mainstream of esoteric, mystical, psychical experience and/or spirit phenomena at the roots of the Christian experience.

Pagel's work, together with the Nag Hammadi texts and the work of a few other scholars, could begin to change this situation. From insights gained from new material, it may be possible for theologians to reconstruct once again a clearer picture of the primitive Christianity which was indeed not only quite compatible with but also drawn from the soil of that Primordial Tradition of spiritual intuition and psychic insight.

From Pagels' study, and from the Nag Hammadi texts themselves, we can now see that the early Christian church was " . . . far from the unified body we have assumed it to be," and that " . . . it was deeply split from the beginning" between those who believed in esoteric and exoteric forms of Christianity.[4]

The gnostic Christians believed in personal psychic and mystical experience, in " . . . the presence of the Divine within the human," and that "the way to salvation was through self-knowledge."[5] They challenged the priestly authority of the emerging (exoteric) church leadership, which insisted upon an outward succession of bishops and their exclusive regulation of the only valid worship of God. They characteristically denied that Christ returned in his ordinary physical flesh, opting for conceptions of a "spiritual body," (the *soma pneumatikos* of St. Paul), and stressed the centrality of various psychic visions and apparitions thereof witnessed by true disciples, saints and mystics.[6] They denied that Christ appointed Peter as his sole successor in the worldly sense, which was claimed by the nascent, "orthodox" church. They rather believed and practiced a very democratic form of church government and liturgical participation in which the various functionaries were sometimes selected from among the laity.[7] They stressed the equality of women, even asserting the androgynous nature of God as both Father and Mother. Women played a central role both as charismatic Church leaders and prophetesses.[8]

The main consideration in this study is that the evidence now clearly indicates that the "gnostics" were those who, like the ancient shaman and modern psychic and mystic, believed in an "open doorway" between heaven and earth, in the possibility of continued revelations and visitations between this and higher worlds, and in a hierarchy of angels and spirits who might encounter the enlightened faithful in dreams, visions, at prayer or in meditation, offering either symbolic or literal forms of instruction and guidance.

As Pagels has said, the " . . . gnostics considered original, creative invention to be the mark of anyone who becomes spiritually alive."[9] And, as we know from contemporary studies in Jungian psychology and the symbology of dreams, visions, and myths, the vagaries of personal interpretations and the expectations of the unconscious levels of the self can and often do condition and color the form of such personal psychic and spiritual revelations and prophecies.

The result was, as Pagels has said, that the gnostic believer saw his other mystical communion with Christ, Mary, angel or saint in psychic experiences " . . . as a continuation of what the original disciples enjoyed."[10] This then often prompted him to write spiritual or mystical "dialogues" in which the ultimate revelatory authority of the former is claimed for works which are then attributed to the latter. The end of this process is the production of a vast literature (i.e., "gnostic" gospels and epistles) in which it becomes exceedingly difficult to distinguish between the historical experiences of the original disciples with Jesus and the psychically derived, mystical and symbolic experiences arising from the spiritual lives of a number of later gnostic Christian leaders.

It was a protest against this kind of perplexing situation, together with the demands of the increasing institutionalization of the Church and its more exoteric conceptions of salvation, which led to the final confrontation between the bishops of the official church and the various gnostic schools or traditions and their leaders both within and without the church.

On the one side, those representatives of the generally non-psychic, non-charismatic, official (exoteric) church discipline and theory, who would eventually emerge as "orthodox," would hold that membership in the official church was the primary qualification for salvation. This official Church was the one governed autocratically in each place by a bishop of the physical succession from the historical Apostles, who had themselves received their authority by witnessing Jesus' physical resurrection from the dead.

On the other side, the gnostic Christians were those who generally held that mystical identification with the eternal, resurrected Christ, the Logos, was all that mattered to salvation. The gnostic Christian "knew" of his own immediate relationship to this eternal Christ because he could regularly "experience Him within." The gnostic Christian believed in his own soul as a "spark" of the Divine Logos, and thus knew that the Christ lived within him. He experienced inner and higher worlds of spirits and angels, visions of heaven worlds, and prophecies, and sensed the heavy oppression and ignorance around him in the political and social world in which he lived, which included at times the increasingly institutionalized "outer" Christian church.[11]

The problem was that Christian gnosticism, as a predominant movement within early Christianity, began to run afoul of certain elaborate pre-Christian, Asian and Hellenistic gnostic mythological and philosophical conceptions concerning the evil nature of the physical world and the "lesser" God or gods who were—they speculated—responsible for the defects in its creation.

Some gnostic Christians—like Marcion, the prominent Roman presbyter of the 2nd century A.D.—identified the God of the Old Testament Jews, Yahweh, with such a fallen or "lesser God." Like gnostics in most traditions after him, Marcion saw the necessity of identifying the God and Father of Jesus Christ in the New Testament with the "God behind God," i.e., the Father of lights, the Hidden Sophia or Wisdom, the Ultimate Spiritual Source of all Creation . . . which was only revealed and known in the Eternal Son, the Logos. Such a cleavage between the "God and Father of Jesus Christ," and the "God of Abraham, Isaac, and Jacob" was, of course, unfortunate, and ultimately to prove quite unacceptable in a tradition which, like the Christian, found its roots in the Hebraic soil. As a result, gnostics were expelled and nearly all of the gnostic beliefs, practices and literature purged from the institutional church.

Another factor which contributed to the distrust of live psychic and spiritual channellings during the 2nd century of the institutionalizaton of the Church was Montanism. Tertullian and the Montanists claimed that a direct revelation and inspiration from the Holy Spirit gave their doctrines a priority over the pronouncements of the "uninspired hierarchy" of the rest of the Church. They then proceeded to use this presumed authority of direct revelation (1) to condemn harshly what they considered to be the laxity of the rest of the Church in faith and morals, and (2) to condemn all pagan philosophy and religion as if it had nothing whatsoever to do with the universal revelation of divine wisdom to all peoples.

Most of the other Fathers of the early Church, following Justin Martyr, Clement of Alexandria, and Origen, knew better than this. For them, the *logos spermatikos*, or "word in germinal form" existed, in part at least, in the inspired writings of the pre-Christian pagan philosophers. But with the final rejection by the Church of Montanism, an understandable hardening of attitudes against personal psychic and spiritual channellings, like those which the Montanists had misused in the service of fanaticism, established itself within the Orthodox Church.

iii. how the gnostic christians were eventually excluded from the church

James M. Robinson, the general editor of the Nag Hammadi library, has provided a plausible statement of the process by which the original gnostic elements of Jesus' own teachings were gradually excluded from the emerging "orthodox" church structure of early Christianity:

"*Primitive Christianity was itself a radical movement. Jesus called for a full reversal of values, announcing the end of the world as we have known it and its replacement by a quite new, utopian kind of life in which the ideal would be the real. He took a stand quite independent of the authorities of his day . . . and did not last very long before they eliminated him. Through a remarkable experience of his vindication, his followers reaffirmed his stand—for them he came to personify the ultimate goal.*

"*Yet some of his circle, being a bit more practical, followed a more conventional way of life. The circle gradually became an established organization with a quite natural concern to maintain order, continuity, lines of authority, and stability. But this concern could encourage a commitment to the status quo, rivaling, and at times outweighing, the commitment to the ultimate goal far beyond any and every attained achievement.*

"*Those who cherished the radical dream, the ultimate hope, would tend to throw it up as an invidious comparison to what was achieved, and thus seem to be disloyal, and to pose a serious threat to the organization.*

"*As the cultural situation changed with the passage of time and the shift of environments, the language for expressing such radical transcendence itself underwent change. The world of thought from which Jesus and his first disciples had come was the popular piety of the Jewish synagogue, focused in terms of John the Baptist's apocalyptic rite of transition from the old regime to the new ideal world whose dramatic arrival was forthcoming. In this way of thinking, the evil system that prevails is not the way things inherently are. In principle, though not in practice, the world is good. The evil that pervades history is a blight, ultimately alien to the world as such.*

"*But increasingly for some the outlook on life darkened; the very origin of the world was attributed to a terrible fault, and evil was given status as the ultimate ruler of the world, not just a usurpation of authority. Hence the only hope seemed to reside in escape . . . And for some a mystical inwardness undistracted by external factors came to be the only way to attain the repose, the overview, the merger into the All which is the destiny of one's spark of the divine.*

"*Christian gnosticism emerged as a reaffirmation, though in somewhat different terms, of the original stance of transcendence central to the very beginnings of Christianity. Such Gnostic Christians surely considered themselves the faithful continuation, under changing circumstances, of that original stance which made Christians Christians.*

"*But the 'somewhat different terms' and 'under changing circumstances' also involved real divergences, and other Christians surely considered Gnosticism a betrayal of the original Christian position [on the issue of a basically good creation and the necessity not to escape from it but to redeem it].*

> *"This was the conviction not just of those who had accommodated themselves to the status quo, but no doubt also of some who retained the full force of the original protest [against the present fallen condition of the world] and ultimate hope [of its restoration to the ideal state].*
>
> *"But as Christianity became organized and normalized, this divergence between the new radicals and those who retained the more traditional Christian language [from Hebraic sources on the basic goodness of the creation and its Creator] became intolerable.*
>
> *"Gnostics came to be excluded from the Church as heretics . . ."*[12]

It is important to note that Robinson's scenario lays on the heretical gnostic Christian side a correct stress on the original transcendence of Jesus, and a correct radical rejection of the world as it is in favor of an ideal state of existence. But—in Robinson's picture—these gnostics were heretical because they went too far in identifying the world in itself with evil and its Creator with a fallen, lesser god. This identification had already been made in various pre-Christian gnostic mythologies which were incompatible with the Hebraic, Egyptian Hermetic, Platonic and Neo-Platonic mythologies. On the other hand, the majority of Christians seem to have lost the original fervor of Jesus' radical transcendence, and his stress on the ethic of the "Kingdom of God," which brings about the ideal state, beginning from the inside out. It is these Christians who accommodated the status quo and institutionalized the Church, in alliance with the few who had retained *both* "the original protest" *and* "the ultimate hope" for the world, who now condemned the heretical gnostic Christians and pushed them out of the Church.

Unfortunately for Christians ever since, something very precious went out of the Church with the gnostic Christians. That is the tradition of live psychic and spirit experience which they, like Jesus, James, John, and Paul, had lived by. For although they had become involved with exotic, world-denying Asian mythologies and an utterly passive stance of inward-looking mysticism, the gnostic Christians of the late 1st century and the 2nd century A.D. were undoubtedly in contact with a living tradition of psychical and spiritual phenomena. This included dreams, visions, heavenly apparitions, and healing experiences which continued to feed their faith in a transcendent order behind the physical universe. It was just this kind of live psychic and spirit experience and mystic vision which had fed and nurtured the wellsprings of the faith of the Fathers of the Judeo-Christian tradition. Abraham, Moses, the Prophets, Jesus and Paul, as well as the entire Primordial Tradition of psychic intuition and spiritual insight of the ancient world, are depicted in the Bible and in pagan writings as having been motivated by divine initiative through such paranormal psychic and mystical experiences.

iv. *primitive christian orthodoxy's "gnostic" elements*

A leading Protestant theologian and philosopher of religion, Dr. Geddes MacGregor, Emeritus Distinguished Professor of Philosophy at the University of California, is another scholar who would support the idea proposed in our present series of books, *Toward Recovery of the Primordial Tradition: Ancient Insights and Modern Discoveries*. In a recent book, *Gnosis: A Renaissance in Christian Thought* (1979), Dr. MacGregor has declared that only a recovery of an understanding of the ancient gnosis in the light of contemporary psychic research and conscious-ness studies can revitalize our own understanding and appreciation of " . . . the message that Jesus brought to the world," and "exhibit the inner meaning of Christian orthodoxy."

Dr. MacGregor writes:

> *"The Gospels are full of allusions that imply special attitudes of mind that are not ordinarily to be expected of people of any race or class at any period of human history . . ."*[13]

He then alludes to the account of the meeting of the disciples with the risen Christ on the road to Emmaus, and elsewhere such stories as the meeting of Mary Magdalene with the resurrected Christ in the Garden before the empty tomb, the story of Jesus' sudden appearance in the midst of the locked room, his encounter with the doubting Thomas, and the story of Paul's conversion on the road to Damascus, accompanied by the phenomenon of the "blinding light" and the symbolic opening of his eyes.

MacGregor calls attention to the non-recognition by the disciples on the road to Emmaus of their Master, even when he had taught them the inner meaning of the scriptures " . . . beginning with Moses and the prophets, showing why Christ had to suffer and what had befallen him." Only afterwards, in the familiar ritual action of the "breaking of the bread," did the recognition occur as their eyes were opened and "they knew him; and he vanished out of their sight." MacGregor rightly concludes:

"Only in the light of the gnostic presuppositions in which the Christian faith emerged do such accounts become intelligible at all, and then they at once captivate heart and mind.

"Plainly, stories of this kind presuppose a climate in which what we now call parapsychological phenomena are part of the scenery, a climate in which people are expected to be unsurprised by clairvoyance. We are being told that the two disciples, in their crestfallen mood following the tragic experience of the death of their Master, were still spiritually myopic and were then raised to a higher level of consciousness, able to penetrate another dimension or reality."[14]

MacGregor emphasizes a point which I have also tried to make by illustrating the relevance of parapsychological facts to religious studies and to Christian theology. He writes:

"Such a story (the Road to Emmaus account) to such hearers (ancients familiar with the widespread Primordial Tradition, under the form of Gnosticism) would not in itself raise eyebrows much higher than ours would be raised today by accounts of well-established phenomena such as hypnotism, telepathy, and thought-reading.

"That is not at all, however, the way in which either uncritical hearers of the Gospels or learned Biblical scholars have traditionally read narrative of this kind.

"On the one side, the skeptics have dismissed such stories as the folklore of an ignorant and superstitious people; on the other, conservative piety, 'Catholic' and 'Protestant' alike, has called for the exercise of blind faith, thereby raising a vast network of philosophical problems about the nature of faith and how it is to be distinguished from knowledge and belief."[15]

In the same chapter (VIII) on the "Peril of De-Gnosticizing Jesus," MacGregor writes:

"The whole New Testament literature, to say nothing of the vast non-canonical literature of early Christianity, is written by and for people who have attained considerable sensitivity to psychic phenomena. For most people today, blinded by their positivistic tendencies and empiricist presuppositions, the apostolic kerygma or proclamation is difficult because grasping its meaning entails such sensitivity and such experience.

"In the first century the difficulty was of a different kind. The difficulty was not that such 'paranormal' events were occurring, but that they were occurring in such a way as to focus upon him who had been discredited by the ignominity of the Crucifixion.

"It was the latter that made the paranormal events point to the

validity of the apostolic claim that Jesus was the uniquely divine Being who had pitched his tent among men and was now to be hailed as Savior of the world, the full and final revelation of God to man."[16]

MacGregor then expresses the same point that we have been trying to make, in past and present writings, concerning the importance of prior personal experience of psychic phenomena, and an understanding of the universal principles or metaphysical laws by which they operate. To those who would attempt to read the New Testament, or to understand the language of the historic church and sacraments with any kind of comprehension, he says:

"The apostolic message put the whole jigsaw puzzle of their experience of psychic realities in place and gave direction to their spiritual quest. Yet as you cannot put a jigsaw puzzle together until you have the pieces, so you could not possibly see Jesus as the answer, in the way the first Christians saw him, unless you had the preliminary psychic awareness and the flashes of clairvoyance.

"Without the complex spiritual scenery that gnosis enables its initiates to perceive, who could see Jesus as the answer to anything? The appeal of Jesus is strong in proportion to your spiritual awareness. Einstein would not impress you if you knew absolutely nothing of either physics or mathematics, nor would Joyce if you knew nothing of literature."[17]

In one way or another, the sharp distinctions between "faith" and "knowledge" made by most modern Christian theologians are usually spurious by-products of the deadly schism between 18th-century Enlightenment philosophy on the one hand, and the various 19th-century, fundamentalistic "leap-of-blind-faith" attempts to defend God and the Gospel on the other hand. MacGregor has called attention to the crux of the matter when he points out that the early gnostic Christian conception of "faith" did not radically contrast it with, or separate it from, "knowledge" at all. The gnostic and primitive Christian conception of "faith" included the faculty of psychic and spiritual perception, and the uses of a trained high intuition (in the Platonic sense), which enabled the "believer" to ground himself in "reality" and "realities" rather than in illusions or distortions.

MacGregor points out that the New Testament concept of "faith" implies a higher form of psychic and spiritual perception which grounds one in the "knowledge" or "gnosis" that Christ is real and his promises reliable. This is far from a blind leap of faith made on the basis of merely hearing the external words of a preacher. Yet, as

MacGregor observes, modern Christian theologians are regularly accustomed to separate "faith" from every kind of "knowledge." He writes:

> *"Paradoxically, the New Testament calls this (psychic and spiritual) awareness 'faith,' which contemporary theologians sharply contrast with every kind of 'gnosis.' Yet faith is a kind of knowledge. According to the New Testament writer of the letter to the Hebrews, it is faith alone that 'can guarantee the blessings that we hope for' and is able to 'prove the existence of the realities that at present remain unseen.'*
>
> *"But if by 'unseen' we are to understand 'empirically unseen,' what the writer is calling faith (pistis) is really a kind of spiritual perception, a clairvoyance that enables those fortunate enough to enjoy it to grasp a dimension of existence that neither the largest telescope nor the most powerful microscope could penetrate, any more than a slide rule could measure time.*
>
> *" . . . What it (faith) means entails sensitivity to realities inaccessible to physicists, chemists, and botanists as such. (Faith is) . . . inductive gnosis.*
>
> *"Academic theologians, medieval and modern, have often been so alienated from the (psychic and spiritual) perception of realities of that other dimension of being that they have by-passed the fundamental nature of the life of faith.*
>
> *"Christian mystics, however . . . have all known in their own way that from their point of view the traditional distinction between faith and knowledge is but a matter of degree.*
>
> *"Jesus, to whom is so much attributed the language of faith, reproaches those who are willfully 'blind' and proclaims that he has come into their world 'so that those without sight may see.' Those 'of little faith' are indeed the spiritually blind."*[18]

Thus, MacGregor correctly insists that by employing the metaphor of "sight," which is perception, to describe "faith," Jesus himself has implicitly told us that "knowledge" (gnosis)—which comes through perception of either psychic, spiritual, intuitive or empirical varieties—is itself intrinsically involved in, contained within, and inseparable from, the New Testament conception of "faith."

Finally, MacGregor says that Christianity was, from the beginning, a God-given answer to the "gnostic quest." That quest is seen today as the quest for the meaning and goal of a Primordial Tradition of psychic intuition and spiritual insight from the ancient world. He would agree, it seems, with this writer's premise in *From Ancient Religion to Future Science* that although we have by the 20th century moved ahead in the knowledge and methods of the physical sciences, it will quite logically take longer for mankind to master the far more sophisticated psychic and spiritual sciences upon which the Primordial Tradition, or the ancient gnosis, was built. MacGregor says:

> "Need we be much astonished, then, if the gnostic quest that was in progress in the Mediterranean world at the time of Christ, with its attendant awareness of psychic phenomena and the apprehension of other dimensions of being, should need at least as much time for its development of a satisfactory methodology of its own?
>
> "If, as I am suggesting, Christianity was from the first an answer to that gnostic quest, and if gnostic speculation provided the creative element in Christian thought, would it be astonishing to find that the full appropriation of such wisdom should take even longer than the development of medical knowledge and scientific method?"[19]

We are left with some clues, says MacGregor, provided by Jesus himself, if we would move ahead in the development of that methodology and knowledge of psychic and spiritual sciences:

> "I cannot but think that what Jesus so constantly deprecated was lack of spiritual vision, and what endeared man and woman to him was that clarity of spiritual perception that we may call clairvoyance. That it was to be achieved, according to his teaching, not through the study of hermetic literature or of any kind of elaborately conceived chemistry of the spirit, but, rather, through that loving disposition of forgiveness and the openness to new truths, makes it not at all less a gnosis. On the contrary, that is the very nature of all true gnosis.
>
> "We find it difficult in discerning the divine not because God is too complicated for our human brains to fathom, but because he is too simple for our highly complex brains to grasp. Jesus established himself forever in the hearts of his followers by showing them that the purity of a truly loving heart gives us that kind of knowledge that no amount of learning, rabbinical or otherwise, can ever provide.
>
> "Nor can there ever be anything static or smug about such a gnosis, for the purification of the human heart goes on until all its brass is turned to gold, and that is a very long process indeed . . . "[20]

MacGregor is prophetic and undoubtedly correct. It is the excessive adulation and idolization of the ratiocinative, analytical intellect alone— at the expense of the Spirit, and of the superconscious mind in which psychic intuition and spiritual insight occur—that has since the Age of Reason and the Enlightenment led Western civilization down the philosophical path of rationalism, with its concomitant reductionism, materialism, and a mechanistic, dehumanizing conception of mankind and its potential. An all-pervasive philosophical rationalism has pervaded our educational systems and our media of social communication. And this same idolatrous rationalism has too often infected Western religious institutions with doctrinal and institutional substitutes for the primary psychic perceptions and spiritual intuitions of the "Kingdom of God," and its very gnostic promises of eventual renewal in a "new heaven and a new earth."

v. the "son of man" in hellenistic judaism and the canonical new testament, and the "man of light" in iranian sufism

Perhaps it is possible even today to shed light on an enigma and to find the missing key to understanding the way that the earliest gnostic Christians—including Jesus, John and Paul—thought that the pre-Christian "Primal Man," "Son of Man" or "Heavenly Redeemer" figure was related through salvation to the soul of Everyman, through the historical Jesus.

We do know that the "Son of Man" figure (Hebrew: "Ben Adam" Aramaic: "Bar Nasha"; Greek: "Ouios Anthropou") in pre-Christian Hellenistic Judaism (found in the Apocryphal books of Enoch and Daniel) was a divine figure borrowed from the Primal Man concept of ancient Iranian origin. It was this Hellenistic gnostic, Jewish concept which formed the background of Jesus' own reference to himself as the "Son of Man" in the synoptic "Logia," or sayings.

Rudolf Bultmann has located the basic features of a pre-Christian Heavenly Redeemer myth in an early oriental gnostic tradition which is reflected in Mandean texts. Its characteristics are as follows:

1. In the cosmic drama a heavenly "Urmensch" or Primal Man of Light falls and is torn to pieces by demonic powers. These particles are encapsuled as the sparks of light in the "pneumatics" of mankind.
2. The demons try to stupefy the "pneumatics" by sleep and forgetfulness so that they forget their divine origin.
3. The transcendent Deity sends another Being of Light, the "Redeemer," who descends the demonic spheres, assuming the deceptive garments of a bodily exterior to escape the notice of the demons.

4. The Redeemer is sent to awaken the "pneumatics" to the truth of their heavenly origins and gives them the necessary "gnosis" or "knowledge" to serve as passwords for their heavenly re-ascent.

5. The Redeemer himself re-ascends, defeating the demonic powers, and thereby makes a way for the spirits that will follow him.

6. Cosmic redemption is achieved when the souls of men are collected and gathered upward. In this process the Redeemer is himself redeemed, i.e., the Primal Man who fell in the beginning is reconstituted.[21]

Bultmann and others have argued that New Testament writers, including the Fourth Evangelist and St. Paul, have interpreted the historical Jesus in terms of the language and metaphors of this widespread pre-Christian gnostic myth. They would have seen Jesus as its fulfillment. In the non-Christian, Mandaean versions of this gnostic Redeemer myth one even finds parables characterizing the gnostic Revealer as "the good Shepherd" and "the true Vine."

E. Kasemann has also seen the gnostic origins of the New Testament image of the Church as the "Body of Christ." He says that the figure of the "Heavenly Man" appears in Ephesians 2:15 as "the New Man" and in 4:13 as the "perfect Man," and that the idea of the solidarity between the gnostic Redeemer and the collected souls of redeemed men is expressed in Ephesians 5:22ff. as the "heavenly marriage" between Christ and the Church.[22]

Thus, Bultmann and his disciples would allow for the existence of a pre-Christian, universal tradition of human gnosis or wisdom. This pre-Christian wisdom tradition would have had to have come through a kind of universal divine revelation picked up in the mystical reflection, intuition and insight of pagans.

In various Iranian and subsequent Hellenistic Greek and Jewish mythological accounts of the Primal Man, the latter was the Divine Source Principle in Humanity, or the human principle in Divinity itself. The Divine Source had—in the beginning—projected its Image, or the Primal Man (Hebrew: "Adam Kadman") which was as Father of Mankind or Archetype the pattern upon which all humanity was formed. This Image or Divine "blueprint" was thus in everyman by virtue of creation as the authentic core or center of his being. By virtue of his creation, everyman ("Adam") was potentially the whole human race.

Humanity on earth represents then those sons (reflections) of The

Primal Man who were informed with matter and descended into the earth plane, i.e., incarnated. The one "Primal Man" was all the while thus in his earthly reflections divided into the many sons of men. But at the same time, because he was himself part of the Godhead as its second principle, he was undivided and transcendent to the whole Creation, and distinct from his extensions, outside of all worlds.

It was this "first creation of mankind," or the "first Adam," which progressively "fell" from the realm of light into denser and denser matter and ultimately lost its way in the darkness, forgetting its identity and becoming deaf, dumb, and blind to the spiritual light and insensitive to the divine ethical laws of the creation.

At this point, a "second Adam" was projected from the Primal Man and sent to the rescue of his lost brethren of the first projection. This was the (gnostic) "Heavenly Redeemer" figure, who descends, incarnates into matter, witnesses to the Light, suffers, is rejected by most of humanity, is killed by wicked men, and then rises again to new life while revealing his identity. Those who "recognize him" identify with him, follow him, and are remade after their own perfect original image as "beings of Light." They are refashioned, by acts of their own volution and divine grace, after the original divine image of the Primal Man/God. In Iranian Zoroastrian tradition this figure was known as the "Gayomart" or "Kaiomart," the "one who raises himself up."

Now Bultmann sees from such Iranian and Hellenistic myths where the ideas behind the New Testament came from.[23] Jesus identifies himself as the "Son of Man" ("Bar Nasha," i.e., Son of the Primal Man) sent by his Father, who is God and the Source of all Mankind. He is "Son of 'Man' " and as such, Son of God, Son of the Father. Paul explicitly identifies Jesus as the "Second Adam," i.e., the projection or "Son," the incarnate form of the Primal Man, or second person of the Godhead.

Jesus and his followers undoubtedly came out of gnostic circles in Hellenistic Judaism which were familiar with and believed in these myths. Jesus sees his own mission as the "Son of Man" who is to awaken his "sleeping," "blind," "lost" brethren of the first "projection," i.e., the first "Adamic" descent, to awaken them to their own true, inner nature as sons of the Primal Man, i.e., sons of God, in whom the "Father" dwells. This is the "second birth." Every member of the human race is called to become new creatures, new men in the One Primal Man through accepting, identifying with, and following the words and deeds of the "Son of Man."

The term "Christ" is the Greek rendition of the Hebraic term Messiah, which was—in the expectation of the Saducees, Pharisees and Zealots—not a divine figure at all. In fact, the popular Jewish expectation of the Messiah was that of a political or military figure who, like Judas Maccabeus four centuries earlier, had led a revolt to overthrow pagan domination of the state of Israel.

Both Jesus and Paul, following a pre-Christian Jewish mystical tradition like that of Qumran, have spiritualized and allegorized the meanings of the terms "Israel" and "Messiah." For Jesus, and Paul, "Israel" is not the physical state of Israel or the Jewish race, but rather the universal spiritual people of God—whether Jewish or pagan— who respond to the universal, human, metaphysical and spiritual Person, message, and work of God. The "New Israel" is, thus, that people of God ("Q'ahol," "Ecclesia," "Church" or "Body of Christ," "Soma Christou") which recognizes the Son of Man in his physically hidden, humble, incarnate state by finding in him the "Power of God," the quality or notes of the Divine Nature, in his redemptive words and deeds. The "Christ" is now not a Messianic deliverer of the state of Israel, but the "heaven-sent god-man" who is a "spiritualized-type" of "Messiah," i.e., the "bringer" of the "Kingdom of God" (which is "within you"), and the "Deliverer" of all Mankind from its "collective Sin" and its "Fall" into spiritual blindness and evil deeds.

The Gnostic Conception of "Recognition" of the Divine through Psychic-Spiritual Faculties of Perception

Now the question that we must ask is: How does the recognition of the divine qualities, the Divine Light, in Jesus occur in the earliest New Testament writings? How does one "recognize," "accept," and "identify" with Jesus as the heaven-sent Son of Man, or Heavenly Redeemer?

The answer is obvious, even from a cursory glance at the New Testament. The "recognition" of Jesus as divinely appointed, as "Lord" and "God," occurs in a thoroughly gnostic fashion. "Their eyes were opened and they beheld him" (Lk. 24:31-32). "Let those who have eyes to see, see, and ears to hear, hear! Others, seeing will not see; and hearing, will not hear" (Mk. 4:12). The implication throughout is that a very mystical awakening is involved, and an inner process of knowing, the opening of "spiritual eyes" and "spiritual ears," i.e., subtle faculties in the soul of man, brings about "recognition" of the true nature of the "Man" Jesus and his works as one with the Divine Presence, the "Shekinah," which had been known in the Temple and in the lives and works of the prophets (Is. 6:9-10).

It is most interesting to observe that in the pre-Christian esoteric traditions of Iran and the Hellenistic world there is evidence of a whole gnostic phenomenology for describing the "recognition" of eternal truth and of divine credentials in the world through "awakened" human subtle faculties of psychic and spiritual perception. This resembled the Platonic theory of knowing and recognition of higher truths through *nous*, or the spiritual, intuitive mind. Man is not limited—in this Primordial conception—to physical sight and hearing, etc., but possesses in his ideal state a whole set of subtle, psychospiritual faculties for perceiving higher and higher frequencies, dimensions, and worlds, as well as higher and higher realities within and beyond the individual consciousness.

The medieval Sufism of Iran claimed to be the inheritor of these ancient Zoroastrian and Hellenistic maps of "ways of knowing" (gnostic epistemologies). In *The Man of Light in Iranian Sufism*, Henry Corbin has described the fascinating phenomenology of the "Man of Light" in ancient Iranian religion, in Hellenistic Judaism, and in Hermetic Platonism, which found its way into medieval Sufism.[24]

In this model, there was the "earthly Adam, the outer man of flesh (*sarkinos anthropos*), subject to the elements, to planetary influences and to Fate." Then there was the "Man of Light" (*photeinos anthropos*), the hidden spiritual man, the opposite pole to corporeal man. "Adam is the archetype of carnal men; 'Phos' or 'Light' is the archetype, not of humans in general, but of 'men of light,' the '*photes*.' "

The "Man of Light," is the archetype of all "men of Light" who are oriented toward the Light and have subtle, psychospiritual faculties which are open. Those who are carnal men do not have such open or operative subtle faculties, hence they cannot "see" or "hear," "sense" or "recognize" the "Man of Light" when he comes into the world as "Heavenly Redeemer." How does he come into the world? The "Man of Light" comes primarily in the form of one's own "Guide of Light" in various theophanies, visions and apparitions, but only when the time and occasion in the life of the individual are correct. That is to say, only when the seeker is ready will his or her spiritual Guide of Light appear. The "seeing" of the "Guide of Light" will thus depend upon one's state of consciousness and spiritual development. The seeker must be sufficiently awakened within before the "Guide of Light" will appear.

The interesting fact—from the standpoint of the reconciliation of dualism with non-dualism in religion—is that the "Guide of Light" appears as if "out there," i.e., another being in time and space encountering one, surprising one, and revealing the way to higher realms, higher stages of development. But this figure which encounters the seeker on the spiritual Path is in fact not really just "out there." He is also "in here," in the center of the seeker's own being as the image of God, a Primal Man archetype upon which both the individual and all mankind are created.

This is the "Christ who lives within," encountering one as the "Christ figure without" in theophanies, visions, and apparitions, as the eternal "Guide of Light" to "Everyman-Adam" who accepts to become the "Man of Light."

Corbin illustrates this concept as it appears again in the *Pistis Sophia*, the gnostic "New Testament of the religion of the man of light," in the words of Mary Magdalene in an initiatic conversation between the disciples and the Resurrected Christ.

> *"The power which issued from the Savior and which is now the man of light within us . . . My Lord! Not only does the man of light in me have ears but my soul has heard and understood all the words that thou hast spoken . . . The man of light has guided me . . . "*

And again, in the angelology of Valentinian gnosticism:

> *"Christ's Angels are Christ himself, because each Angel is Christ related to individual existence. What Christ is for the souls of light as a whole, each angel is for each soul."*[25]

The "Son of Man," or in an allegorized spiritualization of the term the "Christ," as the Primal Man of Light is—as the Divine blueprint within each soul—both the "witness in Heaven" and the "supersensory personal master," revealing itself to whoever is ready as one's own "Perfect Nature," the origin and goal of one's own whole psycho-spiritual evolution and pilgrimage.

The "gnostic" on the spiritual path is described as oriented toward his "true country of origin" by "supersensory phenomena" which are progressively "visible" to him in the subtle spheres or dimensions of reality. Corbin cites descriptions of a "concrete world of archetype-Figures," a heavenly, supersensible world between this physical world and the "world of pure (formless) spiritual lights."

> "Between the world of pure spiritual lights ("Luces victoriales") . . .
> and the sensory universe . . . there opens a "mundus imaginalis" which
> is a concrete spiritual world of archetype-figures, apparitional forms,
> Angels of species and of individuals."[26]

This ability to "see" or be otherwise aware of this dimension or sphere of higher reality depends on spiritual-psychic development in a holistic sense. It is interesting that it is said to occur through what Corbin describes as " . . . the visionary apperception of the active imagination of such psychically and spiritually awakened and developed persons."

The compatability with the yogic and Vedanta traditions of India of the Iranian Gnostic Man of Light and Hebraic-Christian "Son of Man" traditions should be obvious. Thus the Vedantic statement that the "Atman-Brahman is One" recalls Jesus' statement that "the Father and I are One." The "Primal Man" would be "the One," or "Atman-Brahman," issuing as "Purusha" toward the creation to awaken "sleeping" mankind to its true Divine Nature, the "Atman" or "Kingdom of God," within. In Hellenistic Gnosticism the "Man of Light," "Son of Man," or "Heavenly Redeemer" appears as the Perfected Divine Human Being to men on the Path as if "out there," but in fact is already unconsciously (and then becomes consciously) the "Real Man" inside, the "Atman," or the "Christ" living within.

And indispensible to the whole process is both active and passive "gnosis," knowing through direct psychic, spiritual, mystical apprehension by every individual involved in the process of redemption and transformation ("metanoia").

Thus, the arcane traditions behind Christianity as a world-religion knew—just as did earliest Christianity—of the necessity of personal psychic and spiritual development. But rationalized and institutionalized versions of Christianity have dispensed with such necessities and frequently held out the illusory promise of "entrance into heaven" without Jesus' own precondition of "metanoia," or getting "beyond the finite mind." "Metanoia" is the capacity to go beyond the physical senses and logical mind to the Spiritual-Self within by identifying with the Divine, Primal God-Man, the Man of Light, the New Being.

vi. "heavenly cities" and "beings of light"

Corbin has described the Iranian Sufi's conception of "a supersensory world," which was perceived only by awakened souls whose subtle faculties were opened. This description of the Sufi's supersensory world corresponds with the conceptions of heaven worlds, high astral worlds and paradises everywhere, from similar descriptions found in Plato and his ancient successors, to the "heavenly city" described in the canonical Apocalypse of John, to modern descriptions provided by Spiritualist mediums and contemporary psychic seers who claim to "channel messages from the Masters."

> *"This, Sohravardi declares, is the world to which the ancient sages alluded when they affirmed that beyond the sensory world there exists another universe with a contour and dimensions and extensions in a space, although they are not comparable with the shape and spaciality as we perceive them in the world of physical bodies."*[27]

The point we should like to make here is that these astral "heaven worlds" or higher, supersensory worlds are perceived only through human psychic and spiritual faculties. Thus it is manifestly ridiculous to say, as many modern traditionalist religionists do, that psychic development and the possession of supersensory faculties have nothing to do with spiritual development. To the contrary, the two have, in fact, characteristically been inseparable in the lives of most of the founding prophets, saints, and seers of the world's religions. The sacred literature of the world is filled with claims of such supersensory visions as an essential part of the process of divine revelation during the initial establishment of religious traditions.

It is only those religious "reformers" who have been confronted with a plethora of confusing and extravagant claims to "supernatural" signs and visions who have turned away from psychic visions and spirit experiences in describing the authentic spiritual path. Thus Siddharta Gautema, the original Buddha, confronted with what he viewed as the degenerate ritual practices and magical superstitions of 7th-century B.C. Benares, turned his disciples away from the whole psychic area as a dangerous trap. And, some 23 centuries later, St. John of the Cross, living at the end of the Middle Ages (with its multiplication of miracles and the Babel of rival claims of various monastic orders on behalf of their chosen saints) also turned away from visions, apparitions, and miracles as of "no importance" to "true spirituality." But such a position was certainly not characteristic of the founders of the Hindu epics, nor those of Christianity—Jesus or St. Paul, or St. John on Mount Patmos. Psychic experience has always been a vehicle of transcendent experience inseparable from the origins of religious traditions. Subtle psychic and spiritual faculties of perception have always led to traditions of intuition and insight—whether about God, gods, angels, devas, man, or the cosmos—which have found their way into the sacred books of mankind, East and West, ancient and modern.

vii. conclusion: rediscovering psychic and spiritual experience at the root of primitive christianity

In the light of the phenomenology of human psychic experiences it is possible to conclude that an esoteric or occult corpus of natural psychic experience, knowledge, and a universal tradition of intuitive spiritual wisdom lies behind the original formulation of Christianity, and is far more deeply rooted in the Western religious tradition than the modern Christian is prepared to see or acknowledge. For modern Western man has accepted, in an *a priori* fashion, a whole host of reductionistic, materialistic, and rationalistic assumptions from the so-called Age of Reason and the 18th-century Enlightenment which has prevented him from rediscovery of the reality of those "spiritual and psychic sciences" with which ancient civilizations were familiar.

But within the Yogic traditions of India and Asia, the Egyptian and Greek mystery rites, the classical Greek metaphysics of Plato, Pythagoras, Plotinus, and the Hellenistic philosophy standing at the threshold of ancient Western civilization, such a Primordial Tradition of intuition and insight postulating the existence of real spiritual and psychic faculties had been recognized, examined, classified, and codified. Its legitimate heir was now lost "esoteric Christianity" of the "Cosmic Christ." It is this alternative reality tradition in the West which Robert Ellwood, Jr., Jacob Needleman, and others have seen re-emerging today in new religious and spiritual movements influenced by Eastern religions and hithertofore underground Western esoteric or occult traditions.[28]

And it is this "alternative reality tradition" or Primordial Tradition of the "Cosmic Christ" with which the Christian Church must now come to grips in the 20th century, before any authentic universal approaches to human spirituality can be developed—in transcultural terms—for mankind in the emerging "global village" civilization of tomorrow.

Chapter 5

Recognizing Our Essenian, Gnostic, and Hermetic Forebearers

i. recovering the Cosmic Christ in the psychospiritual roots of the judeo-christian tradition

The Church in most of the modern world is undergoing a silent shaking of its very foundations through a failure of many of its clergy, theologians, and faithful to understand the existence of its classical, supernatural dimension. Scripture, church tradition, and the entire Primordial Tradition intuited such a supersensible realm to be real, and declared that it surrounded and supported the very foundations of physical nature.

Such an intuition provided a common experiential groundwork for most of the world's major religious traditions. Such intuition of awakened and disciplined psychic and spiritual faculties could endow religion once again with an aura of universal validity. The supernatural dimension of Christian tradition could then conceivably be restored to the Church's imagination, where since earliest times it has stimulated the development of classic esoteric themes which have fed the deepest aspirations of those on the spiritual path.

Scholars must be prepared to explore Christian origins with a new openness, for there is evidence that primitive Christianity was indeed founded upon the psychic and spirit phenomena which gave rise to the later prophetic and mystical traditions of Israel, and then to the world-view of the historical Jesus. The world-view of Jesus—in its New Testament portrayal—included knowledge of a oneness with a pre-existent "Cosmic Christ," who was both the archetypical "Anthropos" or "Heavenly Man," and his active Hierophonic image incarnate on Earth, the "Son of Man." Such spiritual perceptions, derived through visionary experience and psi phenomena, constituted a Christian form of "gnosis." Centuries of mystical, psychic, and spiritual experience in the ancient world lay behind the New Testament writers' claims to their original "recognition" of Jesus as "the Son" of the "Heavenly Man." The general understanding of such a Primordial Tradition of universal gnosis was gradually diminished and lost by Christian leaders from the second through the fourth centuries of our era. Christianity at first grew and spread in a Jewish-Hellenistic mystical milieu within the Roman Empire. But after Constantine and the imperial appropriation of the Church as the state religion, widespread, personal mystical experience was deliberately discouraged in the face of various exotic heresies and the Church's own increasing institutionalization and codification of its doctrines.

Scholars engaged in a contemporary quest for the esoteric elements in a "lost Christianity," i.e., a genuine, primitive Christian gnosis, must be aware of its inseparability from primary, universal forms of psychic and spirit experience, and mystical reflection, found in all of the ancient religions. Such scholars should also be aware of the fact that similar psychic and spiritual experience can and still does happen, simply because "man and the world are made that way." Ordinary people can once again revive and relive suh experiences in order to authenticate for themselves the roots of religion, and of the Western religious tradition in particular.

ii. the characteristic mistake: to separate Jesus from the primordial tradition

There is a characteristic mistake made both by some early Christian apologists (Tertullian, for example) and by many contemporary Christian theologians, a mistake tragic in its consequences for any dialogue between Christianity and other world religions.

This mistake is the well-meaning but in fact wrongheaded attempt to defend the uniqueness and importance of the (Christian) revelation by separating Jesus from the rest of the direct psychic, mystical, and spiritual experience of mankind. The effect of this is, in fact, to separate Jesus from the Primordial Tradition.

The Christian gnostic would say that it is only on the basis of that universal experience and knowledge (gnosis) of God, and through its potential natural operation in the whole human race, that one could ever hope to establish the valid "credentials" of Jesus as an authentic reflection or incarnation of the Divine in human terms. The Christian gnostic would say that it is only through experiences of "higher consciousness" that anyone (or "Everyman," i.e., "Adam") can recognize Jesus in the depths of his or her own soul as the authentic embodiment of the "Word" of God through the Gospel message.

It is precisely this "proto-gnostic" experience which is at the heart of all true "conversion experience," which alone paves the way for "illumination" or the true gnostic "knowing" through direct apprehension of the "Divine Light." Such a description of this universal human process would hold true in many of the world's "higher religious traditions." And "recognition" of the "Christ," in the classical Christian terminology of the New Testament itself, is likewise a direct and immediate experience within the soul of the believer. The believer is the "New Man," the "Second Adam."

And the "believer" through this experience becomes the "knower," i.e., the gnostic. This experience of "metanoia"—according to the canonical Gospels and Saint Paul—is not just for Jews, but for Greeks, and for the then-hated Romans and all others as well. By extension of this principle, we must affirm that this potential experience of metanoia or "gnostic illumination" is eventually for all humanity to undergo, and is not the exclusive property of "Christians" in the institutionalized or fundamentalistic sense.

Yet, to this day many would-be Christian apologists, including modern Western fundamentalists and "neo-Orthodox" zealots, would mistakenly work to separate Jesus from the Primordial Tradition of such universally accessible gnosis. Even careful traditional scholars have fallen into this trap. They often argue against Reitzenstein's and Bultmann's case for the existence of a pre-Christian Gnosticism. They would prefer to convince us that all of the early gnostic heresies were derived from misunderstandings of Christianity, rather than accept that the latter, as well as the former, arose out of a common background and ultimately from a Primordial Tradition of pagan intuition and gnosis which was shaped differently by various groups.

My point is that when psychic and spiritual channels "between heaven and Earth" remain open, people of all cultures and traditions can and do experience "God," or the Divine Ground of Being and Transcendence. Recognition of the authenticity of the message of Jesus occurred among those mystical Jews (Essenes, Therapeuts, Zaddokites, Nazoreans) who were familiar with primary psychic and spiritual experience as well as with great pagan symbols, myths, and archetypes of religion, which allowed them to affirm the idea of the Messiah, or "Christ," as cosmic "god-man," and the model for human psychospiritual evolution. Universal, higher psychic and mystical experience, together with appropriate myths, symbols, and rituals, must always have been an essential pre-condition, a *sine qua non*, of the recognition of the Christian message which we find enshrined in the canonical New Testament.

iii. *what is "gnosis"?*

In Greek *ginoskein* " . . . denotes the intelligent grasp of an object or situation, or the ingressive experience of becoming aware." This contrasts with mere perception (*aisthanesthae*) without an accompanying understanding, or with merely " . . . holding an opinion or idea without any guarantee of its truth."[1] *Ginoskein*, then, means "grasping things as they really are," the "being" (*on*) or "truth" (*aletheia*) of a thing or situation.[2] "Gnosis" as a noun, therefore, denotes the act of knowing a thing or situation in its reality, having "true knowledge" (*episteme*) as distinct from mere opinion, theory, or intellectual belief.[3] The word "gnosis" comes to mean among the Greek philosophers (Plato, et. al.) personal acquaintance, or reliable inner knowledge of the reality of a person, thing, or situation, rather than theoretical, secondary, mediated knowledge or opinion (*doxa*). Thus we have Socrates' famous charge, *gnothi seauton*, or "know thyself."

As Rudolph Bultmann has said, "Ultimate truth for the Greeks means the reality which underlies all appearances." For the Greek metaphysical philosophers " . . . reality belongs to forms and figures, or to the elements or principles which they embody."[4] The true philosopher or student must encounter, grasp, and understand the latter, within himself or herself, if there is to be true knowledge (*episteme*) of anything, even in the external world. The act of doing this is "gnosis." The "gnostic" is thus the true philosopher, the true student, the true knower of realities, as distinct from the mere holder of opinions, beliefs, and theories.

Consequently, in religious usage it would be and was natural to use the term "gnosis" to distinguish between an authentic knowing of divine realities, as distinct from a mere assumption or opinion formed from the testimony of others, or through traditions, books, or institutions.

In its original religious application, the word "gnostic" meant someone who encounters and directly intuits a divine reality or truth through the higher rational-intuition, or "spiritual mind" (*nous*). Subtle faculties of psychic and spiritual perception and understanding must be awakened and operative in such a person. In other words, the "gnostic" is someone capable of deriving truth through "inner channels," including primary psychic, mystical, and spiritual experience.

In early Greek Christian usage, from the New Testament itself to Justin Martyr, Clement of Alexandria, and Origen, "gnosis" was a perfectly acceptable term to describe the proper approach to spiritual knowledge of the Christ by the ideal Christian. It was only as the term was increasingly employed in the 2nd century A.D. by persons and groups developing exotic, heretical theological doctrines that it came primarily to denote, among the Church Fathers, varieties of world-denying religion to be avoided by the "orthodox" Christian.

Modern scholars influenced by modern Jewish or Christian tradition have characteristically identified the term "gnostic" more or less with such world-escaping and world-denying dualism. Yet there is another, more positive meaning to the terms "gnosis" and "gnostic" in the history of Western civilization which the Christian churches, and other institutionalized religions, can neglect only at their own peril. There is no doubt that that heretical or distorted form of gnosis which Hans Jonas has called the "gnostic religion" did exist as an anti-cosmic, world-denying religious attitude in many sects of Jewish Hellenism, in 1st- and 2nd-century Christianity, as well as in the pagan world. And there is no doubt that the strange doctrines reflecting this world-denying attitude are quite incompatible with both Jewish and Christian orthodoxy, as well as with classical Greek metaphysics in the Platonic and Neo-Platonic traditions. But the point which must now be stressed is that such kinds of nihilistic, "gnostic" existentialism which alienate the "inner man" from the "natural order," and then condemn the latter as the root of all evil, is not what authentic "gnosticism" and "gnosis" was, and is.

The terms "gnosticism and "gnosis" have also carried the implication of other, good things in the ancient world. Chiefly this was the reliance on direct, inner perception and on awareness of psychospiritual realities—an immediate mystical apprehension of truth by the "divine spark" or "image" in man, rather than through a reliance upon external, mediated authority, in the pursuit of religious truth. "Gnosis" was primarily a certain knowledge of transcendent realities gained through personal psychic, spiritual, and ethical development. It involved also the idea of awakened subtle faculties of psychic and spiritual perception and of the formless ground of Being which lies entirely beyond the physical level of existence. As such, "gnosis" was the core experience of all religion as transcendent experience. It yielded a Primordial Tradition of intuition and insight throughout the ancient world that originally included many of the best Hellenistic Jewish and primitive Christian writers.

It was unfortunate that many who called themselves Jewish and Christian "gnostics" became involved with overly pessimistic, world-denying attitudes and mythologies, which were described by Jonas in *The Gnostic Religion*.[5] These were rightly opposed by the Fathers of the Church in the 2nd-3rd centuries. But it is important that contemporary New Testament scholars not condemn and abandon altogether the idea of gnosis, of a Primordial Tradition, and of personal spiritual awakening, and of the apprehension of high, supersensible realities because of a long standing confusion between various heretical mythologies and the original meaning of the term "gnosis" itself.

iv.   *"optimistic" versus "pessimistic" forms of gnosis and orthodox versus heterodox forms of christianity*

There is an essential distinction which must be made between "optimistic" and "pessimistic" forms of pre-Christian esoterism. The "optimistic" gnosis views the whole world as good, as a divine and living world because animated by the divine effluvia, and capable of being activated by man as a co-Creator with God and as a priest of Nature. In this world, man's function is not to "escape the world" but to awaken and activate persons, places, and things in Nature to become "temples of the Divine Spirit." Man himself develops gnosis in order to "become or re-become a god," in order to "know God" in the existential sense. Like the "magician" or "theurgist" in the iconography of the Egyptian tarot card, man is to "bring down" the divine power and light in order to impregnate and fill the objects of the physical world with their appropriate form of divinity.

This "optimistic" form of gnosis may be identified with the ancient Egyptian "religion of the world," according to Frances Yates.[6] It was such a positive "Hermetic" conception of a good, God-given creation (which is to be redeemed and divinized rather than discarded) which indeed may have provided the Egyptian background of both the Hebraic and Mosaic concepts of the creation in Genesis, and a source for the classical Greek metaphysics of Pythagoras and Plato. This earlier Egyptian understanding of gnosis pre-dated the later Hellenistic, world-denying "religion of Gnosticism" in the early Christian era.

This later "pessimistic" type of heretical gnosticism viewed the whole creation as utterly lost in darkness and under the government of fallen "archons" or angels of the planets. In this version of gnosticism, the principalities and powers which governed the atmosphere ("air") of earth, and the density and darkness of material existence itself, were so inimical to the "man of light," i.e., the true gnostic, that the latter could only think of redemption in terms of escape from the body, matter, and time.

It is interesting to note that "pessimistic" forms of gnosticism have certain similarities (in their conceptions and prescriptions of an ultimate escape from matter as the only way to salvation) with various Iranian and Far Eastern dualistic philosophies. The latter traditions have—in popular and debased forms—often turned their backs on matter, time, and history. It has taken the giants of the modern Hindu Revival, such as Sri Aurobindo of Pondicherry, to re-establish the implicitly positive, world-affirming and redeeming principles of India's "integral yogas" in the popular consciousness of modern India. It is likely that the "pessimistic" gnosticism of the later Hellenistic world can be traced to various Oriental—rather than Occidental or Egyptian—sources. But this is not our primary concern here.

The role of the "optimistic" Hellenistic gnostic's "Heavenly Redeemer" was, according to the Egyptian Hermetic tradition, to bring the divine light down, through incarnation and the divine work of the heavenly "Magician" or theurgist, and thus sanctify the physical world as the Temple of God, for the "recreation of a new heaven and a new earth."

During the Renaissance, Ficino and Giordano Bruno believed that this "optimistic" variety of an earlier Egyptian "proto-gnosticism" had found its way into original Mosaic tradition, and into the works of the New Testament, in the positive metaphysical philosophies of Jesus, John, the author of the 4th Gospel, and Paul. It also found its way into the Neo-Platonic Hermeticists of the early Christian centuries.

The "pessimistic" forms of gnosticism had found their way into the various heretical forms of pagan and Christian gnosticism, and these followers believed that the primary function of the Gnostic "Heavenly Redeemer" was to rescue the sparks of the Divine from man and from the earth plane, where thy had been imprisoned, thus abandoning the world itself to perdition.

The Fathers of the early Church contended against this world-denying form of gnosticism, asserting that the Creator was God and that the Creator and the Redeemer of the world were One Being, that the physical incarnation and the redemption of man's spiritualized body, of the earth itself, and of time and history were essential to the divine plan through the Son of Man–Christ figure.

While certain notes of pessimistic gnosticism found their way into both Plato and the New Testament, these were sub-dominant and not prevalent themes; for example, Socrates asserts "the body is a prison" and looks forward to his release from it into the heavenly places. But the overall Platonic appraisal of nature and of the world is positive; it is a divine theater for the working out of cosmic purposes in which man's role is—through higher self-knowledge—to re-create the ideal existence, the utopian society.

Similarly, in the Fourth Gospel and in several New Testament Epistles, we may read of the evil "principalities and powers" that govern the "air" of earth. And we read that the "world" ("cosmos") is enveloped in a darkness in which the sons of men are lost and subject to the power of the principle of opposition to the divine will (i.e., "Satan"). But the overall picture presented by all of the canonical Gospels, Acts, the Epistles, and Revelations is a positive one. The physical world of time and space was created by a loving God, and is good. Although led astray and temporarily subjected to fallen angels and an aura of darkness, it awaits a glorious redemption, a complete transformation by the Cosmic Christ, the Original Light, in the Man of Light (Son of Man—Messiah) who has re-entered the world, in the flesh, to transform and spiritualize all matter, so that the heavenly Father's will is done "on earth, as in the heavenly places."

The central point is that in the "optimistic" gnosticism of the "Egyptian type" found in the New Testament, Christ and his Church, or "Mystical Body" fulfill the role of the divine psychospiritual "Magician," or Theurgist–Sacramentalist, who brings the power of God down from Heaven to earth, in order to redeem the latter, to fill it with the Holy Spirit, and ultimately to make it over and transform it into the "new Heaven and the new earth" of Revelations.

This "Great Work" of the Divine Plan is, essentially, a psychic and spiritual work, a work of the highest form of divine "Magic," with a very worldly objective, i.e., to infuse matter with spirit, and to infuse the human with the divine. In the process of accomplishing this Work, first Jesus, then later his Apostles, are portrayed as performing all sorts of "miracles," "nature miracles," "healing miracles," "soul-miracles," (the forgiveness of sins and the casting out of "evil spirits" and negative forces of all kinds). Then there is the miracle of the giving of life again to the dead, including the Resurrection, or reappearance and reclothing, of the Son of Man in a transformed body of flesh which becomes the marvelous *soma pneumatikos* or spiritual body of the Resurrection (St. Paul). This is promised to Everyman who will undergo the *metanoia*, the "new mind," the "second birth" in the One Restored Model, the Heavenly "Son of Man."

It should be noted here that "resurrection of the body" implies far more than mere survival of bodily death or immortality of the soul as understood in Platonic and Neo-Platonic philosophy. But, as H. Wolfson has shown, the two conceptions are complementary and interdependent.

The conception of "resurrection of the body" in Hellenistic and Pharisaic Judaism seems to have been developed against the background of ancient esoteric traditions in which, as Robert Crookall has shown [*Psychic Investigations*, London], there were various "levels of the self," various "sheaths" or "bodies," including the "physical body," the "soul-body" (or "psychic body"), and the "spiritual body." In this division, the "soul-body" was indeed not ultimately immortal or imperishable, although it was said to survive the death of the physical body for a time. It was only the "spiritual body" which, because it was made out of "divine stuff" or the imperishable Spirit, was truly immortal.

This background should make it possible to see that our usage of the term "soul" (in exoteric terms) has been very ambiguous. For, if one is describing the "soul-body," (*soma psykikos*) or the personal "mind" of an individual, there would be nothing inherently immortal in these, according to the ancient esoteric conceptions. But if one intends to describe the "spiritual body" (the "jiv-atman" in Sanskrit) by this term, then it is indeed immortal according to both Eastern yogic and Western Platonic usage. Aristotle, as well as St. Thomas Aquinas and modern Protestant fundamentalists, apparently have not known enough of the terminology of the esoteric distinction between the psychic and spiritual "bodies" to steer clear of this semantic difficulty.

The net result has been a loss of understanding among exoteric Christians concerning what the "soul" (psyche) is, and how it develops its potential under the guidance of the immortal Spirit of God (Atman) immanent in "Everyman."

vi.   the early loss of esoteric comprehension of the "son of man" figure

From the canonical point of view, the difference between heterodox or heretical gnostic Christian schools of thought and the originally orthodox but still gnostic Christian school of thought of the 1st century, which began with Jesus and Paul, would have been found in the insistence of the latter that the heavenly, cosmic "Primal Man" or "Son of Man" had been "grounded" or incarnated in history within the earthly experience of man, in the person and work of Jesus.

Those Hellenistic Jewish gnostics who would not accept Jesus as the physical incarnation or "hierophany" in time, space, and flesh, of the "Primal Man" (or Ouis Anthropos or "Son of Man"), as well as various pagan gnostic schools of thought (drawing upon extremely dualistic Greek, Egyptian, and Iranian sources), would have shared with heretical Christian gnostics the tendency to avoid statements which—like those of canonical New Testament writers—emphasized the centrality of the incarnation as a historical event. The canonical Gospel of John's insistence that the Eternal Word ("logos") "became flesh," and the Synoptic writers' insistence on the physical death, passion, and resurrection of Jesus as heavenly Son of Man incarnate, would have been unnecessary and even offensive to those kind of gnostics who conceived of the "Primal Man" or "Son of Man" only as a "Heavenly Revealer" whose appearance on Earth was simply to disclose eternal truths.

As Frederick Borsch has said:

> "Eschatological statements about the Son of Man would have been of little value to groups who saw no meaning in the historical process and who looked for salvation, not in the future, but in another realm. Similarly, statements about the Son of Man as a historical earthly figure would have been relatively meaningless to those who saw the

savior primarily as a heavenly revealer whose visit to Earth was only
for the purposes of disclosing eternal secrets and not to forgive sins (as
Mark 2:10 par.) eat and drink (as Matt. 11:19 par.) and have no place to
lay his head (as Matt. 8:20 par.). Finally the idea that the savior should
actually suffer would have been tantamount to blasphemy to many
gnostics.[8]

But even the orthodox Christian usage of the title "Son of Man"
originated by Jesus himself and found in the canonical New Testament scriptures was certainly gnostic in the broadest, non-pejorative
sense of that term later employed by Clement of Alexandria. This
usage of the "Son of Man" figure was gnostic in the sense that it
implied knowledge of the Primal Man, Son of Man concept from pre-
Christian gnostic sources, including Jewish sources such as the apocryphal Enoch and Daniel.

The original gnostic Christian orthodoxy of Jesus and his Apostles,
including Paul, would have represented the continuation and for the
earliest Christians the fulfillment of the Primordial Tradition of intuition
and insight of antiquity, which understood implicitly the necessity
and role of the awakened human psychic and spiritual faculties for the
recognition of the divine in human form, or of God as he comes into
this world in any encounter with man.

But even this orthodox, incarnational form of the original Christian gnosticism of Jesus was to pass out of popular comprehension
within the Church by the 2nd century. Along with the less frequent
usage of the term "Son of Man," there also gradually passed away the
original implicit understanding found in the New Testament of the
significance of the awakened human psychical and spiritual faculties,
and the importance of visions, heavenly apparitions, and dreams to
divine revelation and to the processes of illumination and sanctification in the life of the individual Christian and the Church.

The orthodox church fathers of the 2nd to 5th centuries generally
substituted the terms "Christ" and "Son of God" to signify the
"heavenly Redeemer" concept originally designated by the term
"Son of Man," which was said to have been used by Jesus himself in
the earlier writings of the canonical New Testament. At the same time,
they did emphasize—in continuation of the canonical tradition—the
importance of physical incarnation, historicity and "this world" in discussing the process of human salvation. But the pendulum was to swing
so far in the direction of the "grounding" of salvation in the concrete-
ness and institutionalization of the authoritative Church and the

established Scriptures that nearly all room for the living psychical, spiritual, gnostic encounters which had originally fed the New Testament portrayal of Jesus and his closest apostles was practically eliminated. Indeed, this truly gnostic tradition of psychical and mystical "encounters with heaven" did and does continue to occur in the lives of the great saints and mystics of the Church to this day. But the clergy and laity of the institutionalized churches have, for the most part, walked another and more rationalistic, non-gnostic path, one that does not understand the revelatory power of dreams, visions, apparitions of saints and angels, spiritual healing, and the living encounter between this world and the heavenly places.

Today it is only outside of the institutional churches, for the most part, that seers, mediums, and prophets combine psychic channelling and spiritual healing with faith in the transcendence of God and the idea of a transformative awakening to the Kingdom of God within the inner consciousness of every man.

vi. *the gradual loss of esoteric understanding*

There is some evidence to suggest that the original pre-Christian gnostic doctrine of the Primal Man—Redeemer, which lay behind the Jewish apocalyptic "Son of Man ("Bar Nasha") portrayal of Jesus in the New Testament, was generally no longer understood by most of the Fathers of the early Church by the end of the 2nd century A.D. Saint Ignatius of Antioch, whose anti-gnostic zeal was obviously overdone through partial ignorance of the original gnostic context of Jesus' own teachings about himself in the canonical New Testament, was able to shout in his "Letter to the Ephesians" that he accepted " . . . Jesus, not as a son of man, but as son of God." It is obvious that Ignatius is unaware of the full mystical and divine content of the "Bar Nasha," or "Son of Man" figure, both in late Jewish Hellenism and in the canonical gospels.

As Frederick H. Borsch has said in *The Christian and Gnostic Son of Man*:

> *"We find it difficult to overstate the impression left by our survey. Out of what is a relatively large body of Christian literature which can be dated or, with some probability, traced, at least in part, to the middle of the second century or earlier we find astoundingly few uses of a title (Son of*

Man) which tends to dominate in the Synoptic Gospels and which is well represented in the Fourth Gospel. Though Jesus in these Gospels is reported to have spoken of himself almost solely with reference to this designation and employed it at crucial junctures in his ministry, the later New Testament writers, the early Fathers and bearers and creators of tradition seem almost unconcerned with it.

"Apart from Justin the references to the figure could be counted on one's fingers and are outweighed far by contexts in which the Son of Man designation is deliberately or unconsciously avoided.

". . . although the Gospels unanimously and unequivocally witness to the fact that Jesus alone was reported to have spoken of the figure, . . . very few if any vestiges in the tradition of a more orthodox Christian variety passed on to us from the subsequent period.

"The Son of Man designation occurs with much more frequency in second-century materials of a decidedly gnostic character than it does in Christian writings which do not appear to be under this gnostic influence."[9]

Unless one's scholarship is biased by contemporary exoteric Christian traditionalism, the conclusion should be fairly obvious. Jesus uses an esoteric term, Son of Man, which has its mystical antecedents deep in Iranian, Hellenistic, and pre-Christian Jewish gnostic—perhaps Essene—circles, and which can only be understood by other "gnostics," i.e., by his apostles after the Resurrection, Ascension and Pentecost. Later New Testament writers, and the Apostolic Fathers of the 2nd century, have already almost completely departed from the occult Hellenistic Jewish milieu in which this kind of original "Christian Gnosticism" was shared.

That original milieu must have also been one in which direct psychic and spiritual perception through the awakened subtle faculties of man were commonplace experiences. The recognition of the Son of Man figure as fulfilled in the life and person of the historical Jesus was something which would obviously have depended in the first instance— beginning with Jesus himself—upon the operation of such awakened subtle faculties of psychic and spiritual perception within the context of "familiarity with the visionary symbols of the "Heavenly Man" traditions of the ancient world.

This is a point which is particularly relevant to our contention that the full gnostic psychic and spiritual experience of Jesus and the original apostles conveyed in the canonical Gospels was to be found after the late 2nd century, not primarily in the writings of the (by-then) "orthodox" Fathers of the institutionalized Church, but rather only for the most part in the writings of various heretical gnostic schools and sects. The unfortunate part is that many of the latter groups, while keeping to the original spiritual, mystical and psychical world-view expressed in the cosmology of the Son of Man—gnostic Primal Man— Redeemer concepts of Jesus and Paul, had by then departed from the positive theology of a "good" creation and a divine natural order which had characterized both the classical Greek metaphysics of Plato and the Hebraically-rooted New Testament itself.

Thus, the rejection of now-heretical, world-denying varieties of Gnosticism, plus the rejection of Montanism, led by association to a hardening of attitudes against all of those people still in the Church who—like the heretical Gnostics and Montanists—were visible charismatics claiming direct personal psychic visions, apparitions, dialogues-in-spirit with ascended saints and the Christ. These factors, plus the general tendency to lower the standards required for the Christian initiatory experience (which had originally involved psychospiritual transformations, a *metanoia* toward a "second birth" in the Spirit), eventually led to the all-but-complete shutting-down of inspired psychic channelling from and to the heavenly places within the exoteric institutional Church.

From the 2nd to the 4th centuries, but especially after Constantine's recognition of Christianity as the state religion, a new breed of hierarchy, presbyters, and bishops had flooded the Church. Most of these men quite obviously had not participated in mystic circles and developed psychically or spiritually into "sages" in the classical Oriental sense, at least not to the point where their own subtle or intuitive faculties could guide them in recognizing and separating real from unreal elements in the once living tradition (*paradosis*) of gnosis (faith and knowledge through direct psychic-spiritual experience). An increasing dependence upon the "frozen tradition," and the need to list and refer to a gradually approved New Testament "canon" of Scriptures, set in together with an increasingly absolutist conception of the function of the monarchical episcopate.

Even the 1st-century redactions of the canonical gospels and epistles were for the most part shaped by way of reaction to elaborate, world-denying types of gnostic myths, and included passages explicitly designed to emphasize primarily or only the exoteric requirements of salvation, water baptism, profession of faith in the physical resurrection and, in the Epistles, the necessity of worship in union with the duly appointed leaders of the institutional church.

Nevertheless, both the canonical books of the New Testament and the writings of many of the orthodox Fathers are still riddled with the other, non-expungable, essentially gnostic elements of primitive Christianity, such as the primary mystical, psychic, and spirit experiences of the founders—including visions, dreams, apparitions, out-of-the-body experiences, and astral trips "into the heavenly places."[11]

vii. *the importance of dispelling biased traditional christian or jewish conceptions of gnosticism*

The Role of the Discovery of the Nag Hammadi Library in this Process.

In speaking of the Nag Hammadi library, its general editor, James M. Robinson, points out that:

> "...the focus of this library has much in common with primitive Christianity, with Eastern religions, and with holy men of all times, as well as with the more secular equivalents of today, such as the counter-culture movements coming from the 1960s. Disinterest in the goods of a consumer society, withdrawal into communes of the like-minded away from the bustle and clutter of big-city distraction, non-involvement in the compromises of the political process, sharing an in-group's knowledge both of the disaster-course of the culture and of an ideal, radical alternative not commonly known—all this in modern garb is the real challenge rooted in such materials as the Nag Hammadi library."[11]

It is not difficult to observe the similarity between pre-Christian and early Christian gnosticism and those perennial elements of human psychical and mystical experience which have arisen in our day in yoga groups, meditation classes, psychic development programs, and in the study of spirit phenomena and mediumship. And it is within the gnostic traditions of antiquity, including the primitive Hellenistic–Jewish mystical traditions out of which the earliest forms of Christianity arose, that we may find the themes through which we might hope to reconcile primary psychic and spiritual experience once again to the Western religious heritage.

As we have seen in the present study, it is essential to the future of both science and religion that the presently missing link between the sacred and the profane—the psychic area—be restored to its rightful place in Western civilization. This means that the Western religious establishment, Protestant, Catholic, and Jewish, as well as the Western scientific establishment, must be broadened to include this missing psychic area on its maps. And the main historical precedent for its inclusion (the line of Egyptian, Persian, Greek and Hebraic gnosis which influenced the basic concepts of John the Baptist, Jesus the Christ, James, and John the Evangelist, as well as Paul the Apostle) has been so clouded and distorted by 2nd- to 4th-century heresies and their orthodox Christian opponents that we have—until the recovery and publication of the Qumram scrolls and the Nag Hammadi library—not been able to see what it might have before its distortion. Only now can we begin to detect the broad outlines of an ancient, pre-Christian Primordial Traditon of psychic intuition and spiritual insight, cutting across many religious traditions, which formed the background of Hellenistic Judaism in the ancient world and which influenced both primitive Christianity at its roots as well as—in a different direction—the many various heretical Jewish and Christian gnostic sects of the late 1st and the 2nd century A.D.

I would suggest that it is now time for Christian and Jewish theologians to re-educate themselves, and move away from the "heresy-hunting" syndrome which has plagued past efforts to reestablish the Primordial Tradition. This syndrome has characteristically led to the confusion of all gnosis and gnosticism with the particular world-denying heresies rightly condemned by church fathers and rabbis. It has led to an outright rejection of all live psychic and spirit phenomena, and mystical experience, as if they were all "gnostic" in the heretical sense. Persons who do this have not realized that by condemning all gnosis and all live psychic and spirit-channeling, and the systematic cultivation of mystical experience, as heretical or sinful, they are in fact by implication condemning Abraham, Moses, Jesus, Paul, and the very founders of the Western religious tradition itself.

There is no justification today for a biased and uninformed Christian or Jewish heresy-hunting which condemns, out-of-hand, those contemporary movements—whether religious, quasi-religious, or secular—which attempt to recover an understanding of live psychic, spirit, or mystic experience for their adherents. It is time that so-called "orthodox" Christian scholars, and traditional Jewish scholars, began to learn from the more authentic of such new movements and their teachers what personal psychic and spiritual development is really all about. There need be no compromise with one's particular "orthodoxy" in doing this. The ancient psychic and spiritual sciences of yoga, meditation, and the development of natural, God-given psychic and spiritual faculties such as clairvoyance, clairaudience, psychic and spiritual healing, and awareness of the "world of saints and spirits" and the "heavenly host" beyond the "physical veil," all await the sincere seeker, whether layman or minister, priest or rabbi.

As Jesus himself once admonished the intellectually elite clergy of his own day, "Unless you become like a little child, you can in no way enter into the Kingdom of God." Humility will be required in order to go back to basics, to admit that there is something essential in psychic development and primary spiritual experience, and that this is lacking in our rationalistic versions of religion. We must seek out those persons who can provide it, no matter how unconventional or unsophisticated their worldly credentials might be.

viii.   the remnants of the primordial tradition

The great medieval Russian saint, Gregory Palamas, developed a Christian theology of human sanctification and transformation which is thoroughly consistent with the yoga traditions of the East and the Primordial Tradition. He wrote:

> *"It is impossible to possess God in oneself, or to experience God in purity, or be united with the unmixed light, unless one purify oneself through virtue, unless one get out, or rather above, oneself."*[12]

Palamas' theology held that man's knowledge of God could not be purely intellectual, but rather must be direct, intuitive, and experiential. Such direct experience of God is possible because man is not an autonomous being in himself but an "image of God" which is "opened upward." However, no man could experience such a birthright in actual practice unless he was first restored to his "natural state." Such a restoration to the natural state of "wholeness in being," from which man has fallen through conformity to the existing social and cultural world, could only be attained through ascetical detachment, self-discipline, and an ethical process of de-egotization or self-transcendence.

Man, as he is born into this distorted world, is not really functioning at a truly natural or "human" level until he is so purified, self-integrated, and filled with the Spirit of God. The behavior that we see around us in the world, catalogued as the sociological norm in the media, etc., is not that of "natural" man, nor is it "human" behavior. An awakening, conversion and transformation is required for the restoration of communion with God. Or, one could say that a self-reintegration with one's truest nature within, the "image of God" (or the "Atman" in Indian philosophy), is a prerequisite to man's salvation.

Here, then, is a recognition within classical, Eastern Orthodox Christian theology of the legitimate place and the indispensable need for various technologies of the mind and spirit: ascetic disciplines, and methods of self-control, self-regulation, and self-integration. According to the Hesychast tradition, these must be found and used in order to open the soul "upwards" to the Divine Spirit before man can be restored to his truly natural, human state. In such a higher state alone can man be reached by God. Only in such higher modes of functioning of the human consciousness, or more spiritually attuned states, can man indeed hear the still small voice of God speaking from within him.

Thus, we come to discover the relevance of various kinds of psychical studies both to Christian theology and Christian life in our day. Indeed, not all kinds of Christian thought will accept such things as courses in yoga, mind development, psychic self-development, intuitional awareness, or courses in mediumship, OBEs, NDEs, apparitions, and spirit-contacts as relevant to Christianity. But such a position is an unfortunately restricted view of the matter. It is usually based upon rationalistic-doctrinal *a priori's* which have nothing to do with either an experience of psychic or spirit phenomena, or with an authentic, living, spiritual experience of any kind.

Those who are well grounded in the spirit of the Jesus of the Gospels, and who have explored such areas as Yoga-Vedanta, consciousness research, mind development courses, psychic unfoldment, or the spirit phenomena of the Modern Spiritualist Movement and the conceptions of 19th- to 20-century Theosophy in a first-hand manner will know that the techniques, practices, concepts, lifestyles, and worldviews fostered by such New Age groups and movements are really much more akin to those of the ancient Christian mysticism of the Gospel and of the Catholic Church than the latter is to the rationalism, materialism, and logical positivism of the rest of secular Western civilization today.[14]

But it is equally important that New Age people learn that all varieties of Gnosticism are not alike, and that some of them are potentially destructive of their own aspirations to rebuild the planet for a New Age.

ix. *dangers and strengths in esoteric versions of christianity*

(a) World-Denying Approaches to Life

Some "neo-gnostic" religious movements—like the heretical versions of ancient Gnosticism described by Hans Jonas—have tended to create attitudes of despair of the reform of this world, or even of its basic worth. Spirituality can take on the unhealthy approach of the "flight of the alone to the Alone," the "getting to Heaven" in Christian terms, the disengagement of the soul from Nature or God's Creation, rather than a loving commitment to natural order and the redemption of the physical and social worlds.

(b) Elitism

Some versions of "neo-Gnosticism" and "neo-Montanism," including some "charismatic" versions of Christianity, have tended to by-pass or condemn "outer humanity" or even the rest of the Church as uninspired or lost. Such an elitist attitude can be based upon a combination of naivete, ignorance, and old-fashioned pride in one's special revelations. It can result in harsh, judgmental attitudes toward others as outsiders, in contradiction to the clear injunctions of Jesus in the Gospels. This can lead to a fanaticism which does more than anything else to turn people in our day away from religion altogether, and from Christianity in particular.

(c) Authentic Esoteric Christian Theurgy: Transformative Mysticism and Sacramental Approaches to Living

There have also been *authentic* esoteric versions of Christianity. These have combined a transformative participation in mystical experience with holistic, sacramental approaches to living. We have reviewed in this study some of the esoteric conceptions which lay behind the concepts of Jesus as "Son of Man" and "Christ" in the New Testament, and seen that these rested upon the belief in the existence of valid, subtle faculties of psychic and spiritual perception through which metaphysical and spiritual realities could be apprehended and grasped by human beings.

Later we will review the psychic solidarity conceptions of the ancient world, including those of the Old Testament, and relate these to the primitive New Testament Christian conceptions of the Church as the "Body of Christ" and of the sacraments as psychic and spiritual extensions of the life, person, and work of the historical Jesus as the Christ. We shall see that such an understanding of the function of the church and sacraments is not institutional in the pejorative sense, but rather depends upon the recognition of live psychic and spiritual encounters, across the boundaries of physical time and space, with the resurrected and ascended Jesus, together with the entire company of heaven.

x.   conclusion: a continuation of the earliest christian gnosis in the parapsychology of religion

We may observe that the gnosis and sacramental mysticism of Orthodox-Catholic Christianity has as its ancient antecedent the positive, world-affirming cosmology of a Primordial Tradition of intuition and insight. This Primordial Tradition had been reflected in Egyptian Hermeticism and the Greek mysteries, and in classical Greek philosophy from Pythagoras and Plato to the Neo-Platonists. In this world-affirming mystical tradition, a divine "theurgy" had as its objective the bringing down of the "uncreated energies" of God into the temple of flesh and of the earth and the transformation thereby of the human body into the Temple of God. In this respect, Jesus as the Christian "high priest" was seen as the fulfillment of the work of the Archetypical God-Man, known to pre-Christian Hebrew and pagan mystics alike as the supreme Divine Theurgist. The Church's liturgical re-enactment of his life and work in the sacramental order was seen as the historical extension and hierophony of this divine work in the many times and places of succeeding human history.

Awareness of the underlying principles of psychic and spiritual action—which is available to us today through primary experience of psychic and spirit phenomena—could potentially open us toward the personal rediscovery of the Primordial Tradition of intuition and insight which lies at the roots of this kind of primitive Christianity.

My own conclusion is that in spite of the real pitfalls and dangers involved there are real strengths and benefits to recommend the pursuit by balanced individuals of studies in (1) personal psychic development programs, (2) spirit phenomena and mediumship as practiced in the modern Spiritualist movement, and (3) the esoteric stream of consciousness in the Judeo-Christian tradition. In view of the dominant threat to Transcendence in our culture of rationalistic materialism, the pursuit of studies in these three areas may be recommended to those who are ready to take up the challenge.

We live in a culture today in which, on the one side, skeptics with no real experience of psi deny its existence for fear of allowing what they consider to be pre-scientific superstition. Along with parapsychology and its claims they would also deny the very possibility of any spiritual world-view in which such basic religious axia as God, angels, life-after-death, prayer, or the existence of the human soul could conceivably find meaning.

On the other hand, we still live in a 19th-century religious environment in which, as Bromley and Shupe have pointed out, some fundamentalist Christians " . . . openly attack the claim that mystical experiences or meditation constitute an authentic spiritual experience."[14] In this kind of a context, the urgency of the need to rediscover what we have called a Primordial Tradition of intuition and insight about God, man, and the universe should speak for itself.

It is for this reason that a comprehensive study of the various psychic and spiritual practices, concepts, and movements extant today could offer to the Christian scholar and the apologist for Catholic thought a ready-made area of exploration for experiences and insights, to be used in the potential construction of a natural theology for the New Age, or a new Christian "gnosis" from the Primordial Tradition.

From a Christian perspective it is absolutely essential, as has been said by St. Gregory Palamas, that those who would attempt to launch themselves successfully onto the road of inner discovery through psychic and spiritual development must sooner or later come to the point where they "accept God" and undergo conversion to the central reality and power of love in and beyond the universe. That power is the One whom those who call themselves Christians have described as "the Cosmic Christ." But those in other traditions have actually described the same and/or similar experiences of some divine reality in other language.

In Eastern Orthodox theological terms, it will only be through the power of the Divine Spirit that such natural experiences of the potential of the human psyche and spirit will come to fruition. The Spirit can only fill us when we have been purified and emptied of selfishness, and have transcended our mundane existence and its attachment to the priority or finality of things of the flesh, i.e., ego, greed, and insensitivity to the needs of others.

That fruition, to be real, can only end in the bringing to birth of the "New Being" in every creature. The goal of human spiritual evolution was, according to the blueprint of the Christian orthodoxy of Greek Fathers from Clement, Origen, and Justin Martyr to Irenaeus and Gregory Palamas, nothing less than the bringing to birth in Everyman of the very mind and spirit that was in Jesus the Christ.

In this perspective, if the ethic of the "Kingdom of God" in which Jesus lived, moved, and had His being is ever to come to reign "on earth, as it is in Heaven," the peoples of earth must first be convinced through a new science of total consciousness affecting the soul, as well as the mind, that that Kingdom of God really exists *as a dimension for potential discovery within themselves.* Infinite love—with the real power of creation and redemption at its command to redeem the earth, and human affairs with it—will be required for this task.

Christian scholars must begin to direct themselves once again, with "right-brained" knowledge and skill, to explore those authentic "inner spaces" of "higher consciousness" in which alone the experience of the "New Birth" of the "Cosmic Christ" in Everyman is to be found. An awareness of the reality and power of those "inner spaces" has been lost in our materialistic and rationalistic civilization. It has been the present writer's experience that we can rediscover some of that awareness through the exploration of the potential of human psychic and spiritual experience in universal terms, in new, but very old, "technologies" of mind and spirit, transpersonal psychologies, and various new religious movements. These might be described as modern rediscoveries, or as a renaissance of authentic gnosis from a Primordial Tradition of ancient insights and intuitions known in a number of cultures throughout the ancient world.

Chapter 6

Precursors of the Cosmic Christ
Prophets, Saints, Magi and God-Men
in the Major Salvation Myths of Western Civilization

*i.   the transformative function of civilization's shamans
and their salvation myths*

The purpose of this chapter is to illustrate the important point that many of the central mythical themes of the Bible, in both the Old and the New Testaments, including the major salvation themes of the "Cosmic Christ" and the Son of the "Primal Man" as "Messiah"— were taken from earlier pagan sources and adapted to suit the needs, respectively, of the Hebrew cult of Yahweh and the Christian cult of Jesus.

This is an important point for us to grasp for two reasons:

(1) We have come into a new situation in the history of human development in which it is absolutely essential for the attainment of world peace and a higher consciousness that all people on the planet— including Jews and Christians—come to realize that God has spoken and continues to speak through and to all people everywhere, regardless of their religious and cultural traditions, through a variety of names, forms, symbols, myths, rituals, and customs.

(2) Simultaneously and for the first time in recorded history, we now have the capacity to understand, through comparative studies in religion and culture, that there was a higher, "evolutionary message" described in the code-language of ancient religious myth and magic, and particularly [for us] in the Judeo-Christian forms of ancient religious myth and magic.

Myth and magic have been very important in the formation of the guidelines for all of the great civilizations of humankind. And they are not subjects which we can afford any longer to leave to those who see in them no more than "pre-scientific superstition."

Civilization's shamans—including the prophets, wonder-working saints, and hierophant priests, rishis, magi, and the various god-men and -women of the major salvation myths of world history—have provided us essential material for understanding the ancient psychic and spiritual experience and the ideas of ancient culture on the subject of the future evolutionary goal of human consciousness. And from the heroes of myth and magic in Mesopotamia, Persia, Israel, Greece and Rome we may discern the broad outlines of a portrait of a "new humanity," as it were, which was ahead of its time on this planet.

Myths in the ancient world were creeds, or statements of a community's beliefs, in the form of a story. The great, perennial questions of human existence were answered in these stories. Sometimes the stories were historical, or historical in part; that is to say, in some cases they were based upon a historical incident or incidents, or upon the life of an important person who exemplified the values and lived out a drama illustrative of the values of the community.

Sometimes the stories of several persons' lives contributed to the myth of a single hero. At other times, the focus of the myth was not a single hero, but a series of persons who played different roles in the development of a people, nation, or cultic group. Sometimes myths were imaginative contributions which had little or no basis in history, but were created or inspired, much as are ballads or historical novels, to illustrate values of spiritual, moral, cultic, tribal or national importance to the group. These would have been used in conjunction with various rituals, or as an enacted religious drama, to illustrate and inculcate shared values in the participants in such ceremonies.

All of the religions and cultures of antiquity used myths in these ways. The ancient Israelites were no exception. The "national history" of Israel was put together by connecting a series of "events" and incidents in the lives of legendary heroes which illustrated theological and moral points which the storytellers were inspired to make. Original composition was usually transmitted orally and committed to memory before being written down and edited by official court scribes, often long after the "events" or individuals so commemorated had passed into history (if indeed they had ever been "history" in the first place).

As in the case of the holy scriptures of many of the great world religions, it is usually claimed that both the original heroes whose lives enacted the archetypical dramas, and the storytellers or editors who committed them to writing, were somehow inspired to perceive, then to understand and adequately transmit, the story of the events with its implicit *authoritative* interpretation.

"Revelation" was thus dependent upon a double inspiration. The "will" or "truth" of the deity was first revealed through the heroic action of the chief protagonist(s) of a drama who was inspired, guided, protected and empowered to "overcome" opposition and manifest a "truth," or the divinely determined outcome of the event. Then it was transmitted through the inspiration and enlightenment of storytellers and later editors of scriptures, so that they could successfully transmit the "truth" to succeeding generations of the faithful in a religion or culture.

The primary point which will be presented for the reader's consideration in this chapter is the interesting fact that, under all the often confusing details of ancient religious mythologies, there is often an implicit desire to communicate a vision of the origins and destiny of the whole human race, and the processes by which it can be transformed into something "better" than it is. This goal is always described in terms established by a particular people's highest vision of a "divine plan," or of various abstract "metaphysical" realities which are believed to govern an ideal state of human existence.

In many of the great world religions, the saints, prophets, seers, gurus or teachers, and god-men who are the central figures in their scriptures, are implicitly presented to the faithful as great spiritual and ethical exemplars or role-models. What happens to the central hero either does or should happen—in some form—to all. The trials he or she endures, and his or her victories, should be shared, or participated in, by "Everyman." And the glorified state which such heroes of spirituality achieve is held up as the goal of the human spiritual evolutionary process.

The stories of the lives of the patriarchs, Moses, and the prophets, as well as Jesus as the "Messiah of Israel," were meant to be read in this light in the Jewish and Christian scriptures, respectively. In the Judeo-Christian Bible, consisting of the Old Testament and the New Testament together, "orthodox" Christian scholars have generally perceived a "sacred history" which has relevance to all humanity.

But it has not always been perceived clearly by Jewish or Christian readers that their Bible is, in fact, an ancient mystical tradition's conception of the divine blueprint for human destiny, or a picture of the process of human psychospiritual evolution. The portrait of Jesus in the canonical New Testament is intended by its authors to present Him as the "Alpha and the Omega," the very goal of a Christian's personal human drama and of the whole evolutionary process on planet earth. Also, the faith, obedience, and heroic deeds of the Israelite patriarchs and prophets were to be imitated by faithful Jews.

Other religions, including many of the ancient mystery cults, have done this in varying degrees with the presentation of their godmen, avatars, gurus, prophets, and saviors. Mahayana Buddhism, with its conceptions of an "eternal Buddha," "bodhisattvas," and the future "maitreiya," has clearly presented a central, transformative role-model as the psychospiritual, evolutionary goal for the rest of humanity on the path of the "dharma," or the eternal law of right-mindedness and authentic action. Unfortunately, in institutionalized forms of Christianity the focus on the aspect of the central figure, Jesus, as a realizable role model has been obscured, if not obliterated, by theological overlays which tend to isolate Him from the rest of humanity and its aspirations for itself.

In many religious traditions, particularly in the West, *eschatological myths* tell us about the final transformation of the earth and of humanity. In the Bible, for example, Isaiah's passages about the Messianic Age in which "the lion shall lie down with the lamb, and there shall be no harm in all of my holy mountain," and the vision of the "new heaven and the new earth" seen by John on Mount Patmos in the Book of Revelation in the New Testament, both illustrate the ideal final state of the earth and of human society after the Divine Plan for this planet has come to fruition.

Individual human destiny, however, is portrayed in pagan stories of the final "divinization," or "apotheosization" of the heroes, or "godmen," in *soteriological myths*. It is to this latter category of myths that we must look if we are to find the "blueprint" in ancient religions for the steps that we (e.g., ordinary humanity) must take in order to become what "God," the "gods," "Nature," or "History" want us to become. In other words, the pictures of the "transfigured" [i.e., transformed], "resurrected," and "ascended" god-men in ancient religions and cultures are really graphic revelations of the ideal future-state of Everyman, the "target," as it were, toward which all of us should strive.

There is thus a "divine anthropology" and a "divine cosmology" implicit in ancient sacral mythologies of East and West. This is expressed in varying degrees in the great world religions, and is quite central and inescapable in Christianity. Nevertheless, many fundamentalists, ecclesiastical institutionalists, and rationalistic liberal theologians have missed this point in their presentations of Christianity.

This flaw has developed primarily because the former two parties often do not know how to read "myth" in general, and the latter party is often too reductionistic to concede that there could be such a sublimely inspired *universal* wisdom under the myth that we should take seriously. In traditionalist circles, there is also an ancient reluctance to Jesus being in any way related to the "god-men" of the ancient pagan mysteries, to Avatars in Hinduism like Krishna, or to the Eternal Buddha or Bodhisattvas in Mahayana Buddhism. This is quite misguided thinking which removes Jesus entirely from the context of the Primordial Tradition, and deprives modern Christian apologetics of its strongest argument for the divinity of Jesus. For, in today's rationalistic and materialistic cultural milieu, Oriental mysticism provides us with the missing keys to understanding this ancient concept.

Finally, the reason that many modern Christian theologies miss the seriousness of the message of the Biblical myths concerning the goal of human psychospiritual transformation into a "new being" is simply that most people today do not know very much about the hidden, divine-human potential to manifest transformation and transcendence in the "gifts" and "fruits" of the Spirit.

The failure to understand highest states of consciousness and being, the failure to understand higher mystical states and divinely inspired spiritual and psychical faculties, results in an inability to accept the archetypical gospel portrait of Jesus and His "supranatural" powers as in any way potentially depictive of the rest of the human race. The very idea that ordinary people are meant by God to develop into "new Christs"—with all of His miraculous powers as their divine and natural birthright—is simply preposterous to most Christian clergy. The result is that they do not tell their people about it.

This, in turn, creates a vacuum in traditionally Christian cultures. No "divine blueprint" for the human evolutionary process is held up before the people. No "divine anthropology" or "divine cosmology" is postulated. Secular "scientism" rushes in as the new religion governing political and social theory. Its ideal state is to be engineered without regard to the attainment of any higher state of consciousness or being by humanity at large. The brave new world replaces the vision of a "new humanity," or of a new heaven and a new earth, portrayed in ancient soteriological and eschatological myths of religion. This has happened, in part, because our "wise men" today have turned away from the yogas and other psychospiritual technologies of psyche and spirit to flat-world, linear, cybernetic computations in the "left-brain," where the great mysteries of God, man, and the cosmos are not to be found. And the people suffer the loss of the vision of the "Kingdom of God." It has been replaced, in fact, by the vision of the status quo, the various normative modes of human behavior that have turned our planet, from Beirut to Belfast, into a Hell.

Perhaps a first step out of this dilemma will be to learn once again to read the maps, the "cosmic blueprint," for the way out written in the arcane code-language of myth, symbol, and magic. Only then will we understand the way back intuited by countless ages of cumulative human wisdom in a global quest for universal human values.

ii. three types of archetypical myth

Anthropologists and historians of religion generally recognize three types of myth which have been used to weave the broad outlines and main features of the Western religious tradition. They are found in the Old and New Testaments and in the subsequent development of the Christian psyche. These three types of myth when taken together provide us with a comprehensive picture of pre-philosophical religious and cultural perspectives in their classical Judeo-Christian form. They have also re-emerged in contemporary, new religious movements (often unconsciously for the adherents of such systems).

The three major types of myth which have helped to shape the Western psyche are: (i) "cosmogenic," or creation myths; (ii) "soteriological," or salvation myths; and (iii) "eschatological" myths, or myths of the End Times.[1]

(i) *Creation myths* are stories that describe in symbolic form the spiritual and psychic origins of the world and humankind. (ii) *Salvation myths* are stories that narrate an ideal pattern or blueprint by which human beings may be "saved" from their "fallen" state, or spiritually and psychically transformed back into "god-men." There is often talk of an invitation to "inherit" a divine or transcdendent spiritual and psychic potential which has either temporarily been lost, or not yet attained on the scale of evolution. (iii) *Eschatological myths* are stories, in highly symbolic form, about the "last things," the "end of an age" or the end of the "old order," and a "final judgment." Often, these stories are not really about the "end of the world" in physical terms— although they use physical imagery. They seem to represent an attempt to tell us about radical changes which must come about before humanity can reach the fulfillment of its divine potential and destiny.

In this study we shall not dwell upon the details of eschatological myth, since it deals primarily with earth changes leading up to a final transformation and a New Order. What we shall be concerned with primarily is soteriological myth, which not only presents the drama which its Hero (representative of ideal humanity) must go through to achieve perfection, but also presents in Him (as apotheocized "God-Man") the true or authentic goal of the human evolutionary process. But cosmogenic or creation myths always provide the necessary background for soteriological myths, and we will have to describe them first.

A. Cosmogenic, or Creation Myths

There are several basic types of creation myths to be found in the world's religious literature, from primitive and ancient-sacral cultures to major religious traditions of East and West. The creation myths found in the Bible represent an integration of several of these types, as follows:

(1) "Anthropomorphic Creator-God Myths"

There are some varieties of creation myths in which a single, Supreme Creator God—often a sky-god—is presented as a universal "Father," the "male" or "active principle," who fashions the world and mankind much as a potter creates objects by fashioning them from clay. He then animates them with his own breath, or life, making them his semi-divine offspring. Thus his own "divine life" or "breath of divinity" is in them. (It is academic error to assume that the Hebrews invented this motif; clearly they borrowed it.)

(2) "Primal Man Myths"

There are other types of myths in which the supreme God and Creator is sometimes depicted as a "Primal Man." In such cases divinity is conceived of in anthropomorphic terms. Thus in India the "Purusha," in Iran the "Kaiomart," in the Hellenistic world the "Anthropos," and in Israel "Metatron"—the "Second Power in Heaven" seen as a man-like figure in the visionary experience of Enoch and Daniel—all represent variations of the mythic image of the Primal Man.

(3) "Divine Parent Myths"

There are, in yet other Creation myths, a pair of Divine Parents, Male and Female, or Primordial Father and Mother, who give birth to the whole created order, including mankind. In some cases, there may be only one Parent who produces the creation and mankind out of the substance of his or her own body. In ancient Babylonian myth, it is out of the body of the primordial Goddess Mother that Creation springs. In the canonical Biblical myth, the "Primal Parent" figures, Adam and Eve, are simply transposed from heaven to earth, and demoted to the status of mortals from that of immortals which they generally hold in older, pagan myths. There are also persistent Jewish mystical traditions about a cosmic being, a sort of "Adam before the Fall," called "Adam Kadmon," similar to those in earlier pagan myths.

(4) "Mother/Earth Goddess Myths"

Just as the primal "Father" God is a sky-god represented as coming from the heavens, and ruling over its elements, including the lightning bolts and clouds which invade the atmosphere of earth, so is the primal "Mother Goddess" portrayed in many Cosmogenic myths as representing the fecund and fertile earth, or "Mother Nature" herself. She alone, when impregnated by the Sky-God "Father," gives birth to all life. Isis, Cybele, Demeter, and in a reduced mortal form the Hebrew "Isha," or "Eve," were such figures.

(5) "Evolutionary Creation Myths"

In some creation myths, there is even an evolutionary perspective. Some very primitive peoples in Africa and Australia have developed a rather sophisticated evolutionary schema in which the lower-to-higher orders of creation gradually emerge out of the earth in stages from the inanimate to the animate. Worm-like figures, who emerge out of the earth gradually, are said finally to stand upright and eventually take on human characteristics. These kinds of primitive "evolutionary" myths stress the stages of development of the created order, and emphasize that an innate principle of life or intelligence from within the order of nature itself is reflected in the divine process of Creation.

The canonical Hebrew myths of Genesis, in spite of their primary emphasis upon an act of creation as the voluntary fashioning act of a supreme, man-like Creator, nevertheless incorporate this primitive evolutional mythic schema. They do this by means of the device of the six days of creation, during which "mythic time" there is a serialization of the appearance of order from chaos, and of life-forms in a sequence from the emergence from the lowest to the highest orders. (The idea of "six days" was undoubtedly borrowed by the Jews from the Mesopotamian calendar, in which laborers customarily worked for six days and had the seventh for rest.)

(6) Myths of the "Fall" or "Degeneration" of the Human Race from its Original Perfection: Frequent Appendices to Cosmogenic Myths

In many Creation Myths there are stories included at the end to explain the subsequent loss of the divine nature or loss of earlier presumed spiritual and psychic powers with which humanity, as the semi-divine creature or offspring of a supreme Creator God, began its existence. Such etiological stories of a "Fall of Man" reflect humanity's perennial preoccupation with moral or ethical issues. There would seem to be a universal, and early, perception in human history of the difference between the "intuited ought" and the "perceived being" of things, in both the natural and social orders.

In the Hebrew version of such stories of a fall, we find that Adam and Eve comprise the now sexually separated or bipolarized and earth-bound version of an original, androgynous "Heavenly Man" of a near universal myth. "Adam Kadmon" is the Hebrew version of the first cosmic and divine earthly Man. He and Eve, his now-separate female half, are expelled from a Garden. The latter is an archetypical symbol representing the harmony of the world that "ought to be." But Adam and Eve's ideal habitat is changed into a veritable jungle where they must live by their wits, or by the "sweat of their brows" (i.e., perhaps "left-brain consciousness"). This describes the introduction of disharmony into creation. This disharmony is depicted as humanity's own fault, brought about by its distrust of divine guidance and by its egoic rebellion.

Originally human beings had been put into the Primordial "Garden" not to loll about but to till it and keep it as co-creators with, and as the stewards of, its divine Creator and owner. Even after their expulsion from the Garden, this commission remains, in spite of the Fall. But the work is now obviously impossible without divine help and intervention. This intervention will be necessary to get humanity back into the Garden, i.e., into the harmonious Primordial spiritual condition which it has forfeited. The implication is that without a restoration to its semi-divine spiritual nature and birthright, humanity cannot successfully fulfill God's mandate to share, as co-creators with Him and his stewards, the earth.

(7) In Babylonian and many other ancient civilizations we also find myths of a prehistoric Deluge or Flood connected with a Divine Judgment and a destruction of the "fallen" race and of the old, corrupted order of civilization that had issued from it.

In the Gilgamesh epic, for example, we find a version of the flood story predating the Hebrew version by centuries. In this story, the gods (*elohim*) take council together to destroy mankind as a punishment for its offenses against the heavenly order. But a goddess decides to save one good man, Utnapishtim, as her favorite. (He is a pre-Hebraic, Babylonian version of Noah). She warns him of a coming flood, and instructs him to build a boat, an ark, into which he is to put one pair (male and female) of each species of living being. He and his wife go aboard, the rains and floods come, and the face of the Earth is covered for forty days and nights. He releases a bird to determine whether the waters have subsided. When the bird returns bearing a branch, the Babylonian hero Utnapishtim, like his later Hebrew counterpart, Noah, knows that the flood is nearly over. Finally he lands on top of Mount Ararat, where he performs a sacrifice of covenant with the gods. The features of the Biblical story of the flood appear to be adapted from the earlier Babylonian version.

The basic mythic point, as found in the Biblical version, is that it is the nature of divinity to start with the "one just person," or a "faithful remnant," after the "old order" is destroyed, and to rebuild the "new creation" or "new order" on that single, good foundation.

(8) Appended to the Hebrew Midrashim (mythological stories) of the Creation and Fall there is the story of the "Tower of Babel," borrowed from observation of the Babylonian custom of building "ziggurats" (or artificial mountains) where the supreme god was contacted by a shamanistic high-priest and worshipped by the people only from below, and from afar.

Often the Babylonians and other ancient-sacral peoples built temples on the tops of such structures, where shamanic-priests went into trance states and "contacted the god(s)" for the guidance of the nation and of the people. Later, in *Exodus*, Moses is portrayed as receiving the revelation of the law directly from Israel's god, Yahweh, on Mount Sinai (a real mountain?). Like Shamans, or primitive hierophant-priests of the gods everywhere, Moses is described as ecstatic (in a trance-like state) and "glowing in countenance" from his divine encounter.

The point of the Hebrew creation story seems to be that "fallen" mankind cannot climb or build its way back into heaven (a metaphor for highest states of Primordial bliss and harmony, like the metaphor of the "garden of Eden" itself). The emphasis of the Yahwist editors of Genesis is of course that the way back into Divinity or heavenly states now depends upon the active intervention and initiative of the "I-am" (i.e., Yahweh). It is precisely at this point, in Chapter 12 of Genesis, that the Soteriological drama begins with the story of Abraham. In Soteriological myths, various specialists in the holy— prophets, seers, wonder-workers, teachers and healers, as well as "god-men" in some traditions—come onto the scene of myth-history with the pre-assigned task of getting humanity back to its original state.

B. *Soterological or Salvation Myths*

The function of soteriological or salvation myths wherever they occur in the world's religious traditions (e.g., India, Persia, Egypt, Greece, mystical Jewish traditions and early Christianity) is to set forth, to enact, and to explain the archetypical "cosmic drama" by which "fallen man" regains "his divinity," or "his Primordial status," as an embodiment or reflection "in the earth plane" of the archetypical God-Man ("heavenly man," "primal man," "cosmic man," or "God-in-human-form"). In mystical Judaism, this figure was "Adam Kadmon," the cosmic "divine man" before the Fall. In primitive Christianity, Paul identified Jesus with this figure as a "restored" or "second" Adam.

Thus, soteriological or salvation myths have generally performed the great function of providing a blueprint or archetypical symbol of the "way," or "path" of the "perfected man," or the "apotheocized" or "re-divinized humanity." This is frequently conceived of as the goal of human psychophysical and psychospiritual evolution.

A number of 19th-century scholars (most of whom were "free-thinkers" or skeptics unfortunately bent on embarrassing Christianity) pointed out that there were from 16 to 20 "pre-Christian crucified saviors" or "dying-and-rising god-men" who performed the same kinds, or similar kinds, of functions (in the earlier "pagan" traditions) as Jesus did later in Christianity.

One of these scholars, Kersey Greaves, listed sixteen such pre-Christian mythological "savior figures," or "dying-and-rising god-men," as follows:

Krishna (India/according to some traditions and
  monuments, Krishna was hung on a tree   and put to
death by his enemies)
Sakia Muni (India)
Thammuz (Syria)
Wittoba (of the Telengonese)
Iao (Nepal)
Hesus (Celtic Druids)
Quetzalcoatl (Mexico)
Quirinus (Rome)
Prometheus (Greece)
Thulis (Egypt)
Indra (India and Tibet, see Georgius, *Thibetinum
  Alphabetum*, p. 230)
Alcestos (Greece/Euripides)
Atys (Phrygia)
Crite (Chaldea)
Bali (Orissa)
Mithra (Persia)[2]

Admittedly, one must read Greave's arguments in particular instances and check his sources carefully; but he—and a number of other 19th-century writers in the same vein—do provide at the least massive, cumulative evidence for the general archetype of the "rejected god-man" in the salvation myths of classical antiquity long before Christ.[3] The whole tradition in 19th-century "free thought," which with Greaves postulated the existence of a "Christianity before Christ," should not be overlooked by contemporary scholars.

It is unfortunate that such parallels in the lives of the world's mystical and magical god-men—whether purely legendary or historical figures—have usually been presented in an atmosphere of anti-Christian polemic. There are great truths and important insights on the mythopoeic and psychological levels to be gained from the study of such common or similar myth-typologies. Neither Christian fundamentalists nor their rationalistic and materialistic, skeptical opponents have been sufficiently unbiased to appreciate such insights.

Foremost among the insights to be gained from the study of pre-Christian and pagan salvation myths and their "god-men," or heroes, is that there is a cluster of common ideas, or universal archetypes, which reappear and repeat themselves within the human consciousness and imagination among peoples of many cultures. They seem to have been re-enacted again and again in the history of specific, historical and legendary spiritual figures in all societies.

Specific types of great spiritual heroes are intuitively connected with the process of human psychospiritual transformation. This often involves an "apotheosis" of ordinary mortal human beings into either "god-men" or, at least, into a new (reformed, "spiritualized-type" of) humanity. Spiritual heroes in many traditions have in fact been said to have lived out their lives on earth according to a nearly identical, "divinely established" pattern or blueprint.

iii.   myths of the magus/god-man

Professor W. E. Butler of Cambridge University (*The Myth of the Magus*) has pointed out that the legendary figures of the magician-theurgist or "magus" in occult literature, and of the founders and teachers of many world religions, are often sacrificed savior-gods, saints, or martyrs. They have often " . . . behaved in a similar manner and their lives went according to the same plan."[4]

Butler finds that all of these figures derive ultimately from " . . . that dim past when mythic heroes died to be reborn in kingship or seasonal rites." She says that although such a figure may have gradually become " . . . a creature sealed and set apart in the magic circle, he was originally one of the countless dying gods whose distribution is world-wide."[5]

She lists ten common characteristics in the archetypical life-stories of the magi and/or god-men who become ritual-heroes of myth and/or history. I shall list them, and paraphrase her comments as follows:

(1) *A Supernatural or Mysterious Origin of the Hero:* The hero is usually a half-god, half-human hero, often with one divine parent, usually the father, and one human parent, usually the mother, the latter often representing Mother Earth, or Nature itself. Often the divine, and the royal or kingly parentage of the (divine god-man) child's

father is also stressed. (Sometimes, in the case of god-men rather than merely human magi, the legends also include stories of a virgin birth, to stress the supernatural origin of the hero.)

(2) *Portents at Birth:* These are special signs or miracles given to indicate the supernatural origin and nature of the hero. (We frequently find the arrival overhead of stars, special astrological configurations in the heavens, and other paranormal phenomena among these.)

(3) *Perils Menacing the Infancy:* The powers of evil, represented in the old order, or the establishment of the day, i.e., the existing church and state, frequently conspire to kill the divine child. Thus many centuries or millenia before the New Testament story of King Herod (the "illegitimate," half-Edomite king of the Jews who ordered all of the innocent newborn children of Judea killed in order to destroy the Christ child), we find the story in Indian scriptures of the newly born god-man or Avatar Krishna's wicked uncle Kansa. He is also an illegitimate king who orders the slaying of all newborn children under two years of age in order to destroy the child Krishna.

W. E. Butler attributes such common stories to a universal, ancient literary custom. In order to stress the perils which the god-man must face in coming into a corrupted order on the earth plane, he is portrayed as committed to a self-sacrifice which will later be commemorated in a religious ritual. The remaining common characteristics of the Primordial myth of the god-man/magus and ritual hero are as follows:

(4) *Some Kind of Initiation:* This is often an initiation of the hero himself into the cult about to be proclaimed, or into the new, higher Wisdom or consciousness and supernatural powers to be shared later by him with his disciples. The baptism of Jesus by John the Baptist conforms to this pattern of the initiation, or awakening of the hero to his mission (cf. Morton Smith).

Austerities and temptations, which serve to test and purify his resolve, often occur before and/or after such an initiation. (In Jesus' case, in fact, we find the temptation in the wilderness immediately following the baptism by John in the Jordan River.)

(5) *Far Distant Wanderings:* This is usually in search of, or to teach, wisdom. It may involve the hero, god-man, or magus traveling to far lands which are looked upon by people in his culture as the places where ancient spiritual truths had traditionally been found. (Thus Abraham and Jesus both travel to Egypt.) Or, it may involve supernatural or astral travel into "other worlds" for knowledge (as in the cases of

the Tartan shamans, Hindu god-men and gurus, and European figures like Emmanuel Swedenborg). In some stories both physical travel and "soul travel" are combined.

(6) *A Magical Contest:* This is usually an encounter between representatives of the old order and the hero, in which the hero of the myth represents the new divine order. He wins by virtue of both his superior moral cause and his supernatural powers. (Examples are: the defeat of the prophets of Baal by Elijah; the defeat of the magician priests of Pharaoh by Moses; the miraculous "signs" of Jesus which serve to validate his arguments against the Scribes and Pharisees; the contest between Zoroaster and the priests of older Chaldean tradition; the many contests of this type in Brahmanical literature of India.)

(7) *A Trial or Persecution:* Usually the hero wins the magical contest or encounter with the representatives of the old order. But then, trumped-up charges or a grave injustice of some sort leads to a mock trial or persecution in which the hero is physically taken, convicted falsely, and legally condemned.

(8) *A Last Scene:* This is frequently of a set nature, and involves a sacramental meal of some sort anticipating a voluntary surrender or self-sacrifice to come on the part of the hero. There is often a farewell discourse to the disciples. (We may note Socrates' farewell meal and discourse with his followers, or Jesus' last meal with his disciples commemorated in the Lord's Supper, and the farewell discourses of the 4th Gospel.)

(9) *A Violent or Mysterious Death:* Examples of this are Osiris' death by suffocation and dismemberment; Orpheus' death by being torn to pieces at the hands of the Bacchantes; Socrates' being forced to drink the hemlock by the Athenians; Zoroasters' death at the hands of the old Chaldean priesthood; Jesus' crucifixion by the Roman state at the request of the high priests and the Sanhedrin.

(10) *A Resurrection and/or Ascension:* This often involves a post-mortem (re)appearance to disciples (i.e., a "resurrection"), followed by an "ascension into heaven" (or disappearance into another, higher dimension) by the hero.

Thus, we find similar events in the post-mortem careers of god-men figures like Osiris of Egypt, Orpheus of Greece, and Jesus. And/or in the case of these and other heroes, we find stories of their ascension or translation into the heavens (both Elijah and Mohammed, for example). This idea persists from fictional stories like that of Oedipus in the ancient Greek play down to the 20th-century claim to the "resurrection of Sri Yutkeshwar" witnessed by his disciple Paramahansa Yogananda in *The Autobiography of a Yogi.*[6]

We can surmise that such common features in the lives of classical god-men and/or magi figures result from a combination of (1) actual, historical recurrences of such themes and events in the lives of those who exhibit god-like or mysterious psychic and spiritual powers. Such persons have often attempted to use their gift of such powers as "signs" to reform the old order in accordance with their new vision; and (2) The formulaic, or ritualistic, commemoration of such typical events—whether historical or not—which are "sensed" to belong together with such ritual-hero myths.

Thus, such themes, including those associated with the classical cults of dying-and-rising gods in antiquity (both in fertility rites and kingship rituals), would naturally be linked to one's own special hero by the disciple of an actual, historical religious teacher or reformer like Zoroaster or Jesus. Such patterns of heroic events, stories, and teachings would naturally seem to re-occur in subsequent liturgical and literary histories. Such ideas in fact seem to correspond, as C. G. Jung pointed out, to profoundly embedded archetypes in the human collective unconscious, throughout all ages and cultures.

The disciples of the historical person known to us as Jesus would have recognized these universal, pre-Christian, pagan as well as Hellenistic signs of the archetypical "divine drama" of the classical god-man. Thus they would see their Master, their Teacher, as actually re-living such characteristic or typical actions of the classical god-man figure. They would have thereby recognized him as their promised "savior," and as both God and Man. For them he would have become the actual, historical embodiment, or "incarnation," of the "Primordial god-man," walking the "way of the eternal witness" to his—and their—divinity through death and resurrection.

Like the adherents of the pagan mystery cults before them, they would have wanted to identify with him, psychically and spiritually, through a ritual drama, including an initiation ceremony (baptism) and a communal meal, or mystic supper, modeled not only on the Jewish Passover and fellowship meals, but also on the pagan mysteries.

But this should have shown to Christian scholars with their eyes open that the particular sectarian Jewish spiritual climate which Jesus and his disciples took for granted was deeply indebted to *pagan* antecedents which had already been "baptised" into Jewish mysticism of the Essenic type. There must have been already incorporated into the milieu of Jewish mysticism a recognition of such archetypical signs or the marks of the god-man, and the kinds of things to look for, or expect to see unfolding in his historical life. Certainly the traditional modern Christian portrayal of Christianity as indebted only to the Judaism of canonical Prophets, Scribes and Pharisees for its mystical and magical antecedents is blatantly false.

The Judaism of Jesus, and his mystical and magical forebears in the Jewish tradition (like the Essenes, Therapeutae, and even some of the more esoterically inclined of the Pharisees), had obviously *already* borrowed heavily from the pagan mystery traditions of the East (including Egypt, Chaldea, Persia, India, and Greece), for at least two to three centuries before the Christian era.

Before we examine some of the evidence for the already long-standing practice of borrowing from the pagan religions of antiquity by pre-Christian Judaism, let us first examine the several types of figures, in addition to the god-men and magi of antiquity, who were generally believed throughout the ancient world to have a central role to play in the drama of "salvation," or in the psychospiritual transformation of humanity.

iv. major types of salvation-heroes in ancient religions

All of the following types of figures may be found in the mystical and occult literature of ancient societies. They mark the mystical process of human spiritual transformation from fallen beings to god-men, particularly in the so-called Western mystery traditions. We list them here in more or less descending order of importance in the hierarchy of human spiritual perfection:

The Background to the New Testament Portrait of Christ: Miracle-Workers and Transformers of Humanity

I. Types of "Civilization's Shamans," or "Specialists in the Holy":

Those who act as "Mid-Wives" in the Birth of the "New Being" from the "Old Humanity" (Hellenistic World and Roman Imperial period)

God-Men

Apotheosized or divinized human heroes, thereafter said to be both divine and human, sometimes described as "new beings" (India, Persia, Egypt, Hellenistic Greece, Rome).

Magi

Practitioners of "high magic" or theurgy, or sacramental rites designed to engineer the effects of spirit and mind upon matter (the official Chaldean and Zoroastrian priesthood).

Theurgists

Doers of the "divine work," i.e., bringing the "divine energies" down from celestial realms into the earth plane in order to transform the latter in accordance with divine will. Ritual magic and sacramental rites were used for this purpose, including the invocation of gods and/or angels and higher spirits. (Neo-Platonist philosophers, Egyptian Hermeticists, et. al.) This included a divine "alchemy," the goal of which was self-transformation and the transformation of others toward a divine state of being.

Gurus

Master-teachers, illuminators of their disciples in India and Asia A similar relationship came to exist between Greek philosophers and their pupils, and between popular Hasidic Jewish Rabbis and mystical teachers and their disciples).

Prophets

Proclaimers of the divine will and plan, particularly in specific instances for specific people and events. This involves the element of precognition of the future as one of its components. Prophecy is done in an ecstatic or trance state in which the prophet is possessed or inspired by the God whose words are thought to be uttered (Judaism, Christianity and Islam and their derivatives are said to be "prophetic religions").

Seers

Clairvoyants, clairaudiants, and diviners of the future. Those who, like shamans, could sometimes "see into" the spirit world and talk to the dead, whether ancestors, saints, angels, or gods, etc. Ancient pagan and early Israelite prophets—before Samuel—were called seers. In modern times, Mesmerist "somnabules" in the late 18th and early 19th centuries, and modern Spiritualist "mediums" in the late 19th and early 20th centuries, performed the functions of ancient seers.

Healers

Religious figures with the "charism" or special gift from God or the gods, angelic beings, or dead saints or spirits to heal the sick, physically, mentally, and/or spiritually.

William James said that healings—whether in body, mind and/or spirit—have been claimed for a vast majority of the founders and principal saints of the world's religions, and that until modern times healing by paranormal means has been an important sign of authentic religious leadership in most traditions.

The medical profession has grown out of priestly schools of healing in Egypt and Greece in the West, and in India and China in the East. The historical origins of all medicine are thus found in religious forms of healing.

Exorcists

Those who have the special "charism" or gift to expel negative forces, intelligences, energies, complexes, diseases or disorders of body, mind, and spirit from afflicted persons and thus to prepare them for restoration or healing. Exorcism and healing were thus complementary functions, since in primitive and ancient sacral cultures illnesses and diseases, or mental disorders, were said to be caused by confused or "evil spirits" who either obsessed or possessed a person whose quota of spiritual, mental, and/or physical energy was low. These "spirits" could either be lower non-human entities, i.e., "demons" or "elementals," or confused, deceased human beings trying to live their lives through unfortunate and unsuspecting living persons.

Exorcisms performed an important role in the religion and medicine of Egypt and Mesopotamia in the West, and in India and China in the East. In Palestine, in Hellenistic times, Jewish mystics and healers—the Therapeuts—practiced exorcism, as did Jesus in the canonical Gospels. Healing and exorcism were considered priestly duties in the primitive Christian Church. To this day, one of the "minor orders" on the way to the priesthood in the Roman Catholic Church is the "Order of Exorcist."

II. Several Grades of Those "On the Path" or "On the Way" to Salvation:

Initiates
Persons committed to the "Path" and privy to its mysteries.

Awakened Ones
Those who have had an experience of "awakening" to the primary reality of the non-physical spiritual life and who have gone beyond this to a particular appreciation of the need for a "purification of the psyche" and an appropriation of mystical illumination.

Proselytes and Catechumens
Those under instruction who are committed to eventual "initiation" into a cult.

Hearers and God-Fearers
Worshippers of and listeners to a God, who have not yet committed themselves to a cult.

Seekers
Those who seek after and enquire about the faith, or "Path" that will lead to salvation, truth, or liberation.

Note that all of these "specialists in the holy" are "civilization's shamans," because they represent a division of labor. That is to say, in "pre-civilized," primitive cultures the figure of the shaman combines all of these roles. In addition, s/he was often the leader of the tribe. When nations are forged as the result of a confederation of tribes, the jobs of the shaman are given to several people: the prophet (or seer), the priest, (state-magician and healer-physician) and the chief or king, et. al. Thus, the classic phrase "prophet, priest, and king," used in primitive Christian liturgies to refer to Christ, would mean that he performed all the functions of a shaman.

All of these figures represent the "ascent" in the human psycho-spiritual transformation process from ordinary, "fallen" humanity to the "restoration," or "apotheosis" from "mortal" to "Immortal Being." Such figures are important in the history of religions as sign-posts pointing to the reality of higher forms of being and action.

v. salvation heroes of the old testament: the patriarchal stories

The story of the divine action to restore humankind to its Primordial heritage begins with the 12th chapter of Genesis. It is the metaphorical story of Abraham, a patriarch or type of early Israelite shaman-figure, a leader in touch with God and His guidance, and the forefather of the Israelites (i.e., people who, like Jacob, wrestle with God and win). Abraham is called by God to lead his people out of Ur of Chaldea (an earthly city) to a "promised land," or " . . . a land flowing with milk and honey." As in the case of all tribal shamans, the deity speaks to the shaman in order to reveal His will to the people, and guides the shaman to lead the people in their journeys.

The "Promised Land" was understood both by mystical Jews and by Jesus and his followers to be more than the physical land of Canaan. It was a metaphor—derived from the history of Israel—for the recovery of the "garden of eden," or for the redemption of the true Israelites (or the divinely called portion of humanity) "out from spiritual slavery in the midst of the nations of the world," (i.e., from the "fallen" condition).

Immediately after the stories of the Creation, Fall, and Flood in chapters 1-11 of Genesis, the canonical Old Testament editors have positioned the story of the "Divine Initiative" in the patriarchal narratives. God shows an erring humanity the way to the "promised land," which many Jewish mystics in the Hellenistic period (like Essenes, Therapeuts, and primitive Christians) interpreted to mean "humanity's lost state of union with God and the Divine Order."

Some Hellenistic Jews, early Christian Biblical exegetists, and others, including various gnostics, and later Sufis, characteristically interpreted the "promised land" passages (as found, for example, in the sagas of Abraham and the patriarchs, in the Exodus narratives connected with Mosaic tradition, and in subsequent prophetic and wisdom literature of the Bible) as code words. Rather than taking those words as solely literal promises of "land" to Abraham's descendants, they saw them as allegorical statements signifying humanity's promised re-entry, through divine initiative, grace, and the proper human response, into the "Primordial spiritual state," that inner "Kingdom of God" which would lead to an outer social harmony on earth, or "a new heaven and a new earth."

It is clear from the canonical gospel accounts that Jesus' own teaching is portrayed as having been interpreted on metaphorical lines. It is clearly a mystical teaching. He explicitly rejects the idea that the "Kingdom of God" is synonymous with any earthly kingdom, including that of David or—as Paul was to say—"Israel after the flesh." This major theme is reflected in the speeches of the first martyr, Stephen, by Peter in Acts, in Pauline theology, and in the archetypical mysticism of the Apocalypse of John. Pre-Nicean Fathers, like Clement and Origen, make this allegorical interpretation clear. Later, Augustine picks it up in *The City of God*. But the idea is subsequently rationalized away and almost lost in the development of both the polity of the Byzantine state and in Western church-state settlements throughout the Middle Ages.

Nevertheless, the collective consciousness of the Western psyche, deeply imbedded in the major mythical themes of the past two thousand years, has been subjected to great idealistic teachings which would openly suggest that humanity's "way back" into the "Kingdom," or into the now-lost state of "Primordial spiritual fulfillment," lies primarily in the cultivation of "things of the Spirit," or in a radical, ethical and psychospiritual Transformation, rather than in mere prosperity in the physical realm or in the politics of war and history.

Indeed, for the later mystics of Israel, God's promises did not rest upon His preference for the Jews and their socio-political activity as an ethnic group, nation, or institutional religion. God was not bound to give victory to them (or to any religious group, or nation) over its enemies. According to varieties of interpretation by later Jewish prophets and mystics, prosperity and protection must be the result of an inner spiritual communion with God serving as the source of the individual or group's whole way of life. If the latter was not in line with the divine will, God was not obliged to lead, protect or save the group (or by extension any later group like the Christian Church which claimed to be the successor of the Israelite spiritual tradition). In the estimation of most Judeo-Christian mystics there is even the necessity, at times, of choosing the route of martyrdom in witnessing to divine truths in the midst of a "fallen" world.

vi. moses and the magic of the egyptian priesthood

Sir Wallace Budge, in his definitive historical work entitled *Egyptian Magic*, lists a number of the traditional powers attributed to the ancient Egyptian priesthood.[7] As described by the formulaic lines and phrases in Egyptian religious literature, these include magical and theurgical feats. It becomes obvious that many of these alleged archaic Egyptian "psychic and spiritual powers" are the same ones which are later claimed for Moses by the redactors of the Pentateuch, and even later claimed for Jesus by writers of the canonical New Testament.

The sources of the Egyptian tradition in which these "miracles" are found are older than the Hebrew Bible or the Christian Bible, and it is obvious that the ancient Jews and earliest Christians borrowed the ideas (and the experiences) of such "arcane powers" from the Egyptians, and not vice-versa. This does not mean that these powers were unreal. It only means that the understanding of them, and of the appropriateness of their use, was conditioned by several millenia of Egyptian formulaic usage.

We read in *Exodus* that Moses " . . . was learned in all of the *wisdom* of Egypt." The Hebrew word for "wisdom" is here a known cipher for the traditional "high magic," or "theurgy," of the Egyptian priesthood. And it is also interesting to note that, in the New Testament account of Jesus at the age of 12 discoursing with the "doctors of the law" in the Jerusalem Temple, it is implied that this young Jesus had returned from Egypt wiser than the wise men of the Old Israel.

Budge describes Egyptian magic, in the ancient sacral perspective, as the "transference of Divine power from a Supernatural being to Man, whereby he was enabled to obtain supernatural results and to become for a time as mighty as the original possessor of the power."

Budge describes the purpose of Egyptian magic as " . . . to endow man with the means of compelling both friendly and hostile powers (at times even the Supreme God himself) to do as he wished." He denies that this kind of ritual magic was—as modern Christian and Jewish theologians often try to make out—readily distinguishable as less noble than a hypothetically "higher," or "religious" kind of miracle found in the Jewish Old Testament.

Here are several of the characteristic types of divine magic or "miracles" performed by the traditional Egyptian priesthood, as described by Sir Wallace Budge:

It was believed that almost boundless Divine power could be obtained by pronouncing certain *words* or *names of power* in the proper manner. It was said that such invocations could be used to accomplish the following feats:

(1) To heal the sick.

(2) To cast out evil spirits.

(3) To restore the dead to life.

(4) To bestow upon a dead man the power to transform his "corruptible body" into an "incorruptible body" wherein the soul might live to all eternity (note in this regard St. Paul's description of the divine power of Christ to "raise the dead" or to "clothe" his disciples with an "incorruptible body").

(5) To project souls into animals (as Jesus cast evil spirits into bodies of swine who then ran into the sea).

(6) To command life into inanimate figures and pictures or command them to perform at his behest (i.e., to speak, move, cry real tears, bleed, etc., as has often been claimed for saints' statues in Catholic and Byzantine Christianity).

(7) To command the powers of nature, i.e., the wind, the rain, the storm and tempest, the river, and the sea, to obey his behest (as Jesus did in the gospels).

(8) To cause disease and death to work evil and run onto one's foes, and upon enemies of those provided with such divine knowledge (as Moses did to the Egyptians with the several plagues he invoked upon them).

(9) The world itself was said (by the Egyptians) to have come into existence by the power of a *word* uttered by Toth (Hermes). (In India, the Primordial divine utterance of the sound "Om" was said to have called all things into existence. Later, the ancient

Hebrew writer(s) of Genesis had Yahweh, the God of Israel, uttering such a "word of power" in the biblical Creation story.)

(10) By the means of such a "word of power": (a) the world could also be "rent asunder," and (b) " . . . the waters, forsaking their nature, could be piled up in a heap" (as Moses is said to have done in Exodus, to allow the Israelites to go through the Red Sea), and (c) " . . . even the Sun's course in the heavens could be stopped" (as later seen in the story of Joshua).

(11) No god, spirit, or devil could resist the "word of power" spoken by an accomplished Egyptian priest-magician. (Note: Compare with the identical claims made for Jesus' power of exorcism in the New Testament.)

(12) The future as well as the past was open to the skillful priest-magician. (Note the claim made for Israelite prophets to be able to read the future and the past.)

(13) Neither time nor distance could "limit the operation of his power, and the mysteries of life and death were laid bare before him." He was said to be able to "draw aside the veil which hid the secrets of fate and death from ordinary mortals." (Note the claims made for the ascended Christ's cosmic powers in the New Testament.)[8]

Budge says that these traditional psychic and spiritual powers of the Egyptian priesthood were encoded as well into the elaborate symbolism and ceremonies of the temples. They had a deeper significance by presaging the potential of humanity for sharing in divinity. But, as Budge believes, after the Old Kingdom the "higher" meaning of earlier Egyptian sacramental magic was not understood by the priesthood. It was at this point, Budge suggests, that the theurgical "high-magic," or sacramental liturgy of the Egyptians, degenerated into sorcery and superstition. Others have suggested that reformers—from Akhenaton to Moses— attempted to do something about this situation.

vii. *osiris and christ: egyptian religion,*
      the new testament kerugma, and the nicean creed

Some scholars have seen the Osiris cult as the prototype of the theme of the dying-and-rising god-man in classical antiquity. Sir Wallace Budge has composed an eloquent description of the lofty salvation-myth and the accompanying mystery cult of Osiris as it was enacted in the Egyptian temples of antiquity. He emphasizes that the ancient Egyptian who participated in it, affirmed that it contained a profound transcendental truth. He believed in:

(1) ... one God-Almighty, eternal invisible ...

(2) ... who created the Heavens, the Earth, and all beings therein ...

(3) ... the Resurrection of the body in a changed and glorified form

(4) ... in which he would live to all eternity

(5) ... in the Company of the spirits and souls of the righteous.

(6) ... in a Kingdom ruled by a Being of Divine origin (Osiris)

(7) ... who had come down to live on earth,

(8) ... had suffered a cruel death at the hands of his enemies,

(9) ... and who had risen from the dead

(10) ... and become God and King of that World which is to come, beyond the Grave.

One can see the striking similarities between the framework and content of this ancient Egyptian creed with the whole structure of the Christian "Proclamation" or "Message" ("Kerugma"), both in its canonical New Testament form and as an official, creedal affirmation. The latter was to take shape by the fourth century A.D. in the "Nicean Creed" (325-381 A.D.). This marked a victory of the Christology of the Egyptian patriarch St. Athanasius of Alexandria over the perhaps less "mythically informed," rationalistic theology of the presbyter Arius. Arius appears to have missed the archetypical significance of the "dying-rising god-man myth" and opted in favor of a "watered down" version of the Christ message. In his version, divinity itself was not fully identified as the "divine part" of the god-man Christ.

Other pagan "god-men" and "magi," such as the dying-and-rising god-man Osiris, reflected the same salvation-theme as did the orthodox versions of the Christ story. Osiris, as well as other heroes in national traditions of god-men (like Orpheus of Greece), fulfilled this role. He was persecuted, put to death, rose again, and ascended into heaven. In the Persian tradition we find that the figure of Zoroaster conforms in part to this pattern. In Graeco-Roman Hellenism we note the myth-and-ritual connected with the mystery cults of Serapis and Mithra. The latter's birth as a god-man, incidentally, was celebrated at the winter solstice, on December 25th. He was said to have been born of a "virgin rock," (a primordial symbol of the virgin Mother Earth herself), and shepherds were said to have attended his birth. His rites included a baptism and a sacramental meal in which his flesh and blood were consumed as a means of psychic and spiritual union with him as "god-man," and "son of the Sun-god," or the universal Father ("Ahura Mazda," the "God of Light" of the Persians).

viii. was the "joshua-jesus" figure adapted from the osiran tradition?

Was there a pre-Christian, Hellenistic-Jewish mystery cult in which a Joshua-Jesus figure played the role as an archetype in a Hebraic adaptation of the Egyptian Osiris?

A 19th-century skeptic and rationalist, J. M. Robertson, published a book at the turn of this century (1903) entitled *Christianity and Mythology*, in which he attempted to present evidence for a thesis that the Gospel story, including such elements as the Last Supper, the Agony, the Betrayal, the Crucifixion, and the Resurrection, was built up around the classical theme of a pre-Christian, Hellenistic-Jewish "mystery play." Robertson's intention was to debunk Christianity, or at least to disprove the then-dominant fundamentalist versions of it. Because of his polemical attitude, his work never received the attention that it should have by serious Biblical scholars and historians of religion.

Robertson suggests that there was once in more primitive times a Palestinian rite in which a human victim was annually sacrificed. Later, certain groups of mystical Jews in the Hellenistic period may have taken over this more primitive, now-prohibited ceremony and made it into an annual passion-play in which there was a ritual enactment of the death of Joshua, or "Jeshua" (Jesus), the Hebraic equivalent of the dying-and-rising god-men of Egypt, Mesopotamia, Asia Minor, and Greece. He also argues that the cults of such "pagan Christs" as Osiris, Attis, Ammuz and Adonis had themselves allowed for symbolic substitutes for the human sacrifices performed earlier. He argues from various rather circumstantial texts that the name of a putative

Jewish version of this pagan archetype of the "sacrificed god-man" was " . . . Jesus ("Joshua"), the "Son of the Father."

Needless to say, J. M. Robertson's thesis was not met with acclaim in the Christian theological circles of his day. But today, in the light of subsequently discovered documents from Jewish Hellenism, Essene literature, and Jewish Gnosticism, and in the light of contemporary knowledge of the universal functions of myth and ritual in the world's ancient religions, Robertson's thesis would not necessarily be destructive of a mature understanding of Christianity's universal, symbolic origins.

Robertson's hypothesis might in fact be useful to Christian theologians in shedding some light on the positive, universal psychic and mythic roots of the Primitive Christian experience. This archetypal-mythic element in Christianity is very important for us to understand, for there is an urgent need to understand as well the psychic and mythic roots of other peoples' faiths in relation to our own.

Robertson's hypothesis was, at the time he proposed it, tied to 19th-century materialist-rationalist ideas of "progress" in the evolution of religions. Robertson saw an alleged "progression" from earlier, more primitive rites. Human sacrifices gave way to the more civilized mystery-rites of Egypt, Greece, and elsewhere, in which the "earlier savageries" of human sacrifice were mimicked in religious plays and sacramental rites. All of this may or may not be true in specific instances.

We do know that various mystery-rites *were* enacted in Egypt, Babylon, Persia, Greece, and in the Orient in which a symbolic actor or priest represented the son of an archetypical, ancient god-king. He was then mocked and "put to death" in a drama in which he represented the sacrificed son of the king as an archetypical hero. Like Osiris, the god-man, the actor-priest was "put to death" in a make-believe or symbolic mime. An animal substitute was often slain, complete with the out-pouring of blood, to represent his death. A sacramental feast was then held in which the sacred victim's "flesh and blood" were consumed. Sometimes this was done in a symbolic communion rite using bread and wine, which was substituted for the actual body and blood of the sacrificed animal or its human prototype.

Morton Smith has noted in this regard that there are ancient Jewish-Hellenistic magical ritual texts which emulate such an earlier Egyptian, Osiran sacramental feast. Such Jewish magical texts involved a symbolic cup of wine representing the "blood of Osiris," and bread representing "his body." They were consumed in an act of communion performed to "unite the magician to his god."[9] It would have been a short step for mystical Jews before the time of Christ to use such rites and to substitute the name "Yeshua" or "Joshua" for the pagan archetypical salvation hero who in earlier Egyptian circles had been known as "Osiris."

There should be little doubt that the pre-Christian, Jewish mystical and magical traditions using the "Elijah cup" were patterned on such an idea from pagan mystery rites. And there should be little doubt that the writers of the canonical New Testament were also thoroughly familiar with it. However, in the canonical Old Testament we can find no Jewish precedents for the idea of a sacramental cup which represents the blood or bread which represents the body of a dying-and-rising god-man. This was, possibly, a pagan ceremony which was adapted to unorthodox, sectarian Jewish mystical rites. It was possibly taken over in pre-Christian Judaism during the "Inter-Testamental period," and incorporated into esoteric Jewish magical and mystical ceremonies. These ceremonies (like those found in the "Hekalot" books) provide the presently missing Jewish precedents for the ideas of a sacrificial dying-and-rising god-man whose body and blood are to be consumed by his followers. We find such ideas in the Christian Gospel, in the Church, and in the Sacraments, but nowhere in the canonical Old Testament.

ix. pagan "dying-and-rising god-men" as victims of ritual sacrifice and as saviors

We have already alluded to the fact that in earlier times, in the more primitive cultures of the ancient Near East, actual human sacrifices were performed. The victim was often a slave, captive, or a criminal who was released in order to play the role of a ritual king, whether for a day or for a year. Thereafter, he was subjected to a crude ritual passion and slaying—in some cultures by rites of crucifixion.

Robertson suspected there were allusions to this archetypical theme in the mention of a "Barabbas," in the crucifixion story of the canonical Gospels.[10] Here we are told that, at the annual feast of the Passover, it was the custom in Jerusalem to release a prisoner.

Robertson saw this as a carried-over "literary fragment" from an earlier, pre-Christian Jewish "passion play" in which the audience was told that a "Jesus Barabbas," or "Joshua/Jeshua Son of the Father," would be released at the annual feast, and then play the role of the dying-and-rising god-man in the religious pageant, or ritual drama. In the Yahwist cult, an animal would be substituted for the released prisoner in the death scene.

Robertson notes that Origen tells us that the accepted reading of Matthew XXVII, 16:17 in the ancient Church was that the chosen criminal who was released at the time of the crucifixion of Jesus was called "Jesus Barabbas." Literally interpreted from the Hebrew or the Aramaic, this is "Jesus, Son of the Father."

Robertson's hypothesis is that there was an annual Semitic ritual in Palestine present long before the Yahwist era. From this annual ritual, Jews later on developed a mystery play. In this play a mythical ritual hero named "Jesus, Son of the Father" was symbolically sacrificed in mime. According to Robertson, this represented a Jewish form of the widespread practice in the ancient world of ritual assimilation. [Crude human sacrifices would have already been adapted to the symbol systems of Hellenistic myths of a god-man figure, which were then given a Jewish form and content.]

He finds a close resemblance to the Hebrew name "Yishac" (Isaac) in the Syrian form of the name "Joshua," or "Jeshua" (the Syrian form of Isaac was "Yeschu"), and conjectures that in an earlier pagan form of the Biblical myth in Genesis, Isaac (Yeschu) was sacrificed by his father, and that the Abram (Abraham) who did the sacrificing was a divine god-man figure in the earliest, proto-biblical traditions.

All this suggests, according to Robertson, that the Biblical figures of "Isaac" and "Joshua" became united or conflated into the pre-Christian mythical figure of "Yeschu," "Jesus," "Bar Abbas," or "Son of the Father," who was sacrificed in mime by his Divine Father and thereby became the ritual savior of the people who as a whole were named "Israel." Like the Joshua (Yeshua, or "Jesus") of the canonical Old Testament, this figure was then hailed as the one who had led the people of Israel successfully into the "Promised Land."

Robertson sees the conception of a "suffering Messiah" or a priestly "Messiah ben Joseph" (who had to be slain before a royal "Messiah ben David" could inaugurate the Messianic Age) as a mirroring, in the Hebraic psyche, of the archetype found in the Dionysian mystery cult. In this pagan rite the Dionysian prototype (like Osiris, Orpheus, and Attis in their respective rites) is described as the *eleutheros* or "liberator," and as the "savior" who is "sacrificed" and then "born again."

Now if J. M. Robertson is correct in his reconstruction of the possible origins of such a popular, pre-Christian Hebraic cult of a sacrificed, dying-and-rising god-man, then the "Son of the Father" named "Yeschu" or "Jesus" would have already subsumed both Old Testament biblical figures of "Joshua" *and* "Isaac" well before the time of Christ. If accepted, this theory would indeed yield some insight into the mythic background of the Christian crucifixion story in the Gospels. Such a background is entirely missing from the present canonical scriptures of the Jews, shaved back as they were by the "rabbinic council" at Jamnia in 97 A.D. to the time of the book of Malachi (4th century B.C.). After analyzing the literary style of the Gospel story, Robertson feels that it was based upon literary fragments originally intended (before Christian times) to have been enacted in a play rather than merely recited or read, as it was later in early Christian circles.

x. *"Jesus" as an initiatory name for an archetype of the savior*

If all of the above is accepted, even tentatively, I think that we must be prepared to venture even another bold hypothesis. The man whom we know in the canonical New Testament as "Jesus of Nazareth" (or as Schonefield calls him, "Jesus the Nazorean") may have in fact taken or been given the name "Jesus" as an initiatory name. The name could have been given or assumed precisely because he fulfilled, in the eyes of his Nazorean or Essene followers, the existing archetype of Joshua/Jeshua in the Jewish version of an earlier Primordial tradition about the dying-and-rising god-man. The near-universal pagan *and* Hebraic prophecies concerning the role of such a coming ritual-hero would have been fulfilled before their very eyes, not indeed in a ritual drama but in real life. This hero "Jesus" was indeed for them a dying-and-rising god-man, a Son of the Father, who had died to usher in the Kingdom of God as the suffering "Messiah ben Joseph" *and* the victorious "Messiah ben David" in one person.

In fact, one may speculate on the possibility that the name "Jesus" was originally a *title* of an "office," as is the term "Christ" or "Messiah." There was *a* Hermes, *an* Osiris, and *an* Orpheus figure in the earlier Egyptian and Greek mystery rites, and also perhaps a Melchizadek figure in earlier Hebrew traditions. There were mythic, sacramental or ritual "offices" and roles held and enacted by hierophants. Similarly, in pre-Christian Hellenistic-Jewish mystery rites which emulated these earlier rites, there may have been a "Jesus, Son of the Father figure" with a particular office-and-role. Because the man whom we would later know as the "Jesus" of the Gospels re-enacted this typical role, he could have fulfilled the expectations associated with this code-name at his baptism or "initiation," where the "Spirit of the Father" is mystically portrayed in the canonical gospels as saying from the heavens: "This is my well-beloved Son . . . hear ye Him."

Just as Jesus later was to give to his disciple Simon the initiatory name of "Cephas" ("rock") or "Peter" when Simon's "eyes were opened" and he "recognized" in gnostic fashion the true nature of the "Christ," so perhaps had "Jesus" himself been re-confirmed in the pre-Christian messianic expectations associated with the name "Jesus" at his own "initiation" (i.e., the Baptism), or at some other point in his ministry, according to this theory. The canonical gospel's pre-natal prophecies concerning the angelic command to give the expected child of Mary the name "Jesus" and the title "Emmanuel" could thus have been fulfilled not in infancy but in His later life, as He begins to play the symbolic role which His followers saw He had been born to play on the stage of life.

xi. "joseph" ("yuz asaph") as a code name among the essenes

There are rabbinic sources which hint that one of Jesus' earlier names—a "pre-initiatory" name—might have been "Joseph" (as the "son of Joseph"). Hugh Schonefield has claimed that the names Yuz Asaph—coalescing to "Joseph"—are themselves a cipher or code name for a generic figure in the Old Testament epitomizing the archetypical "seer," "healer," or prophet, or the "collector" of the authentic scriptures who represents the true prophetical tradition of Israel.[11] It would be logical to postulate that a holy man once called Yuz Asaph or Joseph might, after his further apotheosis from a patriarch-prophet into a "god-man," be given the additional or "initiatory" name of Jeshua or Jesus in certain mystical circles. This title would have by Hellenistic times designated in common mystical code-language both a "savior" or "deliverer," as well as a dying-and-rising god-man.

Schonefield also suggests that another name for the earlier "teacher of righteousness" or "true teacher" of the Essenes in the 2nd century B.C. (c. 167 B.C.) had been the code-name Yuz Asaph or Joseph.[12] Thus he sees the "true teacher" of the Essenes as a precursor of the "Jeshua" or "Jesus" of the Gospels, as a savior, deliverer, and persecuted leader. Many of this "true teacher's" Essene teachings were subsumed into the Gospel story about Jesus the Nazorean, says Schonefield, because they both represented the same "true" Jewish prophetic and mystical traditions in the eyes of Jesus' followers. Both men opposed the "corrupt" priesthood at Jerusalem, and both men were persecuted for their attempted reforms.

There is indeed a tradition that the Essene "teacher of righteousness" may have been " . . . hung on a tree and stoned." There is also a tradition, as J. M. Robertson has indicated, that another man of the Essene type called Yeshua or "Jesus" was actually crucified for similar teachings in the first century B.C. All of these "Jesus" ("Joshua"/ "Isaac") figures would have been seen by Jews in such syncretistic mystical traditions as attempting to enact the roles of the primordial god-man and savior within the Hebraic messianic context *before* the time of the Jesus of the gospels.

In conclusion, there are a number of extra-canonical indications that the names "Joseph" (Yuz Asaph), "Isaac" (Yitzach), "Joshua" (Yeshua), and "Jesus" may have represented to pre-Christian Hellenistic Jews archetypes of the "salvation-hero" figure. Sometimes this figure was perceived by Jewish "heretics" and their pagan counterparts as a god-man. But he was always seen at least as a "true prophet" suffering in witness to the "Kingdom of God." It is also highly probable, if not proven, that Hebraic mystical adaptations of the pagan mystery rites of a dying-and-rising god-man actually existed. In such rites, for some time before the time of Christ, pious Jews might well have enacted a mystery play. In such a mystery rite or play an actor, perhaps a hierophant-priest using an animal substituted for the much earlier human victim, may have celebrated a religious drama in which the victim was sacrificed, stoned, or crucified in mime.

The substitution of an actor, or a hierophant priest, using a sacrificial animal for the death scene, had already been accomplished in similar rites of Osiris, Dionysius, Attis, Adonis, and Mithra. The "god-man victim" in all of these earlier rites was said to suffer, die, and rise again. By becoming one with him psychically and spiritually, adherents were said to share in his passion and to partake of the fruits of his redemption. In Jewish magical texts dating from the early Christian era, there were also sacramental meals in which the faithful were said to eat the body and drink the blood of a god-man in symbolic form in order to consummate their mystical union with him.

J. M. Robertson's point is that there was probably sufficient precedent for Christianity in popular Jewish mystical and magical traditions, which had adapted early pagan rites to Judaism before the time of Christ.[12] These were distinct from the more formal worship in the temple at Jerusalem, as Schonefield suggests, and would have depended upon popular traditions of "true prophecy" and mysticism. The Essenes and Therapeuts, as we now know, already had freely adapted to their own versions of Judaism various elements from the mystical and magical traditions of paganism in its varied Egyptian, Babylonian, Persian, Indian, and Greek forms.

xii. conclusion: insights of the archetypical myths

What insights can we now claim from a better understanding of the code-language of archetypical myths, particularly cosmogenic, soteriological, and eschatological myths of the Western religious tradition?

(1) In the first place, we might observe that all of these myths were *universal*. That is to say, they took various forms throughout the ancient-sacral world, but their major motifs and themes—and the Wisdom which lay behind them—was of one piece.

(A) Creation myths explained the creation, sometimes by evolutionary means and in stages of development, of the world of plant life, animal life, and finally of humanity (as the crown of the Creation). Appended myths of the "Fall" or "Degeneration of Man" explained why man and woman are not the perfect, divine human beings they were intended to be by their divine parent(s). (The fault was clearly not God's, but rather lay in their own rebellion against the Light.)

(B) Salvation myths explain the paramount role of more perfected men and women, or "specialists in the holy," in getting "fallen" humanity back into a state of divine harmony and perfection. Most of these figures are opposed and persecuted, and often martyred as well in the service of the higher order.

(C) Eschatological myths describe a perfected New World Order to come, and the turmoils first required to break up the (fallen) "Old World Order."

(2) The purpose of soteriological or salvation myths was to provide a "divine blueprint" for human improvement, whether involving "salvation," "liberation," or "enlightenment," and

(3) This "blueprint" was exemplified in varying ways and degrees by holy men and women who acted as "specialists in the holy," or "mid-wives" of a "New Humanity" (to emerge from among their faithful followers).

Various prophets, seers, teachers, gurus, healers, miracle workers, magi, and/or apotheosized "god-men" thus acted as the harbingers of, and sometimes the embodiment of, the "new race."

(4) Not only were their spiritual and moral qualities meant to take root in their followers, but also (in the pagan mysteries and in primitive Christianity) the essence of their very ontological being and their miraculous powers were often described as passed on to their followers in sacramental rites.

(5) Primitive Christianity, which appears to have arisen out of Hellenistic-Jewish mystical groups like the Essenes and Therapeuts, was no exception to this general ancient tradition.

(6) Soteriological or salvation myths of the Jews began with the stories of Abraham, the Patriarchs, Moses and the Prophets of Israel, and extend into the Christian New Testament stories of Jesus the Messiah, as well as into heretical Hellenistic Jewish gnostic groups in pre-Christian and post-Christian times.

(7) Most of civilization's great "shamans," whether god-men, gurus or prophets, and the salvation myths of the higher religions of the world which feature them, perform an effective transformative function by holding up role models for the spiritual, ethical, and

psychological metamorphosis of the people devoted to their cults.

(8) Conversely, "villains" and "anti-heroes" who represent the opposite of the higher values of the heroes and saviors seem to perform the function of "exposing" and "guaranteeing" the views of the latter, as long as the authority of the Salvation myth holds sway over the faith of the people. However, when the people's faith in the myth and its hierarchy of positive values weakens, then negative values or "vices" are accepted into the culture more freely and become widespread under the guise of expediency, relativism, or rationalized survival tactics. (This can be seen in contemporary as well as in past instances of the failure or collapse of "Christian values" in Western civilization.)

(9) Primary mystical and psychic experiences are all important components of the lives of the heroes and "specialists in the holy" of the great Salvation myths.

In fact, it is precisely through such experiences that they obtain or derive the multi-dimensional views of cosmos and of the human person which characterize their special teachings and their authority as "world teachers."

In conclusion, the dilemma of persons conditioned by modern Western rationalistic and reductionist models of reality is precisely that often they miss the significance of many of the above-listed points. The result is that the "secular mentality" which dominates much of the scientific and established Christian theological thinking today cannot appreciate the importance of the "mythical and magical worldview" to the recovery of an understanding of a universal Primordial Tradition of higher intuition and insight, or to the recovery of a lost esoteric Christianity of the "Cosmic Christ" at the roots of primitive Christian gnosis.

Chapter 7

Jesus as Cosmic God-Man:
the historicization of a primordial archetype

i. guiding images of incarnation and immortality
in the western tradition

*T*raditional versions of Eastern Orthodox and Western Catholic Christian incarnational theology have, since the 4th-century publication of the definitive tome *De Incarnatione Verbum Dei* by St. Athanasius, Archbishop of Alexandria, asserted that God, the "Immortal One," "the Eternal Word of God, Light from Light, Very God from Very God," was both *uniquely* and *historically* united to the stream of human evolution in the person and work of Jesus of Nazareth, "true God and true Man." Subsequent Christian thought has consistently proclaimed this message in its encounters with the faiths and philosophies of mankind throughout the ages. It is the bedrock of Christian spiritual tradition.

But many Christian thinkers have, unfortunately, not also understood that this incarnational emphasis does not do away with (1) the universality of the process of personal, divine inspiration and guidance in persons functioning in non-Christian religious, philosophical, and cultural traditions: (2) the essential unity of the entire human family in experiences of psyche and spirit; and (3) the potential "immortality" of Everyman, who is created in the divine image or *Imago Dei*.

Thus most Christians (after the primitive period) have tried to take Jesus outside of the wider context of the ancient Primordial Tradition of intuition and insight, which originally provided him with the symbolic—and psychic and mystical—credentials by which he was recognizable as both "God and Man" by his earliest disciples.

Contemporary fundamentalist, institutionalist, and liberal Christians should especially note that primitive Catholic Christian thought proclaimed that God had acted at sundry times and in diverse manners, both through the psychospiritual experiences of the Old Testament prophets of Israel *and* in those of the great pagan Greek philosophers, many of whose insights and inspirations were "baptized" into Christian thought.

From the days of St. Justin Martyr, when Christianity was struggling to come to grips with the many pagan faiths extant throughout the Roman Empire, and in more recent times in the Declaration of the Second Vatican Council ("On the Church and Non-Christian Religions"), it has been formally acknowledged that God has spoken to and guided men and women of all traditions. In straightforward contemporary terms, this means Hindus, Buddhists, Moslems, Jews, and even those of no faith, agnostics or atheists, who open themselves to divine grace and inspiration. For, in the words of the Fourth Gospel, "He was that Light which lightens everyone who comes into the world" (John 1:9).

In other words, what Orthodox-Catholic Christians are talking about when they speak of "Jesus" or the "Christ" is related, whether they know it or not, to the innermost divine core, or the immortal *"Imago Dei" within every human being.* It is to the awakening of our awareness of this "immortal core," and of the infinite and divine inner potential in everyone, that the historic Christian proclamations of faith were directed.

ii. *archetypical salvation myths of pagan antiquity and primitive christianity*

In the Orthodox-Catholic version of the Christian *kerygma* or message found in the canonical Gospels and Creeds, there is a proclamation of one "divine blueprint" of the Immortal One at the core of every human being. This is the "Archetypal Man," or "Son of Man" within, to which you and I must be awakened. Christians would declare that this "logos" assumed a *full, historical* birth in the Man Jesus, in whose earthly life there was worked out an archetypical, divine blueprint for humanity. This was perceived as a glimpse of immortality under the dynamic conditions of finite time and space. This was understood by the founders of the Church as the fulfillment of an eternal pattern or process which previously had been perceived by ancient seers and prophets to be operating in the human psyche on the inner plane. It was recognized as already enacted in part by great heroes in the myths of previous pagan faiths, from Osiris/Horus and Orpheus to Zoroaster and others.

iii. immortality and myths of the god-man/magus

The new religion—Christianity—now prescribed, in its canonical and Pauline form, an awakening to a universal consciousness of the Divine Life. It saw this as expressed in human terms by an archetypical, symbolic message. As in previous stories of dying-and-rising god-men, this message included a descent from Heaven of a Divine Son, a supernatural birth, the witness to a new/old truth of primordial order, opposition by the established worldly powers of the old church and the established state, a magical contest between the two in which the heaven-sent One wins the moral point by both argument and miraculous occurrences testifying to his authentic credentials, the inevitable false accusations, an unfair trial, and a condemnation to an unjust death and the execution of the holy One as innocent victim, followed by his "resurrection" or reappearance to faithful witnesses on earth. There is then an ascension to the heavenly places, "at the right hand" of the deity or Supreme Being, where the Divine Son rules as King of the world to come. This myth-structure—derived from ancient mythologies of a divine priest-king—was in reality a psychospiritual map of the potential destiny of "Everyman," i.e., any who would freely identify with it. And it was borrowed, largely, from pagan sources.

In many traditional versions of the myth of the god-man—such as that found in Orthodox Christianity, mystical Judaism, messianic movements in Islam, and in Mahayana Buddhism—there is also a "second coming" of the archetypical divine human being at the end of the historical age or epoch, or at the end of the world itself. Various apocalyptic imagery is associated with such a future event, including that of judgment and destruction of the "old order" through fire, flood, plague, warfare or earthquake, as well as a separation between the "sheep and the goats" or the "children of light" and the "children of darkness." Finally, there is the recreation of a new heaven and a new earth, or "new cosmic order" in which the image of heavenly things is established at last on the earth plane, and a reign of peace, justice and divine perfection is seen among a "new race" of human beings re-made after the divine image of the immortal or archetypical man. This future-oriented phase of such major salvation-myths describes a biographical and evolutionary schema for the destiny of the human race as a whole.

It is, incidentally, important to observe that such myths of the god-man, magus, priest-king, and ritual-hero are of one piece with not only some of the most ancient maps of consciousness, but also with some of the contemporary "New Age" expectations of the "higher evolution" of human consciousness, and a "new world order" being suggested in many of the new religious movements in the West.

The writers and editors of the canonical Gospels of Matthew, Mark, Luke, and John, like the compilers of many of the works we now know as the "gnostic Gospels," were the "new religionists" of their day. But the emerging "orthodox party" in Christianity, unlike some of their world-denying "gnostic" counterparts, understood full well the impact on Jesus' original companions and followers of the *historical* enactment by Jesus of the universal, archetypical and cosmic salvation myth. As they perceived it the historical man Jesus had *actually re-lived* the entire salvation myth, the "divine blueprint," of antiquity.

For them he *was* the "myth of the heavenly magus" incarnate (or the "archetypical God-Man" and "savior"), a myth which had been present in the various legends of Egypt, India, Greece, Persia and other ancient lands. The canonical Gospels might thus be said to represent a quest for a historical Christ, or better perhaps as an attempt to historicize an archetype in the flesh-and-blood person of Jesus of Nazareth, in contradistinction to extant gnostic literature and its often world-denying visionary revelations.[2]

We must also note here Professor Morton Smith's reconstruction (in *Jesus the Magician* and *St. Clement and the Secret Gospel of St. Mark*) of the relationship between Jesus' baptism to the various Hellenistic-Jewish and pagan conceptions of initiatory death, out-of-the-body experience, ascension through the celestial spheres, and "resurrection," (i.e., return to the physical body), and to subsequent New Testament (particularly Pauline) language concerning the "death and resurrection" of the individual Christian. We will deal with these issues more fully later on.

iv.   primitive christianity as a "blueprint"

It is quite obvious that the canonical New Testament writers have changed the sequence of initiatory death, ascension of the spiritual body, and Resurrection, to physical death, Resurrection, and ascension, and added something new and distinctive to it. They did this in order to present the full picture of the life, death, resurrection, and ascension of Jesus as a "blueprint" or map of historical human psychophysical and psychospiritual evolution.

This new, distinctive "historical" element is, in particular, the claim that in Jesus' death, "descent into Sheol" and "resurrection on the third day," there was an exceptional"transmutation" or transformation and assimilation of the matter of Jesus' physical body into his "spiritual body." In the canonical Gospels, there is an implication that Jesus' "resurrection body" involved some kind of higher form of physical matter and spiritual energy. This *soma pneumatikos* or "spiritualized body" could express itself perfectly in the physical dimension for short periods of time. The portrait of Jesus appearing and disappearing beyond closed doors suggests that he, as the "lord of matter" itself, could change the vibratory frequencies of his "bodies" and go at will into "other dimensions" or "other worlds." But even this exceptional transmutation of the physical body into a numinous, higher "energy-body" is something that St. Paul describes as a gift awaiting the perfected ones, the "new race," or the new species of human being to come at the culmination of a process of psychospiritual evolution. Jesus is thus seen as the "first fruits" or first example of a "new creation," i.e., a higher order of human being. This idea is similar to Hellenistic conceptions of a new, "gnostic race" of spiritually transformed individuals. It is, incidentally, also similar to Sri Aurobindo's conception of a "new race" of "metamental beings" into whom the highest, divine consciousness can descend. Aurobindo describes the bodies of quasi-material light and energy which the future "Man of Light" will inhabit.

An overview of some shamanistic phenomena, ancient esoteric psychic traditions, modern psychical research on mediumship, and contemporary studies in the phenomenology of out-of-the-body and near-death experiences strongly suggests that the experiences of the witnesses of Jesus' Resurrection, and the language which they borrowed from existing Hellenistic Jewish and earlier Pagan traditions to describe those experiences, were of a piece with the language of extant gnostic and psychic groups. In other words, Jesus' Resurrection would have been recognized in the psychic and mythic milieu of Hellenistic religions, and of Jewish Hellenism, as conforming to a known pattern and fulfilling the criteria of an archetypical "apotheosis," through the "ritual death, ascension, and Resurrection" experience, within the great Mysteries of pagan antiquity.

The one essential difference, or addition, would have been the "historicization" of this apotheosis in the physical death and "resurrection" of Jesus in a "spiritualized body" (*soma pneumatikos*), and the universalization of this previously private or secret sign or pledge of a similar destiny or future in a "new heaven" and a "new earth" for a new human race. Through this historicization of an archetypical experience Jesus became what St. Paul was later to call him, i.e., the "pioneer of our salvation," or the "first fruits of the new creation." Primitive Christianity thus presents a historically realized and therefore realizable "blueprint," or "map," of psychospiritual evolution for the whole race, rather than just the few select initiates of the ancient pagan mysteries.

v. *the nicaean christianity of st. athanasius*

It was under the impetus of this drive to universalize and historicize an archetype that the orthodox Catholic Christian Fathers of the early Church went on in succeeding centuries, especially during the Nicaean controversies of the 4th century A.D., to work out the carefully framed Doctrine of the Incarnation of Christ. Thus it was the later "orthodox" party, and not the world-denying non-Hermetic variety of gnostics, who tried to realize the fulfillment of the true meaning of the pagan mystery-rites in the person of Christ. Needless to say, the rationalist Arius did not understand this point any more than did the gnostics. Some of the "orthodox" party, like St. Athanasius of Alexandria, whose position eventually won the day at the Councils of Nicaea (325 A.D.) and Constantinople I (381 A.D.), would affirm that the eternal Christ (Logos) whom they worshipped had to become both God and Man in one person. Jesus, according to the orthodox party, was to unite in Himself not only the aspirations of the Law and the Prophets of Israel, but also, by implication if not directly stated, the various "god-man" myths and liturgical mysteries of the pagan world.

These ancient myths, and the liturgical mysteries associated with them, had for centuries proclaimed, in sacred stories and in liturgical rites, similar psychospiritual truths about the "Way" of human salvation and transformation. According to this version of the ancient Hermetical, positive-gnostic, archetypical and mythic theme, "Everyman" (who lives in the world and identifies psychically and spiritually with the god-man in his finite drama and struggle) is enabled to undergo a process of psychospiritual transformation, and ultimately to become one with him and to share in his divinity. Both St. Paul and St. Athanasius recognized and fought for this ancient, pre-Christian theme in their versions of Christianity. This orthodox version of the Gospel was challenged from the 1st century to the 4th century A.D. by various world-denying (non-Hermetic) gnostics, and at the opposite pole by non-mystical rationalists.

The basic theme of the Apostolic Message is simply that every human being is called to become a "god-man" by identification with the Cosmic "God-Man," i.e., is called to undergo a process of psychospiritual transformation. The Greek Fathers of the Church, like the Hermeticists, called this process an "apotheosis" or "divinization." But unlike the world-denying kind of gnostics, they stressed the relevance of gaining this immortality to a new higher kind of life while in history, and to the restoration of the finite creation. Since every person in the real, historical world of time, space and matter is himself or herself unique, finite, and physically open to real sufferings and real joys, the Archetype or "Son of Man" (with whom s/he had to identify psychically and spiritually as the "god-man") had also first *to become* quite finite and physical in the Jesus of history. This "Logos" now in human flesh had to undergo a historically real trial, death, and Resurrection *if* He was to be of relevance to ordinary people in the world of everyday finite experience, and if His brand of "immortality" and "eternal life" was to signify anything realizable by them within the earth plane.

The earliest Christians had apparently first interpreted Jesus in the light of archetypical stories of immortal "god-men" in pagan religions, who were usually mythical, or at best shadowy legendary figures whose deeds could not be documented in historical terms. But some early Christian writers were to say that these figures had nevertheless "foreshadowed" or prepared the imagination of mankind for the coming of the *historical* Jesus, who was now viewed as an actualization of the symbolic blueprint or Cosmic archetype of "the Way, the

Truth, and the Life," i.e., of the Divine Plan for the "life, death, and Resurrection" or the psychospiritual transmutation of the "old humanity" into a race of "new beings."

For such writers, from Paul to Ignatius of Antioch, Irenaeus, and Athanasius, the uniqueness of Jesus consisted in his *historicity* as the incarnation of the "Cosmic Christ," "eternal Logos," or "Word." He was the divine-human blueprint for a "new race." His *historical life* was for them both the pledge and guarantee (within their own outer-physical as well as inner-spiritual experience) that the ancient, mythical and spiritual "archetype of immortality" was indeed a truly realizable figure.

The historical reality of the "signs" of Jesus' life, death and resurrection now allowed them to affirm that there *are* real, higher inner processes of the Spirit which are empirically *verifiable in the "Cosmos," or world*. They had, after all, heard his words, seen, handled, and touched his flesh, and witnessed his mighty signs of power including his post-mortem appearances.

Thereafter, the ongoing charismatic experience of that assembly of Jewish mystics faithful to Jesus (now known as an "ecclesia" or "church" after "the outpouring of the Spirit" at the event known as Pentecost) added to their conviction that the awakening, nurture, growth, and psychospiritual transformation of ordinary human beings was indeed possible. This process of human transformation took place according to the "Eternal Image of God seen in Christ Jesus." For Jesus' disciples it was a reality now manifested and incarnated in Cosmic history, first in Him, then in them.

The earliest Christian mystical writers, from St. Paul to St. Athanasius, would thus have perceived that the fruition of that "divine blueprint" of the Cosmic God-Man, is the "Christ-within," and must occur in Everyman in order to bring about the real creation of a "new race," a "royal priesthood" of "new beings," as well as a new social order and a new natural order, i.e., a "new creation." This was the highest form of the ancient theurgy and alchemy. It was both the freely given work of the Holy Spirit, and the magic of the Word and sacraments, to bring the heavenly order down, to transform the earth-plane.

This new, but in fact very old, Primordial and Hermetic "magick" was to be perpetrated within a real, historical group, e.g. "Church," Qahol, or Ecclesia. An ongoing community of persons, this new initiate community of awakened beings was "Christ's Mystical Body," the "midwife of the divine work" and of the "New Age," with its "sacred alchemical process." The Church and Sacraments (viewed, of course, according to the mystical, universal, inner meaning of these "realities") were seen as integral to the psychospiritual evolution of the human race, on this planet and in worlds to come.

vi. contemporary intimations of the same "primordial message" in western esoteric traditions, eastern mysticism, and new religions

Now, conceived of in this light, "orthodox" Christianity should really be the most *inclusive* of historic religions. It should be anything but an exclusivist salvation cult for those who call themselves Christian. Orthodox-Catholic Christianity and those other non-Christian esoteric spiritual traditions which find their historical roots in the more positive, world-affirming varieties of Gnosticism, Neo-Platonism, and Hermeticism have as their common sacramental objective the bringing down into the earth-plane, into matter and into history, that which is already the eternally perfect divine order established in the heavenly places according to the "Father's will." This whole process of bringing down the "divine energy" to the earth is the historicization of both "immortality" and "eternal life" in an archetypical spiritual path, manifested in people and called by early Christians "the Way, the Truth and the Life."

Various Western esoteric traditions have also testified to this theme throughout the ages. In the East, in our century, Sri Aurobindo has interpreted the goal of the classical, "integral yoga systems" of India as a similar "bringing down" into historical manifestation of the "Divine Mind in man," so that the human person may become the "temple of the Spirit."[3] And now, many "new religions" and new spiritual movements in the West have also incorporated such psychophysical and psychospiritual themes about human evolution into their teachings.

Thus both orthodox forms of Christianity and the best of the world's esoteric spiritual traditions might well one day come to recognize as their common goal the historicization of the divine archetype of the eternal god-man in Everyman, as an implementation of "theurgy" or the "divine work" through living psychospiritual experience. Consequently, one might argue that the incarnationalist elements in authentic Christian faith should impel enlightened Christians to support such things as the human potential movement, consciousness studies, psiology, and transformative practices found in other world religions, and to move them toward an even fuller appreciation of both their transcendent and historical implications.

But before this can occur, present-day traditional churches must become aware of and be sensitive to the "divine work" of the "Cosmic Christ" as it is going on under different names and forms both in contemporary "new sciences of consciousness" and in various positive forms of psychic and spirit phenomena in all cultures. This requires a concerted effort on the part of Christians to understand the world's other religions in a positive, non-polemical light and to study non-Christian religious experiences or spiritual-cum-psychical experiences in a similar positive vein.

There is another point to remember that "new religionists," "human potential" people and traditionalists alike must also appreciate. Central to the alchemical "Great Work" is a psychic and spiritual awakening. One of the primary ways that the awakening of an individual to the "divine archetype" of a new humanity occurs is in gradual unfoldment of higher faculties of perception and awareness, or the birth of a higher con sciousness in general. And the creation of saints and sages, or great authentic mystics and adepts of the psychospiritual life, always involves both a "crucifixion" of the ego, or dominant lower self, the birth of an awareness of a higher Self, and the development or unfolding of subtle psychic and spiritual faculties of perception and discernment in a "new being."

Church administrators and theologians, and new religionists alike, have not always been "saints" or "sages" with such developed faculties of psychospiritual discernment! But this *is* an avowed goal at least of many of the more idealistic human psychic-and-spiritual development groups and "new religions" today in the so-called "New Age" genre. Whether the traditional churches and new religious groups will come to respond to this challenge to *metanoia*, or spiritual and moral repentance and conversion, and personal psychic and spiritual development, remains to be seen.

vii. archetypical myths and the rediscovery of images of the western psyche

There are two contemporary scholars whose works have been largely ignored thus far by traditional church scholars, but which are nevertheless quite relevant to the present issue. These are the late Dame Frances Yates, of the University of London, and the already mentioned Professor Morton Smith, of Columbia University. Their works are relevant because of their historical scholarship, which reveals the central role that esoteric magical and mythical beliefs and practices have played in the development of the Western religious and cultural tradition.

Unfortunately, both scholars seem to share the modern rationalistic Cartesian biases and limitations of most of their academic colleagues. Consequently they do not seem to be able to understand or accept the reality of psychic phenomena or "real magic" as the basis for the derivation of the great Primordial salvation myths, whether in the Bible or in subsequent "magical" traditions, that they have described so well. Smith crudely ridicules all psychic and mystical experience; Yates simply seems to assume it to be somehow a mistaken or a misplaced confidence.

But when read together, their works offer many valuable insights into the historical uses and development of magical and mystical beliefs, from the earliest biblical and extra-canonical traditions about Jesus of Nazareth to the "Christian magi" of the Renaissance (Marsiglio Ficino, Pico della Mirandola, Cornelius Agrippus, Giordano Bruno, et. al.) and the fathers of the "Rosicrucian Enlightenment" (Paracelsus, John Dee, Johann Valentin Andreae, Robert Flood, Michael Maier, et. al.).[3]

Scholars in the history of religions today who understand the data of psychic research and recent consciousness studies may legitimately read the works of Yates and Smith in a way which these authors themselves did not understand or intend. The fact that Jesus' earliest disciples and enemies alike may have thought of him in mythic terms as a magician or "god-man" teaching typically shamanistic, out-of-the-body initiatory rites and spirit-magic (Morton Smith, *Jesus the Magician*, 1978) is important to know. But it will be understood in a different light by those who know something about the reality of "OBE's," "ascensions," or "translations" into other "planes of consciousness" or "heavenly spheres," the existence of "parallel or higher dimensions," etc. or "theurgy" in general. It is not correct to label such claims as signs of a "hallucinatory" or "schizophrenic" delusion, as Smith has done. And it is not appropriate to ignore them, as Yates has done. They are, of course, valid and important types of primary psychic-mystical experience from which various religious creeds all over the world have been derived.

And the fact that the earliest impetus toward "modern science" came out of a tradition of "magia" and "caballa" (as Yates has claimed), through such persons as Ficino, Pico, Agrippa and Bruno, will become more significant to those historians of culture who know something about "real-world" claims to "psychokinesis," "ectoplasmic materializations," or paraphysics. Yet, Yates does not relate the magical phenomena and beliefs of the "Renaissance Magi" or "Rosicrucian Enlightenment" to such emerging new sciences in her studies.

(The reader should note that the research done in preparation for my earlier series of books, in which some of the present material on esoteric Christianity first appeared, was undertaken before the publication of Morton Smith's *Jesus the Magician* (1978) and *The Secret Gospel* (1982). Chapter 9 of the present book was written between 1963 and 1972, before the publication of Smith's original *St. Clement of Alexandria and the Secret Gospel of St. Mark* (1973). Therefore Smith's valuable conclusions were not integrated into what I shall have to say in chapter 9 concerning the psychic conceptions of the Church and Sacraments. However, Morton Smith's historical conclusions are quite consistent with my own, and our works are complementary. The difference between us is, primarily, that Professor Smith, having done all of his valuable historical scholarship, can only relate his conceptions of the magic acts claimed for Jesus and his disciples in a reductionist fashion which supposes hysteria, hallucination, self-hypnosis, or schizophrenic delusion.

viii. jesus as miracle-worker and god-man magus

Smith has analyzed what he calls suppressed evidence from 2nd-3rd-century A.D. Jewish and pagan magical papyri, from an allegedly secret longer version of the Gospel of St. Mark mentioned in a recently discovered epistle of St. Clement of Alexandria, and from sources outside of the Christian orbit entirely found in ancient Jewish and Roman manuscripts. These sources collectively would suggest that Jesus was, as a healer, exorcist, and miracle worker, generally perceived as a "magician" or wonderworking "god-man" in the familiar, pre-Christian Hellenistic pattern.

Smith argues that Jesus' disciples claimed for him an equality with God, or that he was a god-man or divine man, after he had had a typical shamanistic "initiatory experience" (during his baptism by John the Baptist) in which, like others in Hellenistic magical traditions, he was "united to the Spirit" and "ascended into the heavens" through the various spheres of spirits and angels to the "throne of God," and then returned endowed with extraordinary powers to perform miracles and to initiate others—by a magical union with himself—into having the same experience.

This, says Smith, was the enigmatical endowment with the "keys to the Kingdom of Heaven" which Jesus passed on to Peter and his closest disciples through a similar shamanistic initiatory rite within the context of a baptism. By shamanistic union with himself, they received the same "spirit" and traveled with Jesus beyond the heavens; upon return they were endowed with grace and new divine powers to help establish the heavenly order on earth, through proclamation, exorcisms, and healing.

Thus, we find in the New Testament the familiar shamanistic pattern of a passage through the "gates of death," an out-of-the-body experience (or "bodily ascension"), a passing into the heavenly places through higher realms of angels and spiritual beings to the Godhead, and then a return to the physical body, or to bodily consciousness, now endowed with new spiritual powers and gnosis.

In Smith's conception, this typical, Hellenistic magical initiatory union with the god-man (who acts as shamanistic guide to the heavens) can be seen in the surviving portrait of Jesus both in the canonical Gospels and in extra-canonical sources. In addition, the materials concerning the "Son of Man," "Primal Man" or "Son of the Primal Man" figure which I have reviewed in the present study are perhaps also relevant to our emerging picture of Jesus.

The "Son of the Primal Man," or "Son of Man" figure (Bar Nasha) of the canonical Gospels is represented in Hellenistic and Jewish magical papyri as typically incarnate in the person of the newly initiated and "apotheocized" or "divinized" god-man. This perhaps would explain the only original term by which Jesus refers to himself (i.e., "Son of Man") in the canonical Gospels. This enigmatical figure of the

"Son of Man" was, in sectarian Jewish mystical circles, naturally equated with the Messiah of Israel, or "Christ," as the "bringer of the Kingdom." But the "Kingdom of God" was for Jesus, as for other mystical Jews in the previous Essenic and/or Therapeutic traditions, not the political state of Israel (as it was for the Zealots and even for many of the Scribes and Pharisees), but was rather the "sphere of influence of the Father," within the hearts of God's people. This was extended, by Paul, to include both Jews and Gentiles who would accept and identify with the Cosmic god-man Jesus and undergo the initiatory death, Resurrection, and Ascension with Him.

The importance of Morton Smith's *Jesus the Magician* is that it provides some interesting historical evidence for the basic premise of the present book, *In Search of the Primordial Tradition and the Cosmic Christ*, that Jesus and his earliest followers understood and used basic universal, esoteric, psychic and spiritual "technologies" of the human mind and spirit. By such sacramental and shamanistic technologies his followers believed that they had united with the Divine Mind that had first manifested in Christ Jesus as "the Spirit" in his baptism. Through initiatory union with Jesus, in their baptisms, the disciples could thereafter partake of that same divine "Spirit."

With Smith's work we may have discovered explicit links for the arguments that I have included in chapter 9 (written between 1965-72) concerning the ancient psychic conceptions behind the Catholic doctrine of the Church and sacraments. Although Smith himself does not seem to understand the reality of psychic and spirit phenomena, the reader of the present series of books should by this time nevertheless be able to make the necessary equations using Smith's excellent historical research while ignoring his often crudely reductionistic and materialistic asides. Smith seems to make wrong *a priori* assumptions about the non-reality or "hallucinatory" nature of all psychic and spiritual experiences in themselves, but he has certainly not been alone in the academic world in doing this, and he is a good and reliable historian nonetheless.

ix. conclusion: the one path to eternal life and to a new humanity as a universal experience

It has been well said that "religions" *per se* do not save, elevate or transform human souls. It is the "eternal Word," present in various forms of authentic psychospiritual expression, that awakens, purifies, elevates, and re-forms the "old man" into the "new humanity." This apparently has occurred in all traditions, regardless of whatever the analysis of various dogmatic religionists may have had to say about it to the contrary. For all of the major religions of the world have been the cradle out of which pioneer examples of the psychospiritual and ethical evolution of a "new" and "divine" humanity have arisen under the influence of the one God. Great saints, and authentic spiritual adepts, are the private preserve of no single, scribalized or institutionalized religious tradition, including the Christian tradition.

The "historicization" of this divine human process has been *mapped* more centrally in the Orthodox-Catholic Christian tradition of the Gospels, and by St. Athanasius of Alexandria. But the living, divine and human process of the transformation of the many into members of the "mystical body" of the one god-man is *not* something that is the private preserve of Christians or of the institutional church, or of Christianity as a religion among religions.

This is perhaps the hardest but most urgent lesson to get through to the average Christian theologian, religious leader, or layman today. It is urgent because until enough religious leaders in all religious traditions understand that the "true God" is no respecter of persons, and that universal forms of psychospiritual experience are the bases of all human faith in—and myths about—immortality, there can be no true dialogue, mutual respect, or learning exchange between religious thinkers in the different world religions.

Nor can there be cooperation between scientists and religious thinkers in the new fields of psiology and consciousness research. For the new breed of scientist coming to birth on this planet will rightly want to study *all* of the great archetypical myths and truly universal forms of psychic and spiritual phenomena suggestive of immortality in all of the world's religions. He or she will not want to be restricted to the study only of those arbitrarily approved "myths" and "miracles" considered as the sole prerogative of "orthodox" Christianity or its sectaries.

My basic point is that our very ideas of "God," "soul," "immortality," and "resurrection," of humanity in a "new, higher life," and the mythology and symbolism we use to describe it, originally arise out of *universal* forms of psychic, mystical, and spiritual experience which have given birth to archetypical myths of dying-and-rising god-men. These are by no means the sole invention of Christians.

In specific, the whole Christian "Kerygma" or "Message" of the dying-and-rising Cosmic god-man rests historically upon such a previously extant Primordial Tradition, with its various *universal* types of psychic, mystical, and spiritual *experiences*. These have been refined and culturally expressed, in myth and ritual, through a particular communal consciousness at given points in history.

Yet the subsequent leadership of the Christian churches often seems to forget this fact when it loses touch with its own basically spiritistic, psychic and mythical sources, and with the general principles of authentic forms of inner, mystical life in general. The historical evidence that primary psychic and mystical experiences formed the basis for primitive Christian belief, and of its myths of "immortality," and "resurrection," and of a multidimensional universe of celestial worlds, is indeed commanding.

Chapter 8

Through "Death and Resurrection" to the "New Being"

i. "resurrection" versus "immortality"

Many Christian theologians in the modern period have debated the difference between the concepts of "immortality" and "resurrection." The late Oscar Cullman argued in a guest lecture at Harvard that the doctrine of immortality was not part of the authentic arsenal of Christian beliefs, but that the doctrine of resurrection was![1] He was correctly refuted in a presentation by Professor Harry Wolfson of Harvard, who pointed out that, on the basis of early Greek patristic texts, most of the Christian fathers not only believed in "resurrection" but also in "immortality." Wolfson pointed out the obvious: the two ideas are complementary, and it is impossible to understand the one without the other.[2]

An *anastasis* literally means in Greek no more than a "standing up again," or "reappearance."[3] Thus it could mean no more than a post-mortem reappearance of a dead person, through psychic experience or by other means, to the living. But quite obviously it had come to mean—in the great mystery traditions of Egypt, Greece, Persia, India, Asia Minor, in Hellenistic cults, as well as in orthodox forms of Christianity itself—much more than just that.

There is a common background to these traditions which incorporates the symbolic-archetypical myth of the death, resurrection and ascension of a god-man or divine person in human form, who is seen as the archetype of the true or "high Self" of "Everyman." We must be awakened to this "Self," and this awakening is described as a "death to the Old Man," as St. Paul put it, and a resurrection to a higher life as a "new being." Such formulae had become ciphers for a higher, psychospiritual transformation of the consciousness, a breakthrough to the truest level of the ontological being of "Everyman," to an "immortal core."

ii.   properties of the "spiritualized body" in esoteric traditions

Both the New Testament and the subsequent orthodox Christian mystical traditions seem, when discussing the Resurrection, to be talking about an all-powerful, Primordial form of life spirit that is able to cause a material organism to take on all of the properties of matter at one moment, and then to dissolve them at another. In reading the Resurrection stories of the New Testament, one is reminded of references from Sri Aurobindo, the great Hindu philosopher-sage of Pondicherry, who wrote in *The Mind of Light* about the man of the future, who is evolved not only physically, but also psychically and spiritually.[4] Aurobindo describes a new kind of human being in whom the physical properties of matter actually react to consciousness differently from the way they react to it in us.

Indeed there are various esoteric traditions in Christianity and in other religious cultures which teach that the dead bodies of the saints sometimes do not rot. In yogic terms, this claim could be said to suggest a particular relationship between the higher kind of consciousness, some kind of spiritually controlled bioenergetic fields, and the physical matter of the body; when such an integral relationship has been established between the higher consciousness and the body during the lifetime of a saintly individual, the very properties of the material of the body are said to be changed. Such stories, together with the New Testament portrayal of the "Resurrection body" of Jesus, are thus possibly very important symbolic keys for any "new physics of consciousness," for these sacred stories and religious ideas convey to us the picture of what the perfected human being might be like if "Spirit" were completely in control of both mind and matter. The New Testament seems to be saying that if we were indeed the "temple of the Spirit" (that St. Paul suggests we should become), many things might be different about our bodies and about our conceptions of human potential in the so-called "real world" of matter, time, and space, or "history."

iii.   biblical accounts of post-mortem contacts with the dead

In the Old Testament and New Testament, one finds stories of visitations of living persons to heaven-worlds, "transfigurations" and various types of shamanistic experiences, which do not make any sense in the language of contemporary philosophy or modern religious history, except perhaps as pre-scientific myths ripe for demythologization. In the New Testament, for example, we encounter the story of Jesus on Mount Tabor in the presence of Peter, James and John. We read that they see him standing there talking to Moses, who had been dead for approximately 1,400 years, and to Elijah, who had been dead for about 900 years. We read very strange, "out-of-another-world-and-context" types of stories of the Resurrection-day and the road to Emmaus. Geddes McGregor has pointed out that these kinds of stories make no sense in the modern, rationalistic milieu of academic arts and science. But he says they *do* make sense in the context of today's parapsychological literature, or within the context of comparative mysticism, and especially primitive gnostic or esoteric spiritual traditions.[5]

I have often reread the passage in Matthew 27:51 ff. New Testament scholars hardly ever comment on it intelligently. It reads: "And behold the veil of the temple was rent in twain from the top to the bottom, and the earth did quake, and the rocks rent; and the graves were opened, and the bodies of the saints which had slept arose, and came out of the graves after his resurrection, and went into the holy city and appeared unto many."

Modern secular rationalists can easily deal with the idea that certain zealous or credulous individuals may have thought that an exceptional individual, a god-man or holy man, was seen in a post-mortem appearance by his disciples. Some liberal theologians can make a "theology of Easter" out of that, somehow. But this passage is considerably more challenging because it says that some of the same kinds of things that were claimed by the disciples for Jesus' Resurrection, on the basis of their inter-subjective experience of him after his death, were also claimed by them about others, e.g. they "saw" other dead people and claimed that their "bodies" too had been "resurrected"!

Here is a bold claim in the canonical New Testament that so-called "saints," or persons who had been deceased, "rose from their graves" and "walked into the city," and "were seen by many." Here we have theophanic literature of a purely psychical and mystical disclosure type. We cannot rationalize and come up with very much else that is "sensible" in modern rationalist terms. It is no wonder that many "higher critics" of the Bible have wanted to do away with this very gnostic passage simply by dismissing it as a late editorial gloss.

iv. st. paul's idea of the "resurrection body"

I have puzzled over this passage because the phrase "the bodies of the saints" is very much in the center of that text. Then I remembered that St. Paul, like most cultured Greeks and Hellenistic Jews, had believed that there were three bodies or "sheaths" in man.

One, the *soma psarkikos*, is the physical body or the outer sheath. The second body is the *soma psychikos*, the "soul body," or the "psychic body." This was the layer in which our consciousness was said to reside, and was supported by the "astral body" or an energy-hologram which shaped our physical sheath at death. And lastly there was the *soma pneumatikos*, or the spiritual body, the true "eternal home" of the inner person.

Thus we find in the funeral narration of St. Paul in Corinthians a very strange reference to being "sown as something corruptible," . . . "first a man of the earth, earthy [*psarkikos*] and then a man from heaven, heavenly [*pneumatikos*]." We also find references in the stories of the Easter appearances to the "spiritualized," or "glorified" "Resurrection body" of Jesus. It is obvious from the Resurrection stories of the New Testament that "spiritualized body"—as we have said in chapter 7—did not relate to the properties of matter in the ordinary sense that we, in the use of our five physical senses, perceive matter to exist in the ordinary or "profane" physical world. There is something more, much more, implied in these stories if we will let them speak for themselves.

v. ancient religious and modern psychical conceptions of the early after-death state, and of "resurrection"

The late Dr. Robert Crookall, British scientist and psychical researcher, has carefully collected data from modern psychical research and from ancient conceptions of the early after-death state and the ideal of "resurrection."[6]

It is interesting to note that, since the beginning of modern psychical research, the collective testimonies of alleged "discarnates" speaking through entranced mediums concerning the early after-death state and the claimed observations of psychics and clairvoyants witnessing the death process square almost completely with various oral and written traditions from shamanistic and ancient sacral cultures. Crookall cites W. Y. Evans-Wentz who:

> "... *summarizes ancient verbally-transmitted teachings and the early after-life which corresponds to essentials with those that are received, through mediums, in Europe, America, etc., at the present day.*
> "*The priests [of ancient Egypt, Tibet, etc.] taught that, when a man dies, his soul normally takes from three-and-a-half to four days to completely separate from the body (i.e., from (a) the dense physical body, and (b) the 'Bardo' Body, which corresponds to what we call the vehicle of vitality or 'etheric body'). The priest helps a dying man to avoid the 'Bardo' 'etheric' realm of dream and illusion 'Hades' and to awaken in 'the Clear Light' (of 'Paradise').*"[7]

Crookall notes: (1) That the "soul body" is variously described in ancient traditions and in modern psychical channelings or observations, as "the body of light," the "radiant body," the "luminous body," and the "astral body." (The word "astral" comes from the Greek word for "star," thus denoting a body made up of light like that of the stars.)

(2) That it is only when this basic "body of light" is still partly enshrouded and dulled in its perceptions by the denser, quasi-physical "etheric sheath" that there is the problem either of "earth-bound" condition, or conditions in the "Bardo" world or "underworld" of dull shadows which gave birth to conceptions of "Hades" or of personal hells.

(3) The "lower astral world" is thus one in which there is dulled perception of reality by the enshrouded "body of light." This is a world in which discarnate spirits can suffer as a consequence and create personal worlds and social situations with similarly dulled beings. Such suffering is, however, the natural consequence of a state of being, consciousness, and not an arbitrarily or externally imposed punishment. All of the ancient mythologies of death and judgment implicitly contain the idea that divine justice works internally. Judgment by a god or God is—in the highest sense—self-judgment, or the law of "karma," i.e., the natural consequence of one's state of being.

(4) One can always "seek the Light" or "go to the Light" whenever one really wants. As soon as the subject is ready to face—see—the Light, the enshrouding "shell" of denser "etheric energies" will drop off, revealing the "body of light" within, like a butterfly emerging from its chrysalis. This process is called the "second death" in eso-

teric literature.

Crookall counts three invisible bodies in the ancient traditions and in modern Spiritualist testimony:

(1) The densest is the "etheric" or "vitality" body, "almost semi-material" and sometimes seen at death by clairvoyants as a "double," "image" or "mist."

(2) The "body of air" (which Crookall equates with St. Paul's "psychical body," or *soma psychikos*, i.e., the soul), and

(3) The "body of light" (which Crookall equates with St. Paul's "spiritual" or "celestial body," i.e., *soma pneumatikos*).

Crookall says that the newly dead person usually "sleeps" in the first, the "etheric" chrysalis, for a very short time, which can vary from no time at all to a few days. Lack of preparedness for death, i.e., the suddenness of death, psychological fatigue from a long, hard life, illness, etc., can cause a longer "sleep." But then the entity will rise from this sleep, shed the denser etheric shroud and eventually even the psychical body, then reveal itself as a "body of light" and ascend in consciousness to the realm of light or celestial spheres.

In ancient literature this was often referred to as "resurrection" and "ascension." Crookall cites an early 19th-century work by John Denham Parsons (*The Nature and Purpose of the Universe*, T. Fisher Unwin, 1906, p. 197), which:

"... *listed a number of religious teachings, including those of Hosea, the Zoroastrians, the ancient Phrygians, Syrians, Chinese and Tibetans, in which Resurrection (in this case meaning entrance into 'Paradise' conditions) took place on the third day and, in addition to correlating the period to certain aspects of sun-worship, said that experience showed that decomposition has generally begun in a corpse by the third day after death, indicating the departure of the soul (in, we would say, the Soul Body) from a Physical Body which could not be re-animated. 'The Spiritual Body of Jesus doubtless rose from his 'natural, here meaning carnal, body' upon 'the third day' in accordance with the belief of the Zoroastrians, and many others, that it took the surviving Spiritual Body about three days to free itself from the dead body of flesh and blood.' The fact that these teachings were not (as so many have supposed) meant to apply merely to mythical solar deities but also to discarnate human beings is shown by the reference (e.g. in the case of the Zoroastrians and ancient Egyptians) to the fact that the three-day 'sleep' was followed by the 'Judgment' and the latter by the 'assignment.' The Zoroastrians said that a man's good and evil works were weighed against each other; the*

Egyptians said that his deeds were weighed in the Scales of Osiris. Moreover, the Zoroastrians and others taught that, after the 'Judgment,' the righteous 'ascend' while the wicked 'descend.'[8]

In the light of such ancient conceptions from a Primordial Tradition of psychic intuition and spiritual insight on the early "after-death" process, it becomes somewhat easier for us to understand the historical antecedents of the conceptions of Hellenistic Judaism, namely, the Pharisaic *and* Essene conception of the "resurrection body." This very same conception is taken over in the canonical New Testament.

Nevertheless the canonical New Testament writers, in addition to building upon such ancient traditions about resurrection of the *soma pneumatikos* into the higher after-death worlds, added something quite new and important to earlier archetypical myths of the dying-and-rising gods. This was in particular the testimony that in the case of Jesus' death, "descent into Sheol" and "Resurrection on the third day," there was a historical "transmutation" or transformation of the matter of his physical body and its assimilation to his "spiritual body." In the canonical New Testament we find implicit suggestion of the emergence of a higher form of physical energy, "body" or sheath which allowed Jesus' spiritual body (*soma pneumatikos*) to express itself perfectly in the earth-plane dimension again as well as to change its vibratory frequencies and to go, at will, into "other worlds." And even this exceptional "transmutation of the physical body" of Jesus into a "numinous higher energy-body" is something that St. Paul describes as an inheritance which God has in store for the rest of the human race at the culmination of the process of human psycho-spiritual evolution. Jesus was viewed by the earliest Christians as the "first fruits" or first example of a "new Creation" of a higher order, a new kind of human being or a "new gnostic race."

The suggestion from ancient traditions and from modern psychical research alike is that the experience of the witnesses of Jesus' Resurrection—and the language which they borrowed from Hellenistic-Jewish mystical traditions to describe it—is one piece with a much older, more widespread Primordial Tradition concerning such issues. And that Primordial Tradition appears to be as true to primary psychical and spiritual experience of mystics and psi experiences today as it was thousands of years ago to magi, prophets, god-men, and saints of antiquity. It is normally, however, the *soma psychikos* or "soul body," itself housing the higher *soma pneumatikos* or "spiritual body"—that "rises" and "appears" to the living in most ordinary post-mortem contacts.

Thus the "bodies of many of the saints that slept" who appeared to many in Jerusalem (in Matthew 27:51 ff.) would seem to have been of this sort. The phrase "the graves that opened" would seem to have been a formulaic way in such ancient mystical traditions of describing the "opening of the portals of death" to allow the reappearance of the dead to the living.

There was, as we have indicated, something apparently different claimed about Jesus' own "Resurrection body" as it is described in the canonical Gospels. It is described as a "rematerialization" of the *soma psychikos*, or physical body, around the other two inner "bodies" on a temporary basis. This, at least, is what the emphasis in the Gospels on "touching," "eating," and acting unlike "a spirit" would seem to be all about.

In other, early-Christian, post-New Testament stories of post-mortem contacts with the dead, however, we are back to the more usual kind of post-mortem phenomena described in Matthew 27:51, ff. (i.e., stories of the appearance of the *soma psychikos*, or "soul body"). The following stories from the early Christian church illustrate what would seem to be post-mortem appearances of such a "soul body."

vi. stories ancient and modern

A. Lucian - Presbyter of Jerusalem

Lucian was a presbyter of Jerusalem in the 2nd century A.D. We read his story in his own account, which is still extant, and in reports by Augustine of Hippo, by the Catholic historian, Baronius, and by the 18th-century skeptic Edward Gibbon.[9] Lucian claimed to have had a dream one night in which he was encountered by the theophonic figure of an old man in white garments, the archetype of a heavenly revelator, who announced to him in the vision that he was Gamaliel, the teacher of one known to history as Paul of Tarsus or St. Paul. He told Lucian that his body was buried in the field next to Jerusalem, and that if Lucian would go and fetch the Bishop of Jerusalem and a party of men to dig in that field they would find three bodies: his own, i.e., that of Gamaliel himself, together with that of the first Christian martyr, St. Stephen, and Nicodemus, the rabbi who in the Gospel story had come to Jesus by night. According to the account, Lucian at first refused to act upon the dream. He ignored his vision and did not follow its instructions. But the vision repeated itself on successive nights until finally Lucian did act on it. According to the story, three bodies were found in the field, one of them allegedly that of St. Stephen, in a state of preservation.

Even that great skeptic of Enlightenment history, Edward Gibbon, tells us that it was on the basis of such experiences of post-mortem contacts with dead saints—or claims to such experiences—that the early Christian movement spread throughout the Roman Empire and overtook paganism in the early centuries of the Christian era.[10]

B. *Potamiaena - Martyr*

There is another such story which is told by Eusebius, the ecclesiastical historian of the 4th century, about a young Christian martyr, Potamiaena, and her captor Basilides. Potamiaena was a beautiful maiden who happened to be a Christian. In the midst of being tortured, she witnessed with charity and love to her torturers. Among them was a soldier, a Greek named Basilides. As she was about to expire in the arena, she told Basilides that she would return for him and bring him into the beautiful kingdom which she was about to enter, for he had in the last moment showed her an act of kindness. According to the story, she did appear to him in a vision three days after her own martyrdom. This so changed his perspective that he was willing to witness to the reality of the new movement, and was soon thereafter beheaded as a Christian martyr himself.

As in the Resurrection accounts of the "many saints had slept" in the New Testament, the point of these two stories is that it was through shamanistic and spiritistic experiences of post-mortem contacts with the dead (according to the accounts of both friends and enemies of the Christian movement) that Christianity spread throughout the Roman Empire. Whatever we may wish to make out of such accounts, I think we must recognize that the earliest chronologies of the church attribute the origins of a great deal of Christianity's early progress to such spiritistic, psychical, and mystical experiences.

C. *St. Seraphim of Sarov and Olga Worral—a Modern Spiritual Healer*

Some time after I myself became involved in the study of religion and psychical research, I had the good fortune to meet a lady who is well known as a spiritual healer, Olga Worral. She brought to me in Montreal a few small shreds of a stole which had been buried on the body of St. Seraphim of Sarov, the last saint canonized by the Czar of Russia before the Russian Revolution. She told me an interesting story about how she had received that relic. Her sister had brought her a brown paper bag one day. Without telling her what was in the bag, her sister placed it into her hands. At that moment Olga said she had a vision of an old man with a hunchback surrounded in light. In the vision, he said to her, "I am Seraphim of Sarov; I was beaten by thieves and had a hunchback, but I forgave my attackers. I served as a spiritual healer. You too will do the same kind of work, and I will help you in it." Subsequent to that, she was told by her sister that an old Russian Orthodox priest escaping from Russia had been given a piece of the stole exhumed with the body of St. Seraphim of Sarov. He had sent it to Olga and that was what was in the paper bag. Of course, Olga Worral herself went on to a great career as a spiritual healer. She says that Seraphim of Sarov has appeared to her many times since during her healings.

These stories are phenomenologically of one piece with the kinds of spiritistic or shamanistic events that we have already encountered in the earlier history of the Christian Church.

vii. insights from gnostic islam: sufism on the awakening of subtle faculties

As we have seen earlier, Henry Corbin has traced ideas held in ancient Persia among the Zoroastrians.[12] These ideas influenced Hellenistic Jews and early Christians, and later the Sufi mystics in the medieval Islamic culture of Iran. In all of these traditions, we find traces of an ancient metaphysical conception that, as man develops and unfolds on the "spiritual path," he becomes open to the awareness of subtle fields of influence and higher super-sensible realities and worlds.

In such ancient proto-gnostic traditions (including the Christian), a form of psychic development, or unfoldment of the individual consciousness, appears to occur as an integral part of the process of spiritual development. Thus, to postulate as many modern theologians have done that "psychic development" has nothing to do with "spiritual development," may, in addition to being untrue, miss one of the central points of salvation-type religious movements, including the earliest mystical forms of Christianity.

viii. the "son of man" paradigm and its pagan antecedents

If we look at the central figure of the New Testament itself, Jesus the Nazorean, we find in him a symbol which speaks of immortality more eloquently than do any of the words that I could use. In the canonical Gospels, Jesus refers to himself only as *"Bar Nasha"* or *"Uios Anthropou."* *Bar Nasha* (Aramaic) and *Uios Anthropou* (Greek) translate into English as "Son of Man." Until recently, especially in the 18th and 19th centuries, many Biblical historians assumed that "Son of Man" referred to the human nature of Jesus alone and that the Greek phrase *Uios Theou* or "son of God" referred to the divine nature alone.

But we do know today, through studies in Hellenistic Jewish, Persian, and Greek literature, that this is not so at all. The term "Bar Nasha" or "Son of Man" refers to the "divine in human form." An archetype of the human creation itself, it is the perfect Cosmic blueprint for all human beings. This was equated by some ancient writers with the "Logos" or eternal "image of God" that was said to be in every man that comes into the world.

ix. symbolic keys to unlocking the canonical portrait of Christ

The enigmatical use of the term "Son of Man," attributed to the historical Jesus in references to himself cited in the canonical Gospels, is incomprehensible without a knowledge of earlier mystical traditions in Indian, Persian, and Hellenistic-Jewish contexts. The *purusha* (Sanskrit) in Indian texts was the "eternal intelligence of the Creator," extended in the creation. This was often referred to in Indian literature as the "primal man."

In Persian traditions, which influenced Hellenistic-Jewish, Essenic mystical traditions out of which the spiritual forerunners of Jesus and John the Baptist came, we find the term *kaiomart* (Urdu). The *kaiomart* was the "one who ever resurrects himself from death, and from his own ashes."[13] This mysterious figure was also equated with the "primal man" and the "son of the primal man." The "son of the primal man," or "son of man" in the Greek New Testament (*Uios Anthropou*) is thus the "son of the primal man" who might be expected, by those who understood the Persian Zoroastrian and Hellenistic-Jewish mystical traditions, to raise himself from the dead, or be raised from the dead by the "primal man," his "Father," or God.

The "Son of Man," or offspring of the Primal Man, is, in these traditions which lie behind the New Testament, the "spark of God" that "lightens each person who comes into the world." It was a code-word for the *Imago Dei* in Everyman, and consequently meant much the same thing that the phrase "Son of God" had meant for some classical Greek writers (i.e., a god, or god-man). In Indian scriptures the term "Atman" (Sanskrit) had already been used for centuries before to describe the highest "immortal self" in Everyman. It is not the empirical [or lower self] "ego," but the "true Self" [or "higher self"] which was declared—on the basis of mystical experience—to be a God, i.e. the "pure, formless, spirit" which is "one with the brahman," or "one with the Father," and hence indestructible.[14]

x. "I and the father are one;" "atman and brahman are one"

In the Fourth Gospel, Jesus says, "I and the Father are one," just as "Brahman" and "Atman" were said to be one (*aham Brahman ahsi*) in the older, Indian Vedantic tradition. In the classical traditions of Yoga and Vedanta, we find a universal testimony to the idea that the highest part of every man is immortal because it is forever in union with its divine source. This divine source, or "Brahman," is often referred to in metaphoric language as "the Father." Vedantic language also describes a process of "awakening," or "new birth in the Eternal Spirit," to become aware of the divine self within the empirical self, or within the everyday, "sleeping" physical consciousness and within the mundane conscious mental processes. A whole psychophysical and psychospiritual trans-formation into the "new being" is said to manifest on the earth-plane whenever such a divine "self-realization" occurs. The canonical New Testament must be read within the context of such a wider, Indo-Iranian religious milieu, which had, prior to Jesus, already influenced Hellenistic Judaism.

xi. conclusion: insights into the language and concepts of mystical religion on the issue of immortality

A. Subjective Factors and Code Language in Historical Affirmations of Immortality Must Be Understood

Immortality and various perceptions of it have been expressed in various mythic and symbolic code-language. Its recognition depends upon subtle faculties and other subjective experiences which most modern Western academics have characteristically not cultivated or developed. These include an awakening, and a movement along a path of higher or divine consciousness and awareness. For its adepts there dawns, in the immortal words of the yogi after Samadhi, the recognition that "I am not the body, I am not the mind; I am (pure) Existence, Consciousness, and Bliss" ("Sat, Chit, Ananda").[15]

Obviously this does not mean that such self-realized yogis would disclaim the fact that they have a physical body or that they inhabit a mind-and-body instrument. Their challenge is rather to make the latter into "the temple of the Spirit" by various disciplines or sciences of self-integration known as "the yogas."

In Western traditions, such an awakening to a "higher consciousness" in which one's share in the divine immortality is perceived is often related to the conception of participating psychically and spiritually in the "resurrection" of dying and rising god-men, or saviors, in pre-Christian mystery cults (Osiris, Orpheus, Adonis, Mithra, etc.) as well as in Pauline descriptions of the Christian's "participation in Jesus' death and resurrection."

By the study of comparative concepts in the ancient world we come, I think, closer to an appreciation of just where the conceptions of "immortality" and "resurrection" merge. "Resurrection," then, in both Christian tradition and pre-Christian mysteries, is a code-word meaning either the sudden *or* gradual transformation of those kinds of consciousness which limit us solely to the egoic perception of our empirical self, a transformation yielding finally that kind of higher or "cosmic consciousness" that make us feel immortal and one with the Divine, as well as integrally related to all living things.

At the point of entry into this "resurrection life" one is also said to see the face of God or the "*Imago Dei,*" both within oneself and in all others in the world. The individual who is reborn through such a psychic and mystical participation in the resurrection of the archetypical God-Man recognizes in himself or herself that very "logos" or "word" which St. John said was "in every man as the light that lightens every man that comes into the world."

It is the "saints," i.e., those who have achieved such a "resurrection-life" through word and sacrament, who then talk of "seeing God," or "Christ," in the face of even the most hardened criminal, or the most degenerate example of the human race. It has been a specific gift of the saints, who are in fact spiritually progressed individuals, to perceive or discern something higher, something divine, in every instance of ordinary humanity, no matter how debased. This is something that mere logical reason alone will not account for. It is out of psychospiritual unfoldment that the saint's "mystical" or "gnostic" recognition of the divine occurs. It is out of spiritual progression alone that "self-realization," or realization of one's own share in the divine immortality, seems to occur.

B. Intuitive Psychospiritual Awakening—Not Logical Analysis Alone—is Required of the New Being

Metaphysical realities, including the fact of human "immortality," may not be proved or disproved through the use of *logical* and *analytical* mind-functions alone. A higher, *intuitive* form of *spiritual* mind-function is required to trigger the kind of psychic, shamanistic, and mystical experiences which generate the *raw data*, or existential facts required for anyone to be able personally to affirm immortality or the reality of a personal experience of life after death.

This "raw data" takes the form of experience—near-death experience, out-of-the-body experience, mediumistic experience, clairvoyance and clairaudience, visions, dreams, apparitions and the like. These experiences are processed through those higher, intuitive, "spiritual" mind-functions that ancient Hindu rishis and Buddhist sages called the "buddhic" mind-functions, and that Greek metaphysicians like Plato and Pythagoras called "noetic" or "higher-mind" functions. Those who have not attained the experience of such "buddhic" or "noetic" functions of the higher, "spiritual mind" can at best only *believe in* immortality, or in various forms of life after death, *on the basis of a rational faith in traditions, or testimonies of others* who were themselves seers, saints, sages, masters, or adepts. These figures have "been there." The mere "leap of faith" sort of belief on the part of religious persons may be important and good enough for beginners, but will not forever satisfy the God-given spiritual hunger of an evolving humanity for the "new being." A true gnosis based upon personal spiritual *and* psychic experience is required for the higher forms of faith ("pistis") of the spiritually mature person. This is not heretical gnosticism, but sane religion.

We can forever play conceptual mind-games with words, but until a kind of higher-intuitive, psychospiritual awakening process has occurred, or until the Spirit informs the intellect, the existential certainty of a living faith in the transcendent dimension will be missing. And as Henry Corbin indicates in describing Zoroastrian and Sufi conceptions, one's subtle faculties open only as one progresses along the Spiritual Path.[16]

C. The Resolution of Dualism Versus Non-Dualism May Be Found in "Guide-of-Light" Experiences

One of the classical problems in religion is the debate between dualists and non-dualists, i.e., between those people (characteristically of Western religions: Judaism, Christianity, and Islam), who stress that God is another Being "out there," "up there," or "transcendent," and those people who stress that God is "one with the Self," "in here," or "immanent" (characteristically those of Eastern religions, e.g., Hinduism, Buddhism, etc.). But these two poles of emphasis often meet perfectly in the pre-Christian philosophical conceptions of Iran, in Hellenistic Judaism, and in elements of primitive Christianity itself, especially in accounts of Jesus' post-mortem appearances to the faithful.

As we have seen earlier, Henry Corbin says that there is a great tradition among the Sufis, taken from earlier traditions of Persia, that when the "guide of light" appears to the person on the spiritual path, he will first appear *as if* "out there" along the path.[17] He will startle you as if "another being" from elsewhere. But as you progress in your psychic and spiritual development, the "Guide of Light" is suddenly recognized as "in here," in the midst of one's own bosom. St. Paul, one must remember, begins his career with the blinding-light theophany on the road to Damascus.[18] It was an appearance of the "dead" but now really "alive" Jesus whom Paul had been resisting. Later, Paul ends by saying that it is "not I, but the Christ that lives within me, that enables me to do all things."[19] The "guide of light" "out there" has become, because of an opening of subtle faculties of discernment and perception, the guide of light "in here," i.e., one with everything that we *are.* Thus Paul can say, "He is closer than hands or feet."[20]

Chapter 9

Alchemy and High Magick:
Theurgy in the Church and Sacraments

i. a key to understanding the sacraments

T he *Weltanschauung* of the ancient Near East included psychic concepts of various modes of social relationship. G. van der Leeuw has written extensively of the presence of these concepts in the experience of primitive and ancient religions,[1] and several Biblical scholars have viewed such concepts as the basis for the Old Testament understanding of the Israelite Covenant in Semitic thought. H. Wheeler Robinson, Johannes Pedersen, Aubrey R. Johnson, Russell Shedd, Max Thurian, and others have described these concepts in the Old Testament under such headings as "Psychic Extension of Personality," "Corporate Personality," "Realistic Representation," and "Cultic Anamnesis."[2] Some writers have attempted to trace the influence of these concepts in the formation of images employed to describe the Church and the sacraments in the New Testament. J. A. T. Robinson, Russell Shedd, Max Thurian, and others have contributed in this way to our understanding of the Church as the *soma Christou*, and of baptism and the eucharist as instruments of the relationship of the One to the many in the New Covenant community.[3]

But while the establishment of such ancient psychic solidarity concepts as (1) universally present in the ancient Near East, and (2) continuous between the Old and the New Testament does indeed help us to understand the early Christian doctrines, it does nothing by itself to make either these concepts or the later doctrines based upon them any more acceptable in their original form to the modern mind. The philosophical revolution which occurred in the 5th century B.C. in Greece, and the scientific revolution which began in the West during the Renaissance, have removed us from the primarily pictographic and dramatic psychical thought-world of the Heroic Age and of the

Bible. Today, when Biblical scholars and students of comparative religion confront us with evidence that early Christian doctrines of the Church were originally formed under the influence of primitive psychic solidarity concepts, we immediately think merely of the need for demythologization.

Some would feel that the ancient psychic solidarity concepts are completely irrelevant to any modern understanding of the Church and sacraments. But so much of the classical and normative language which is used to describe the Church and sacraments in scripture, theological tradition, and worship is intimately tied to these ancient psychical concepts that little, if anything, remains of the "Body of Christ" concept when they are discarded as the mere "wrappings" of the Kerygma. The Christian Kerygma involves a declaration that many are saved in and through a corporate relationship with one (Cosmic) Man; this would at least presuppose the possibility of a corporate-identity principle akin to that enshrined in the ancient psychic solidarity concepts. Therefore, a more constructive alternative to the abandonment of the ancient psychic solidarity concepts in contemporary explanations of the Church and sacraments is found in the attempt to verify them in terms of 20th-century psychic research. When this approach is taken, the psychic solidarity concepts of the Old Testament which are cited above may be viewed as ancient reflections of timeless truths, or indications of the appreciation in an ancient Hebrew psychology of specific facts generally operative, but not always explicitly recognized, in human experience. As such they may be understood as essential psychic preconditions of the Christian Kerygma of the Cosmic Christ, which were gathered to it during the process of a historical Revelation.

The probability of such a hypothesis depends upon the presence, beneath differing modes of expression, of real parallels between ancient and modern insights into the question of human solidarity. An explication of such parallels is present in recent developments in parapsychology and paraphysics. I believe that such studies—which are often too little understood by contemporary Biblical scholars and philosophers of religion—are making contributions to a rediscovery of the primitive thought-world and its insights into the human psychic faculties, which lie at the root of the Biblical understanding of the Church and sacraments.

ii. *the primitive psychic solidarity concepts of the ancient near east and the bible*

In the psychology which prevailed in the ancient Near East of the 3rd and 2nd millennia B.C., there is the curious but important assumption that every individual human personality, or self, is capable of effecting a kind of intentional or psychic extension of its being in the persons, places, and things which are around it or associated with it in the circumstances of its life. Egyptian, Babylonian, early Hellenic, and Hebrew scriptures afford many examples of such a belief in the extension of a man's personality, most notably towards his messengers or representatives, the members of his family, household or kin-group, and especially his sons, through his name, his words, his spirit, in his material possessions and in places where he has dwelt.[4] Involved in this assumption is the idea that the individual human personality is not limited to what we today should call the individual, physical self, but rather that it is diffused or shared by means of such psychic extensions throughout a group. The group was then conceived, together with the individual, as a larger self.[5] This larger self was seen as psychically embodying the man, plus all of his personal extensions, and the other persons, places, and things with which he shared his life and which were consequently thought to be parts of him. The Biblical writers were convinced that any one individual could, conversely, sum up or psychically embody the whole group of which he was a part, so that he could represent the whole group and the shared personality of its ancestral member either within the group or to those outside of it.[6]

Basic to all of these assumptions, which have respectively been called by Old Testament scholars "psychic extensions of personality," "corporate personality," and "realistic representation," is a primitive thought mode which appreciated the reality of psychic action and could therefore conceive of things "holistically" rather than individualistically. The individual derived his significance from the group, which was itself the basic unit for consideration. The group, not the individual, was viewed first; the individual was considered a real or whole entity only insofar as he participated in a larger psychic totality or sphere of existence. Because the individual never existed, in the full sense of the word, apart from the group, such psychic participation in the whole could be thought of as "extended" or "present" in him/her, and s/he was capable of "embodying" or "summing up" the whole group in him/herself.

A fourth primitive belief in the reality of psychic action is seen in the concept of "cultic anamnesis."[7] In the action of the cultic memorialization of an event, which involved its dramatic representation by persons and material objects, the participant in the ceremony conceived of him/herself as actually participating in the original event. There was thus the possibility of a trans-spacio-temporal, psychic participation in a past occurrence by the members of a cultic group whose intention it was to identify with the original agent(s) of the action so memorialized. Before we can see the relevance of the ancient psychic solidarity concepts to the Christian doctrine of the Church and the sacraments, we must show in greater detail precisely what these concepts were, and how they might have developed into the New Testament presentation of the Church and sacraments. We will then be able to explore those points of contact with modern thought which will meaningfully elucidate the doctrine for us.[8]

iii. *cultic anamnesis in the ancient world*

There is a curious belief which seems to have been fairly well disseminated throughout ancient Semitic and Graeco-Roman cultures that worshippers forming an ethnic and/or cultic community could be united both together and to a common god, lord, hero or other object of worship by means of a dramatic ceremony or ritual in which all participated.[9]

The ancient "mystery rite" consisted first of a cultic "anamnesis," or memorial, in which it was thought that a particularly important or salvation-bearing act, which was once performed by the god or hero, was psychically present for the benefit of the worshippers.[10] The god or hero might be either a historical, a legendary, or a purely mythical figure, but s/he embodied for them a primordial or supernatural being with which worshippers were enabled to share his/her actions, and hence, in his/her life, " . . . its aim is union with godhead, a share in his life."[11]

This primitive concept of "cultic anamnesis" forms the basis of the Old Testament understanding of the Passover ritual, and the New Testament and subsequent Christian understanding of the Eucharist.[12] Because "cultic anamnesis," unlike the other three psychic solidarity concepts, is usually restricted in most ancient societies to operation within a religious perspective, almost all of the Biblical evidence which we have for "cultic anamnesis" is found only within the context of the Israelite "divine Covenant."

iv. cultic anamnesis in the israelite covenant

In cultic anamnesis persons and material objects were employed in the creation of a drama symbolizing and commemorating mythical and/or historical salvation-events. Even when not actually present, members of the group were envisioned as participating vicariously in the "representational" action of its celebrants, who in turn participated psychically in the force of the original life and event being commemorated.[13] Thus, the high priest of Israel bore the names of the twelve tribes on twelve stones affixed to his ephod, so that he symbolically represented all Israelites in "memorial" before God as priest and righteous intercessor:

> "Aaron shall bear the names of the children of Israel in the breast place of Judgement upon his heart, when he goeth in unto the holy place, for a memorial before the Lord continually."[14]

In the case of the celebration of the Israelite Passover, the symbolical embodiments of the psychic reality beyond (present in the Passover event itself) were the unleavened bread, the bitter herbs, fruits and vinegar, the lamb and the blood, etc. These were used in order to recreate symbolically, but also objectively and physically, the original conditions of the first Passover, so that it would be psychically and spiritually present to those taking part in the ceremony, allowing them dramatically to re-live the event as it was memorialized.[15] They were to be involved with all of their senses as well as with the heart and soul. Unleavened bread is eaten because there was no time for it to rise on the occasion of the Israelite's flight from Egypt at the original Passover. Bitter herbs must be chewed so that even the "taste" of bitterness present in the original event would be experienced in its sacramental reenactment by the participants. Fruits and vinegar were to be consumed as a reminder of the mud of Egypt. The lamb that gave its blood to protect the chosen people against the plague was to be slain and eaten. Thurian calls this a "concrete re-living" of the Exodus experience.[16]

All of these objects were used in an action which had been given historical context and symbolic significance by the original event, i.e., the Passover and deliverance from Egypt under Moses. By means of "realistic representation," it was believed that the many could in fact participate with Moses in the crossing of the Red Sea and all that followed in which God had originally acted on their behalf.

The memorial action itself was conceived of as capable of bearing into the present moment the reality or force of the past occasion, or conversely, of transporting the participants back into the time of the original event. This seems to have been envisioned dynamically as a reliving by the participants within the "timeless" moment of the memorial, rather than as a static superimposition of objectified "times." In other words, the worshippers were psychic participants and enactors of real events rather than observers of a dead past. They were participants in a psychic replay of the salvation history taken from a sort of "collective unconscious," one in which they could join as actors now involved in the original drama alongside of its original enactors.

Thurian says:

> "There was in the mystery of the paschal meal a kind of telescoping of two periods of history, the present and the Exodus. The past event became present or rather each person became a contemporary of the past event. It is the redemptive act accomplished once for all yet ever renewed, present, and applied which the Church came to designate by the word 'mystery' or 'sacrament' . . . (it) expresses the Biblical meaning of the 'salvation-history' which was accomplished in time 'once-for-all' but which is equally 'present' at all times 'by Word and Sacrament.' "[17]

v. "cultic anamnesis" and the other psychic solidarity concepts of the old testament

In the New Testament we are confronted with a whole series of images describing the Church which are difficult to understand in modern terms, but which are immediately clarified when interpreted in the light of the foregoing solidarity concepts of the Old Testament. The concept of membership "in Israel" parallels that of membership "in Christ."[18] The concept of the People of God as the corporate extension of its progenitor Jacob, or "Israel," is now to be found in the concept of the "Body of Christ" as the corporate extension of its head, Jesus the Christ.[19] The other images for the Church in the New Testament, such as "vine," "household," and "bride," are taken directly from Old Testament descriptions of the corporate Israel, now conceived of as continued and fulfilled, not according to "the flesh" but by a new psychic dispensation "in the spirit," or in the corporate Christ.[20] No longer a lineal and ethnic inheritance by natural birth, membership in the New Israel is conceived of as gained by a second supernatural "birth" in the spirit, or to use another concept, by incorporation of the many into the person of the one "only begotten Son" through baptism.[21] Such terms were selected by the New Testament writers to describe for the readers in the Hellenic world (who were familiar with such concepts from the mystery religions) the relationship of the many to the one, which was already familiar to these writers from their own Hebraic religious background.

All of the instruments of the psychic extension of personality which we have found in the Old Testament are also present in the New. Thus we have the creedal evaluation of Jesus as the "Word" of God, and the emphasis upon the efficacy of his spoken words.[22] We find in the New Testament the same association of numinous power with the utterance of the "name" of Jesus as we found connected with the "name" of Yahweh in the Old Testament.[23] The "Spirit" is likewise seen as the active extension of God himself in the world and is closely associated with the person and work of Jesus as Messiah and Son of God.[24] The "Spirit" is portrayed as sent by the Christ in the Pentecostal experience in order to extend and continue His messianic presence and mission in the world through the Church.[25]

This principle is attested to in the Book of Acts by the reproduction by the many of the works of the One, and in the proclamation of the Kingdom of God through healing, exorcism, remission of sin, and teaching with authority.[26] As in the Old Testament, physical objects also become the media of the divine presence and of the presence of Jesus ("the hem of His garment," Peter's "shadow," etc.).[27] The story of the baptism of Cornelius' household in Acts mentions all of the instruments of the extension of personality which we see in the Old Testament. Thus Peter, the apostle or messenger, preaches the Word in the words of the Kerygma, and the Spirit is outpoured. Cornelius' household is baptized in the "name" of Jesus and becomes the first Gentile membership of the Church.[28] The principle of the "extension" of the personality of the Christ in individual members of His

Church is explicitly stated in the apostolic commission, "He who receives any one whom I send, receives me, and he who receives me receives Him who sent me,"[29] and in the dominical injunction, "Inasmuch as you have done it unto any one of the least of these my brethren, you have done it unto me."[30]

The concept of "realistic representation" is found in the New Testament in the idea of Christ as Representative Man or New Adam,[31] as well as in the idea of the corporate and representational role of the servant whose sufferings and death are viewed as expiatory on behalf of all.[32] It is because of His "realistic representation" of all men in His life of obedience to the Father, in which the first Adam had failed and likewise implicated all men, that Jesus is viewed as the beginning or "first fruits" of a new creation.[33] His life, death and resurrection are viewed as containing implicitly the key which makes available potentially to all of mankind the new kind of life, or new creation, seen at first in Him alone.[34] It is also because of his understanding of psychic realism and "realistic representation" that Paul can say to his readers that they have died to the old life with Jesus in His death and have risen with Him in His Resurrection to a new life.[35] Pauline theology is firmly rooted in an ancient understanding of the universal laws of psychic action and social participation. One person or event can be participated in or shared ontologically by the many, in many different times and places throughout subsequent history.

The language of a moral transformation incited in the Christian by the example of Jesus is surely not merely metaphorical; it seems to imply an ontological, psychic identification of the many with their "realistic representative," Jesus. In the same way that we have seen the high priest of Israel "embody" psychically the whole nation in his own person and actions in the atonement ceremonies, we now find the New Testament speaking of Jesus in His life, death, and resurrection.[36]

vi.   "cultic anamnesis"—viewed as a psychic "technology"

Max Thurian has written extensively concerning the primitive concept of "memorial" in the Old and New Testaments in relation to the Passover rites and the Christian Eucharist.[37] He finds a continuity in the Biblical understanding of the principle underlying the concept of cultic "anamnesis" in both Testaments. "Azkarath" and "Zikkaron" in the Old Testament and "Mnemosunon" and "Anamnesis" in the Greek of the Septuagint and the New Testament have the effect of the instrumental "Semeion" or "sign" which makes a reality concrete, and are an enactment which "memorializes" or brings an event or thing before the memory—and hence into the actual presence—of God or man. The many times and places are thus psychically transcended in the corporate and cultic "anamnesis" of a once-accomplished event such as the Exodus or the death and Resurrection of Christ.

The concept of "cultic anamnesis" as seen in the Eucharistic memorial continues the pattern, familiar from the Old Testament, of participation of many persons of many times in the one Person in one sacred time.[38] As the many worshippers consume the common loaf and drink of the common cup, they conceive of themselves as psychically (spiritually, mentally, and physically) participating in the one Person ("body") and life ("blood") of Christ given for them in the (once-for-all) event of a redemptive death, and so by virtue of this union share in His Resurrection.[39] The Pauline presentation of baptism as a "dying and rising again with Christ" may also be seen as an embodiment of the psychic principle of "cultic anamnesis."[40]

The dominant modern interpretation of "memorial" is that it is purely a "subjective" or inner function of the mind quite unrelated to external "objectivity." This is not the way the words "recall" or "remember" were characteristically understood by many ancient pre-philosophical peoples. For them, things transpired on the "mental screen" of the "imagination"—even those images or actions invoked or provoked by what we would call "memory"—might be taken on occasion as objective psychic perceptions of quite real spiritual or astral entities not present in the ordinary space-time-matter dimension.

The modern philosopher Henri Bergson has attempted to call attention to something like this ancient view in his concept of "objective recall."[41] In Bergson's conception of "objective recall," actual persons, places, and objects might serve to "awaken" or "call up" within the psyche such past events or persons by symbolic association. Marcel Proust seems to have borrowed Bergson's concept of "objective recall" in some of his writings.[42] Indeed, such an understanding was germane to the Indian and Tibetan conceptions of what is accomplished in *puja* (worship) ceremonies, in which the real spiritual force represented by a deity and its image are thought to be "activated within" the soul, or "jiv atman" (individual self) of the worshipper, through the psychological and psychic actions of the ritual itself.

In the ancient Near Eastern concept of "cultic anamnesis" the actual person or event was "memorialized" and thought to be "called back" from the past or from the "other worlds" to which the departed go. Objects which had either a symbolic or physical psychometrical association with the person or event were frequently used in this action. These ritual actions and objects were accompanied by a story about the person, or a remembering of the person whose spirit was thus, as it were, invoked to be present.

Thus we have seen that, as Thurian has established, there is a unity in the psychic solidarity conceptions of the Old and New Testaments.[43] I would now go beyond Thurian's position to assert that modern psychical research involving particularly mediumistic practices and primitive shamanism might help us to understand these ancient psychic solidarity concepts better in our own age and milieu. There is a dimension of psychic instrumentalism in New Testament language relating to Christ and the sacraments which modern theologians might now profitably explore within a broader parapsychological context.

It is interesting to note that, in the story of the "witch" or "medium" of Endor in 1 Samuel 7:25, the word used in the Septuagint Greek version for the psychic action involved in contacting the spirit of the prophet Samuel is a derivative of *anamnesein* or "to remember." The original Hebrew word would have been *zacher*. This is simply translated in the King James version of the Old Testament as "to bring up" the ghost of Samuel. The basic meaning of both *zacher* in Hebrew and *anamnesein* in Koine Greek is to "call again" or "call up again." In English we use the word "to recall" and/or "remember" interchangeably for the same action.

vii. possible old testament background to the eucharistic language of the new testament

In the King James version of 1 Samuel, the "witch of Endor" asks Saul, "Whom shall I *bring up* to thee" (1 Samuel 28:11). This might be better translated from the Septuagint as "Whom shall I remember (or recall) for thee?" We must take this into account when we read the story of Jesus' institution of the Christian Eucharist at the "Last Supper." In all four of the Gospels he is reported as saying "Do this for a memorial of me" (*eis ton anamnesein mou*). The English version is perhaps a rather weak, modern, interpretive translation of what was intended in Aramaic. Did Jesus institute the fellowship meal as a psychic instrument, i.e., an "objective memorial," in the ancient sense of an actual "recall," a means for his continued spiritual presence with his disciples? Was the action which he instituted at the Last Supper phenomenologically akin to the psychically instrumental actions which the "witch of Endor" had employed centuries before in bringing up the actual spirit of the prophet Samuel to converse with King Saul? Linguistic and phenomenological evidence suggests this.

We do know that psychically and spiritually realistic, not metaphoric, interpretations were in fact placed upon these "words of institution" from earliest times in the primitive Catholic tradition. This conception may be offensive to some persons, but there is a strong argument for the contention that the primitive Christian Eucharist was—phenomenologically at least—a shamanistic exercise or a "mediumistic service." It is interesting to note that when a shaman, medium, or a participant in a seance in a Spiritualist circle wishes to summon the spirit of a particular loved one, he or she is instructed "to call upon" the deceased by a psychic act which consists of thinking about or remembering him/her, and asking mentally for his/her presence. Likewise, when a Catholic or Orthodox Christian prays to a particular saint, he/she "remembers" the saint, and is aided in so doing by a statue or ikon, which thus serves as an instrument of psychic focalization for an objective recall in which the spirit or entity is either actually summoned or otherwise communicated with through the general mediumship of the Holy Spirit.[44] A psychic action or "technology" existed by which the Church, and the entire Primordial Tradition, believed that Jesus (or any saint for that matter) could be psychically or objectively recalled whenever two or three were gathered together "in His Name." In Christian tradition, this was done particularly—but not exclusively—at the Eucharist. The early Church understood the Eucharist to be a memorial giving of thanks for all God's redemptive acts in history, from the call of Abraham through the Mosaic experience to the death, Resurrection, Ascension and promised "coming again" of Jesus. But it was also the place where they "knew Him" now "in the breaking of bread." The earliest Christians claimed not only contact with the eternal Logos or Christ, but with the historical man Jesus, through a realistic, spiritually and psychically delivered presence.

The full paradosis or tradition of Orthodox-Catholic patristic teaching on the "changing of the elements" of bread and wine into the "body" and "blood" of the Christ also implies an alchemical "transmutation" of the essential reality present under the appearances of the matter of the bread and wine. Here we have the clear conception that something happens objectively, within time and space, to the "inner ontological nature" of the material substance present. That substance is described as "transformed," just as the physical body of the man Jesus once was transformed in the Resurrection. It is the *soma pneumatikos* or spiritual-energy body, and becomes a vehicle of the archetype of perfected human nature, which is the *bar nasha* (Aramaic for "Son of Man," i.e. "Restored Adam"), who is, in turn, seen as the universal human vessel housing the "logos," the "Eternal Christ," the "Son of God," and the eternal expression and procession of the "Hidden Father" toward and in the Creation. This was the primitive Christian gnosis.

Anything less than this full psychical and mystical understanding was rejected by Orthodox-Catholic insight as less than the esoteric truth concerning the Eucharist and the sacramental principle itself. This principle demanded a full and realistic participation of many individual human beings, in many times and places of history, in the one archetypical Son of Man/Son of God, as "very members of His Body."

We are approaching the point at which we can see not only the essential unity of the four ancient psychic solidarity concepts, but also the special relevance of all psychic actions to our own better understanding of the "Body of Christ" concept in Christianity, and of the place of the sacraments within that concept. Sacraments are—in this universal ancient as well as in the modern parapsychological understanding—veritable "eternal spiritual happenings" which are psychically repeatable by the faithful for the purpose of mystical identification with the living Christ and His redemptive healing power. Such rites were seen in the Eastern patristic tradition as both tremendous and awesome "mysteries" and at the same time as the simplest of natural occurrences. Like all of the processes by which life, growth, and maturation occur, they may be viewed as part of the holistic spiritual, psychic, and physical technology by which God works through, rather than apart from, Nature to create, recreate, and redeem the human race.

Students of comparative religion will recognize a common language and experience in the mystery religions of the Hellenistic and Roman worlds, and in traditions of pre-philosophical shamanism everywhere. And, as we have seen, these traditions were very much alive in the ancient Israelite conceptions of psychic solidarity and extension, which provided the background of the New Testament metaphors for the ideas of "church" and "sacrament."

The Catholic-Orthodox doctrine of the special nature of the real presence of Jesus, in both His divine and human natures in the Eucharistic liturgy, would thus be found to rest upon a "Primordial Tradition" of intuition, i.e., upon an ancient understanding of the natural human psychic faculties at work in every kind of "objective recall." Only after the loss of such an ancient understanding did the Christian churches lose themselves in endless rationalistic-conceptualist disputes over what was actually transpiring in the Eucharistic liturgy, and in such philosophical theories as Transubstantiation, Transmutation, Consubstantiation, Receptionism, Memorialism, etc. But the Biblical concept of the "anamnesis" involved in the Eucharist was really a corollary of the primitive psychic conception of "anamnesis" which, as may be seen in the work of Dom Odo Casel, was also widespread in the Semitic, Egyptian, and Graeco-Roman mystery cults in antiquity, and as such part of a Primordial belief system pre-dating Christiainity as a specific religion.[45]

viii.   the need for knowledge of parapsychological facts

This study regarding conceptions of human psychic solidarity might give us a better understanding of the historical development of the Christian sacraments, and of the idea of the Church as the "Body of Christ," in ways which overcome the theological and philosophical barriers erected between Protestants and Catholics since the Reformation. But it will still stop short of contributing to a contemporary understanding of these "primitive" concepts in themselves. They are still a strange kind of way to view the world, entirely alien to modern scientific and philosophical presuppositions. Merely to trace the development of ancient psychic solidarity conceptions from the Old and New Testaments to the later Patristic understandings of Israel, Israelite, the Passover, Christ, Christians, the Church, and Sacraments might help us to understand the ideas of prayer and sacrament within a theological context. But it will not help one iota in conveying these ideas to the kind of "modern man" who has always been "profane," i.e., reared on a steady cultural training in rationalistic empiricism and materialistic philosophy to reject the sacred. Neither will subjective explanations impress him. He will retort that there are "better ways to understand things today."

And this could be true from a logical perspective, unless it can be demonstrated that there is indeed a whole missing area of consideration in modern Western man's *Weltanschauung* in which a real phenomenology of psychic phenomena still operates (or could operate). There is such evidence, and we hope to see some of it coming to light as qualified scholars begin to apply themselves to the development of the parapsychology of religion as an experiential science. Needless to say, such a science will provide new and "objective" insights into the universal phenomenology of religious experience in all traditions and cultures, both ancient and modern.

This has obvious relevance to questions concerning the nature and modes of operation of all forms of religion, including forms of Christianity, within the context of an ever-widening religious and cultural pluralism. Discovering universal principles and techniques of psychic action, which seem to run like a golden thread throughout human experience during moments of religious disclosure, is an important first step in the achievement of meaningful forms of communication between men and women who are suddenly thrown together, in our 20th-century global village, from radically disparate religions and cultures.

ix. the role of psychic faculties in ancient religion

It is very likely that such an objective phenomenology of "magic" or psychic action is indeed involved in both pre-philosophical ancient religious and in modern extra-philosophical, occult traditions. Prophecy, divination, revelation in dreams, exorcisms, healing rites, and other forms of miracle tradition are found among them in abundance. Yet modern scholars, who in most established fields are dominated by Enlightenment philosophical and religious *a priori* assumptions, ignore it and are unable to cope with it. Moreover, it will simply not suffice to tell people today—as many historians of religion do—that "primordial subjective realities" are invoked in such religious rites, and then say nothing more. Common sense says that more is involved and that a responsible approach to the history of religion demands its investigation. Explanations are indeed being sought; but to empirically oriented people involved in religious rites in a technological society, academic definitions of the aims of the religious activities of man often appear little more than an impractical, ivory tower intellectualism. What might be more to the point, in the history of religions, is a parapsychological and paraphysical study of similar paranormal occurrences as they may be found today. There is, after all, an abundance of data available on forms of psychic action. The serious scientific study of this data could be a great help to scholars engaged in an open-minded study of the phenomenology of paranormal claims in ancient religious literature.[46]

The classical Greek metaphysical definition of "Reason"—as understood by Socrates, Plato and Plotinus—included what we today should call both "intuitional" or "psychic" as well as "logical" faculties.[47] In this classical metaphysical tradition, which was adopted by most of the fathers of the early Christian Church, "Reason" was thus thought of as an appropriate faculty for what we should term a "rational-intuitional" contemplation, or direct psychic perception of physically invisible but objectively real influences, ideas, entities, or forces, including the Divine.[48] In the ancient world, philosophers had spoken of man's awareness, not only of various abstract truths, but also of the gods and of nature spirits which were believed to be objective entities as perceived through the human psychic faculties. Recognition of the "credentials of the gods" was for them connected with a rational activity integral to the processes of intuitional awareness.

Thus in early Christian theological terms one tested the invisible influences in one's life, whether conceived of as spirits, guardian angels, discarnate saints, demons, or psychological complexes and attitudes, etc., through spiritual and psychical mind-faculties.[49] The art of perception of invisible influences, whether Plato's ideals, various spirit forms, the pagan gods, or discarnate Christian saints, was for most of the ancient world an integral part of a quite rational function of human cognition through an extrasensory form of awareness and evaluation.

Pictorial Symbol from the Tarot.
Design by Pamela Colman Smith from Edward Waite's *Pictorial Key to the Tarot.*

x. the psychic faculties in primitive christianity

At no time in the earliest Christian Neo-Platonic tradition was there a complete break between (1) intuitive reason and claimed psychical-revelatory encounters with God, angels, saints or (2) between ways of knowing so-called metaphysical truths and ways of knowing more ordinary, mundane psychological experience. All involved perception, cognition, and interpretation of the data of experience, whether physically or psychically communicated. If modern scholars are to understand the classical balance between "revelation" and "reason" in the Patristic Tradition, it will be necessary to grasp the importance implicitly attributed to the psychic faculties of the human soul by the Church's founders. And in order to make contemporary sense out of this attribution, it will be extremely helpful to gain some exposure to contemporary facts from experimental parapsychology.

Our modern epistemological distinction between "subjective" and "objective" ways of knowing—based as it is upon *a priori* distinctions between the "physical" and the "mental" forms of perception and social interaction—simply did not exist in ancient and early medieval theology. Such modern distinctions have been recognized as supreme in philosophy and theology since Descartes, Locke, Hume, and Kant, even though they are alien to the *Weltanschauung* both of the Biblical Hebrew and Greek philosophical traditions out of which Christianity was born.[50] These distinctions have made many of the central teachings of New Testament and primitive Christianity quite unintelligible to modern scientific traditions and to many modern Western theological systems alike.

xi. conclusion: the reconvergence of ancient sacramental insights with modern scientific discoveries

Some scholars today would claim that such Enlightenment philosophical distinctions are beginning to crumble under the weight of recent insights from parapsychology and paraphysics.[51] They claim not only that the distinctions between subjective and objective and between mind and matter show signs of inadequacy, but also that evidence suggests that the roots of both Greek metaphysical and pre-philosophical ancient religions may be found in objective psychic experiences of persons and communities.[52]

They also say that, contrary to early modern philosophical and much modern Western theological opinion, the ancient Greek metaphysics of Plato, and the pre-philosophic religions which preceded it, did not initially rest upon rootless speculative interpretations or upon *a priori* conceptualizations at all. In other studies, I have suggested some of the ways in which insights from contemporary parapsychology and psychical events might explain the original forms of experience underlying at least some of the classical Greek metaphysical doctrines of persons like Pythagoras, Plato, and Plotinus.[53]

In conclusion, it will be discovered by the serious and unbiased scholar that the implicit world-views of primitive peoples, the ancient Greeks and Hebrews, early Christians, as well as contemporary non-Western peoples, although perhaps in some cases not philosophically formulated, will also find their origins in various forms of mystical and psychical experiences, or "real magic." In fact, these experiences are grounded in real, not imaginary, universal human faculties of spiritual and psychic perception and interaction—a veritable Primordial Tradition of higher intuition and insight that we in modern times have characteristically forgotten. It is through a careful study of contemporary psychical research and comparative mysticism that modern theologians will gain the insight necessary to understand more fully the religious experience and language of ancient sacral societies and cultures—the now-lost "Primordial Tradition" of both enlightened pagan sages and their Biblical forebearers of old.

Chapter 10

The Loss and Recovery of the Primordial Tradition and the Cosmic Christ

i. the loss of the primordial tradition in the west

*I*t has long been recognized by historians of philosophy and science that Western civilization, from the 17th-century "Age of Reason" and the 18th-century "Enlightenment" to the rise of the 19th-century physical and social sciences, has undergone a radical shift in its basic approach to reality. Even before this period, for at least five centuries since the 12th century A.D., Western philosophers and theologians had been laying the groundwork for the change from a civilization oriented toward faith in transcendental worlds and higher spiritual and ethical dimensions, necessary to any vital conception of a "Cosmic Christ," to our present "modern" civilization, which has considered the "real" to be synonymous with the physical world alone.

In classical and late antiquity, the Greek philosophers Pythagoras, Plato, and Plotinus developed systems of thought based upon the Primordial Tradition of intuition and insight of India, Egypt, Persia and Greece. In this tradition, as summarized by Plato, the material or physical world is but a shadow or projection of the truly "real world" originating in the realm of "Cosmic Mind, Cosmic Consciousness, and the Spirit." The way human beings could know the reality of such a Cosmic Mind "behind," "in," and "under" the phenomenal world was through the use of "Cosmic Vision," e.g. inner faculties of higher or rational intuition, rather than in the mere physical observation and logical computation of data from the phenomenal world. It was generally agreed that only "opinion," based on the partial grasp of half-truths and half-illusions, could be obtained by such empirical methods used without recourse to the higher functions of intuitive consciousness.

But in the 4th century B.C., the 12th century A.D., and finally in the 16th century A.D., three major Western philosophers—and their followers—changed all of this. First, Plato's student Aristotle broke with his master's teachings—and with the entire Primordial Tradition of the higher religions of the ancient East—by asserting that real knowledge of things requires the use of the physical senses. This epistemological limitation laid the foundation for the materialist-rationalist point of view of the modern West.

The philosophy of Aristotle was adopted by the "Schoolmen" of medieval Christianity, led by St. Thomas Aquinas who beginning in the 12th century gradually moved Western Christian thought away from the Greek Platonic and Neo-Platonic foundation laid for a theology of the Cosmic Christ by many of the Apostolic Fathers and Apologists from the 2nd to the pseudo-Dionysius in the 6th century A.D. The Aristotelian denial of the possibility of training of higher, subtle faculties of intuitive perception into "layers" or "hierarchies" of reality in the cosmos led to the great monolithic edifice of Western logic as it was applied to Christian Revelation, from the medieval to the modern periods, in the official Thomistic philosophy of the Roman Church. This development, in turn, paved the way for later, secular forms of materialistic and rationalistic reductionism by conditioning Western culture to the idea that only the physically observable and logically computable is worthy of "scientific" endeavor, whether in the areas of natural and social sciences or in religious studies.

By the 16th century, Rêné Descartes, the so-called "father of modern philosophy," was able to assert that all reality could be neatly divided between (1) the "objective" realm of physical "extension," and (2) the "subjective" realm of "thought." Thus, "mind"—now to be progressively limited to its logical-analytical functions—was believed to be radically distinct and separate from physical objects in material space and time. One could study things "scientifically" only through (1) physical, empirical observation and (2) the logical analysis and computation of data received thereform.

A whole host of Western philosophers of science and religion—from Francis Bacon, John Locke, and David Hume to Immanuel Kant—now proceeded, by way of either affirmation or denial of the reality of the spiritual and transcendental dimensions, to accept this basic Aristotelian-Thomistic-Cartesian limitation of man's "natural" vision to a two-dimensional world of physical observation and logical computation.

ii. revolutionary consequences for western culture

The entire edifice of modern Western science and technology has been built upon this "natural," materialistic-rationalistic and reductionistic assumption. Of course, such a philosophical *a priori* or arbitrary belief is by no means essential to true "science" itself, either with regard to its content or its methodology. In its ancient Greek roots, reaching back into the Primordial Tradition through Plato, "scientia" or "science" included not only the study of empirical forms of knowledge but also use of the higher, intuitive means of perception, yielding "gnosis," or knowledge of the inner psychic and spiritual side of man and the universe. The physical observation and logical computation of material data and behaviors which is modern "science" was only one-half of the original equation. The consequences of this arbitrary limitation of "science" in the West have been terribly dehumanizing, and have created a radical schism between science and religion, or more properly, between our truncated "science" and human spirituality in all of its possible forms.

The only forms of "production" to count in the modern Western milieu, whether capitalist or communist, have been thus far only material production of physical objects. The very idea that man's happiness, fulfillment or success in this world can be created primarily by "intangible" factors such as spirit, truth, beauty, inner peace, joy, love, sharing, forgiving, and victory over selfishness, greed, avarice, hatred and resentment has been largely left out of our textbooks in psychology, sociology, economics, political science, and management. Everyone, secular capitalists and communists alike, seems to assume that physical factors are all that is important in the creation of a perfect society. Seldom in secular textbooks of schools, colleges, and universities in the modern West do essential human spiritual values count as important factors. And yet we are just about at the brink of self-destruction as a civilization for the lack of a universal understanding of such inner human values among the peoples of the world.

The model by which we have looked at reality in the West has not been wide enough to contain a synthesis between modern "science" and universal, common forms of human religious or spiritual experience, whether in Eastern or Western terms. This has caused a kind of schizophrenia in the soul of Western man, one which has also been exported since the 19th century to non-Western, Eastern, and other Third World cultures along with (otherwise good) Western sciences and technologies. Today many people in Third World cultures are not able to reconcile their "scientific," Western-type educations with their own ethnic, cultural, religious, and spiritual heritages.

But as I have said elsewhere, the latest research in the "future sciences" has indicated that the 16th- to 19th-century models for reality that we have used as a basis for "modern science" are simply not good enough to carry psychology, physics, biology, medicine, or religion very much further into this century.[15]

Many feel that, when the new data from these "future sciences" is taken into account, we may well experience what Thomas Kuhn has described as "the structure of a scientific revolution," a radical shift in paradigms or models of reality, both for science and for religion. When the psi data that now waits to be reviewed is finally digested and assimilated by the world's scientific and philosophical establishments, we may indeed experience Arthur Koestler's "Second Copernican Revolution."

But, we might legitimately ask, is this the first time in Western history that an attempt is made to reintroduce the "Primordial Tradition," with its perennial intuitions and insights into the multidimensional nature of man and the cosmos, into a skeptical, reduced, and impaired Western tradition? The answer is clearly "no." There have been other attempts, rather persistent attempts which for various historical reasons have failed.

iii. the survival of fragments of gnosis, and earlier attempts to recover the primordial tradition

When the original Christian gnosis reflected in the "logia" or sayings of Jesus and in the earlier, authentic New Testament writings of Paul failed to take sufficient hold, and the early Christian movement began to move in the direction of codification of the "message" and institutionalization of the Church, the proto-gnostic, Platonic mystical ideas of the Primordial Tradition were gradually lost within the mainstream of the Roman religious establishment. Nevertheless, underground currents of genuine gnosis have survived and persisted throughout the intervening ages, in spite of (1) extravagant heresies on the one side, and (2) a hostile, inveterate, rationalistic skepticism on the other.

Dr. Andrijah Puharich has written a succint resumé of past attempts to resurrect the Primordial Tradition during the subsequent history of Western civilization:

"The Platonic ideas were carried on by the gnostics (excluded and persecuted by the early Church Fathers), and practiced by the alchemists. While the Roman Church ruled Europe with scholastic Thomism and burned witches (remote-viewing and metal-bending practitioners), the more empirically-minded alchemists and astrologers produced Copernicus, Kepler, Bruno, Galileo and Newton. Georgi di Santillana has called Newton the 'last of the Great Babylonian magicians.' The ultimate victory of Giordano Bruno, Galileo Galilei, and Isaac Newton over the scholastic Aristotelian-Thomistic forces of the Roman Church laid the foundations for modern empirical science. But this did not mean that the Platonic idealists had gone into eclipse.

"In the eighteenth century, the great Swedish scientist Emmanuel Swedenborg was doing real-time remote viewing experiments that had such a conclusive quality about them that his friend, the great German philosopher Immanuel Kant, incorporated this data into the formulation of his great Neo-Platonic "idealistic" philosophy. In succession, the alchemists became chemists; the fluid-magnetizers became electricians; the astrologers became astronomers; and the philosophers became physicists.

"For a time it seemed as if the issue between the materialists and the idealists had faded away with the secure triumph of materialistic science. When Clerk Maxwell brought together in a unified mathematical treatment the relation between matter-forces and (immaterial) light waves, and this prediction was experimentally confirmed by Heinrich Hertz and Nikola Tesla in the early 1880s, it seemed that there was nothing left to argue about.

"However, between 1880 and 1900 the materialistic cookie began to crumble in ways not to be clearly recognized until almost 100 years later, with the appearance of the Iceland Papers. What happened is that in the examination of the matter-light radiation physics Max Planck discovered that the energy was emitted in 'energy packets' or quanta. Albert Einstein, in examining events moving at or near the velocity of light, formulated the Special Theory of Relativity, and later the General Theory of Relativity. These two theories (quantum mechanics and relativity) had within them seeds which it is believed will resolve the matter-mind problem.

"But the idealistic camp was not idle during this past century. During the 1880's there appeared 'psychical research' societies in England, France and the United States of America. The methods of empirical science were applied to the study of human 'psychical' behavior. These *efforts are best exemplified by the researches of Sir William Crookes on D. D. Home, a man with paranormal powers. Crookes impeccably documented the ability of D. D. Home to perform action-at-a-distance events, and remote viewing, as well as levitation. With the publication of Sir William Crookes' 'psychic' experiments, many 19th-century scientists rallied to suppress this type of research, just as had happened in the 16th-century Church suppression of the forefathers of the 19th-century scientists.*"[16]

Now, in the 20th century, the Primordial Tradition has resurfaced again, in experimental parapsychology and paraphysics, consciousness studies, life-energies research, investigation of putative psi-fields, and exploration of new paradigms for the convergence of science and spirituality in universal terms. Will it succeed at last?

The outbreak and spread of the Modern Spiritualist Movement in the mid-19th century, and the subsequent birth of attempts at scientific psychical research in North America, Britain, and Europe thus lead to the re-emergence of ancient models of reality and of God, man, and the universe. Evidential communications from deceased spirits through entranced mediums, materializations, levitations, visions into heaven worlds, apparitions of and channellings from alleged spirit masters and teachers of ageless wisdom, etc., were claimed by hundreds and thousands of people.[2]

Some of the leading scientists of the day, crowned heads of European dynasties, a czar of Russia, and an American president, Abraham Lincoln, all gave credence to the "evidence of immortality" from such sources. The co-author of the Darwin-Wallace hypothesis of evolution, Lord Alfred Russell Wallace, was converted to Spiritualism through witnessing convincing, authentic mediumship, including the materialization of ectoplasmic forms. He lived to revise much of his earlier scientific theory—which had been formulated on a materialistic basis—to include the ancient idea of spiritual, mental, and astral forms which serve as the blueprint for the formation of all material life. Lord Wallace, in his book *Miracles and Modern Spiritualism*, was to espouse a doctrine of the priority of spirit and mind over matter much as Harold Saxon Burr at Yale Medical School did over one hundred years later in *The Fields of Life*.[3]

Yet both Lord Wallace and Dr. Burr were to die with their startling work largely ignored and rejected by the world's scientific communities. The revolutionary implications of such discoveries were simply too much for present-day, established, 19th-century versions of empirical "science." Resistance to the recovery of the Primordial Tradition remains strong among scientists conditioned to *a priori* materialistic philosophical assumptions about the limits of reality.

iv. *"the iceland papers" and new paradigms for consciousness and matter*

Burr is not the only scientist in the 20th century whose revolutionary work, in continuation of 19th-century psychical research, has been ignored or suppressed by the scientific establishment. Andrija Puharich describes the suppression, vilification, and neglect of his and other scientists' significant research on psychokinesis with Uri Geller. We have already described that research (in Chapter 11, Book One, Volume I).

British and later Japanese children were able to bend metals through psychokinesis after merely watching Geller do it on television. Puharich says that as Geller went from country to country in Europe, the same effects were created, in Denmark, Sweden, Norway, Finland, Germany, France, and Switzerland. Eminent research scientists like John Hastead of Longon University, Ted Bastin of Cambridge, Friedbert Karger of the Max Planck Institute, Putoff and Targ of the Stanford Research Institute, Astronaut Edgar Mitchell, rocket scientist Werner von Braun of NASA, Nobel Prize-winners David Bohm and Costa de Beauregard, and many others became aware of this research and were convinced of the proven reality of psychokinesis.[4] But, says Puharich, professional skeptics, magicians, and even government agency representatives ganged up to denounce Geller as a fraud and the research as a sham, and thus successfully prevented its acknowledgement by the scientific community as a whole.[5]

Nevertheless, in 1977 the Orb Foundation of London managed to convene a private conference of the top scientists involved in the research at Reykjavik, Iceland. Puharich describes the conference at length in his introduction to *The Iceland Papers*, and we shall quote him at length here in order to convey to the reader something of the magnitude of the revolutionary material involved:

> *"After Hastead gave his paper on over 10,000 metal bending obser-*
> *vations, and Costa de Beauregard gave his paper on 'The Expanding*
> *Paradigm of the Einstein Paradox,' I was so moved that I exercised my*
> *privilege as chairperson to say 'I feel this is a historic moment. It is as*
> *though Faraday had just given us his theory of electromagnetism.' "*[6]

Puharich then reports on several of the major papers given at the
conference, as follows:

1. Elizabeth Raucher's Eight-Dimensional Model
Elizabeth Raucher developed an eight-dimensional model that clearly
shows how information can be accessed from the past (retrodiction) or
the future (prediction) as though it existed in the observers' now.

2. John Hastead on Metal Bending
Hastead's paper on metal bending is a classic example of simplicity
and integrity when it states that children can bend metal without any
physical contact with the metal targets.

3. Will Franklin, Eldon Bird, Ron Hawkes, William Wolkowski, and Ted Bastin on Metal Bending
These (Hastead's) results were reduplicated in other Iceland Con-
ference reports in papers by . . . (each of the above scientists).

4. John Hastead on Teleportation
Hastead also gives preliminary observations of twelve instances
where a piece of crystal is teleported out of a container capsule without
affecting the encapsulation material. This translocation effect if under-
stood and properly controlled by man could possibly provide the solution
to all of mankind's future material fabrication needs, and material
transportation needs.

5. Mattuck-Walker on the Relationship between Mind and Matter
The Mattuck-Walker paper faces the real questions—the relationship
between mind and matter. They clearly put forward the postulate that a
focused consciousness (will) can collapse the wave function of matter.
This occurs without violation of the principle of the conservation of
energy, but does violate the second law of thermodynamics, because
entropy is retarded in the direction of organization due to information
acquisition (non-physical). Their quantum mechanical treatment of ESP
and PK is masterful in that it points the way to verification of some impor-
tant theories, such as the Bohm–Bub hidden variables theory. Most
intriguing is the Bohm prediction that it is only during a complete
measurement (of any physical system) that the hidden variable (gamma)
energizes and dominates the wave function collapse.

6. Costa de Beauregard's New Theory of the Physical Sciences
   Demanding that ESP and PK Exist

Costa de Beauregard's paper is unique in the history of both physics and paraphysics. He argues that the data and the theory of the physical sciences alone demand that ESP and PK exist. He first deals with the Einstein, Podolsky, Rosen (EPR) paradox and shows that the total state vector of the system collapses. This is due to the intrinsic time symmetry of quantum mechanics which demands that retrodiction and prediction coexist. He shows this in the Bohm theory equations by using the additricity of partial amplitudes that both particles and antiparticles exist, even though in practical experience we know only particles and have to resort to extreme measures (high energies) to find antiparticles.

He shows that this energetic symmetry is based on retarded wave functions (for particles) and advanced wave functions (antiparticles).

Therefore, he concludes, the existence of intrinsic time symmetry, and the additivity of partial amplitudes alone would predict the existence of telepathy, telekinesis, and precognition.[7]

We have included excerpts of Dr. Puharich's report on the 1977 Icelandic Conference here because of its extreme relevance to the point of this book. A number of the world's most eminent physical scientists from Sir William Barrett, Sir Richard Crookes, and Lord Alfred Russell Wallace in the 19th century, to John Hastead, Werner von Braun, David Bohm, Costa de Beauregard, and countless others in the 20th century have all testified to the reality of such things as psychokinesis and even teleportation, and have been able to rewrite paradigms for the future of science on the basis of their personal experience and experimentation. And yet the rest of the scientific community—resting secure in its *a priori* materialistic and linear rationalistic philosophical assumptions—for the most part still will not listen, and, at the worst, often resorts to ridicule and active professional persecution of the great minds who have ventured into such "unorthodox" areas.

Puharich is, nevertheless, optimistic—as we must also be—and concludes his report with a prospectus for the future of research in parapsychology, paraphysics, and consciousness studies. He says:

"The experimental data and the theories presented in The Iceland Papers *are only the prelude to a new scientific world-view. The next step in the research must more closely examine the way in which the brain-mind function gives use to a focused consciousness, and a controlled will. What are the boundary conditions for ortho-action of the mind, and for patho-action of the mind? The next step is surely the formulation of a Principle of Intelligent Action (PIA)."*[8]

It is indeed true that we urgently require today "principles for intelligent action" to find our way ahead to the 21st century in science, in physics and psychology, and in the human culture of this planet. But at the end of the Middle Ages some of the greatest minds of the Renaissance had the same idea and, regrettably, failed. We can learn a lesson for today from their failure, which was not a failure in brilliance, truth, or verifiability of data. It was a failure engineered politically, socially, and culturally by the dominant powers of the day, by the established church and state, and by a growing army of determined believers in the pseudo-religion of rationalistic, materialistic and reductionistic skepticism. We face the same opposition—in hardly a new guise—today: "fundamentalist religion" and "fundamentalist science" reinforced by false, hardened versions of the inertia of the status-quo establishment.

v. *the revival of ancient esoteric cosmologies*

The central theme which we have been treating in this book, "Toward Recovery of the Primordial Tradition: Ancient Insights and Modern Discoveries," is not really a new one. The idea of the reconvergence of ancient conceptions of man and the cosmos with the emerging sciences and technologies of the future, through the study of the psychic dimension as a missing link between the Sacred and the Profane, is one which was present at the beginning of the Renaissance itself, and one with which the roots of that great movement were both conceptually and inspirationally intertwined.

The historian Frances Yates has said:

> "New approaches to the history of science have revealed that the scientific advances of the Renaissance and early modern period arose in the context of a tremendous movement of religious interest in the world of nature as a manifestation of the divine, a movement in which influences which today would be labeled "Hermetic" or "esoteric" played a part."[9]

As we have seen in the present series of books, such movements may no longer be separated from questions of scientific advance. Yates has also perceived this point:

"Formerly, such influences were rigorously separated from trends defined as truly scientific, or leading toward genuine scientific advance. If any traces of such influences were perceived in great scientific thinkers, they were ignored or dismissed as unimportant. Today it is felt less desirable to separate the genuinely scientific elements in the minds of thinkers of the past from the context of their outlook as a whole, from one part of which the scientific interest developed."[10]

Catholic Christian faith implicitly rests upon the conception, as Aquinas has said, that there is a "natural theology" of experience of truths about Nature, both physical and metaphysical Nature, which functions of "higher reason" (not just "logic") in man may uncover to some extent through reflection, without the "particular" Revelations which God has given in the Biblical and Ecclesiastical traditions.

Yet St. Thomas himself, by reshaping Western Catholic "natural theology" onto the framework of Aristotelian thought, departed from many of the intuitions of the Primordial Tradition. The earlier, classical-Greek Patristic formulations of Christian Orthodoxy—which relied more heavily on Platonic, Neo-Pythagorean, and Neo-Platonic cosmologies—contained implicit conceptions of the natural human psychic and spiritual faculties in religion and life.

Indeed, the more rigidly empirical approach of Aristotle caused Thomistic thought—and much of Latin Christendom after it—to go off in the direction of that materialistic-rationalism which was later to emerge, full-blown, from the 18th-century Enlightenment. The British historian Frances Yates has made a good case for the argument that (1) the more esoteric and Hermetic elements behind the earliest Renaissance sciences gave birth to the "scientific" impulse itself, and (2) in the 18th century, these elements were then excluded from the emerging natural sciences as "superstitions" by the "Enlightenment" humanists. The esoteric elements of the Primordial Tradition were also opposed by the "Jesuit-Hapsburg" coalition in Catholic Europe, which was under the influence of Aristotelian-scholastic theology.[11]

Yates views the witchcraft hunts of the period as providing a cover under which the Enlightenment was enabled to desacralize science, or to extract and remove its esoteric roots (i.e., the Renaissance magi's insistence upon the reality of higher states of consciousness, psychic perception, and a hierarchically ordered multidimensional universe) by attacking all "occult" psychic techniques as "superstition."

Thus, the inception of the modern atheistic humanism which postulates a linear, rationalistic, materialistic reductionism as the only "reasonable" basis for "science" may be traced to the artful use of a backlash against the superstitions of simplistic religious fundamentalists. This produced a limited and distorted view of "science" bereft of the true sources of scientific imagination and inspiration of earlier, holistic metaphysical systems and cosmologies.

vi. underground occult spiritual traditions in the west

If one who has some knowledge of the history of religious and occult initiatory practices in the Hellenistic world will read Dame Frances Yates' two books *Giordano Bruno and the Hermetic Tradition* and *The Rosicrucian Enlightenment*, and Morton Smith's *Jesus the Magician* and his *Clement of Alexandria and the Secret Gospel of St. Mark*, a quite plausible picture emerges of what may have happened to the shamanistic, or psychic-spiritualistic, magical themes of the ancient world in the earliest Christian experience.

Theurgic rites were performed by the adept for psychic identification of the disciple with himself. He, as the "perfected Man" already united in consciousness with the "Logos," the "Primal Man," and the "Godhead," then became the means through which they, the disciples, could experience "in him" what he had experienced. Thus they could "die" (i.e. leave the physical body in the "soul-body"), "ascend" with him into the "heavenly places," learn the nature of the higher worlds, unite with the Godhead and return to the physical body. They were thus psychospiritually transformed by the initiatory experience of "dying and rising with him." Such language, which is used in the New Testament, could initially indeed have come out of such an ancient occult initiatory context.

This is also a typical, Egyptian-gnostic theurgical experience, and it was believed by Renaissance writers also to have been known to ancient Egyptian priests in the Osiran mysteries, to Greeks in the Orphic and Pythagorean rites, to rishis of India, to Persian "magi" and to Chaldean holy men. Today there is, in fact, evidence to suggest that such occult ideas and practices had indeed entered Palestine and the pre-Christian, Hellenistic-Jewish mystical milieu in the centuries immediately preceding the time of Jesus. Among the early Church fathers, Lactantius and St. Clement of Alexandria viewed such positive (Hermetic), gnostic psychic-and-spiritual experiences as pagan "foreshadowings" of the Christ.

Renaissance figures, from Ficino, Pico dello Mirandola, Cornelius Agrippa and Giordano Bruno to Robert Flood, John Dee, Paracelsus, and others shared this conception of the pre-Christian origins of the role of the Cosmic Christ figure in Christianity. As Dame Frances Yates has so ably documented, these remarkable precursors of modern science understood that the fulfillment of Christianity lay in recovery of a universal, pre-Christian "magical" Hermetic and Caballistic technology of the psyche and spirit, by which the highest divine powers of the "Cosmic Christ" or Primordial god-man in Heaven, could be brought down into the elements of matter—and into the social world of men—in order to transform these into a new heaven and a new earth.

Jesus' prayer, "Thy Kingdom come, on earth as it is in the heavenly places," was something which was very practicable to such Renaissance figures. For some of them (Pico, Agrippa, Bruno and Dee at least) believed and declared that they had themselves experienced the (magical or shamanistic) "death, ascension, and resurrection" in the Hermetic and Caballistic mysteries, which gave them the knowledge ("gnosis") of higher worlds and the secret of the transformation—both spiritually and morally—of this "middle" world of earth.

They viewed the "magic" of the Catholic Christian sacraments in a very naturalistic and instrumental sense, which was anathema to the understanding of those indoctrinated with dogmatic Aristotelian-Thomism, Protestant fundamentalism, and the new humanist-rationalism. It is only through personal conviction born of primary psychic and spiritual experience, of the kinds we have been documenting in this study, that anyone could hope to take their claim seriously. Dame Frances Yates documents some of those claims historically but she does not seem to take them seriously herself. In any event, their esoteric movement failed, largely due to establishment opposition.

x. the debunking efforts of secular humanist scholars of the renaissance

In 1614, the Humanist pedant Isaac Casaubon completed his *De rebus sacris et ecclesasticis exercitationes (XVI)* on commission from James I. He produced a suitable Protestant refutation of Cesare Baronius' *Annales Ecclesiastici*. Baronius had been the foremost authority on the

Catholic miracle tradition, and had accepted pre-Christian, Gentile prophecies of the coming of Christ based on Lactantius. It did not suit Protestant biases against what they conceived to be "magical Catholic conceptions" of Revelation, and of the Church and Sacraments, to allow Baronius' apologetic to stand. It contained things attributed to vast antiquity, which Protestants did not want to accept.

Using a technique familiar to all rationalistic critics of miracle traditions and of modern claims to genuine psychic phenomena, Casaubon consigned the Corpus Hermetica and the Asclepius, which had given birth to the Hermetic tradition of the Renaissance, to the category of fraud. He said they were forgeries in post-Christian times of supposed ancient Egyptian and pre-Christian Greek gnostic traditions. He went so far as to say that even early Christian Fathers perpetrated such forgeries, which showed the foreshadowing of the tradition from Moses and the Prophets to Christ, in order to make the new Christian doctrines more palatable to Greeks and Romans.

For those who believed him, this wrongly and unnecessarily destroyed the credibility of the Hermetic tradition of the Renaissance. With it died the conception that there had been a *priscus theologica* or Primordial Tradition stemming from the legendary Egyptian priest (slightly prior to Moses) called by the Greeks Hermes Trismegistus (Toth), and passed on in Greek pagan tradition in such figures as Orpheus, Pythagoras, Plato, Plotinus, Porphyry, Iamblicus, etc.

Dame Frances Yates documents the manner in which the above-mentioned "Hermetic tradition," which had been revived by the Renaissance figures Ficino, Pico della Mirandola, Cornelius Agrippa, and Giordano Bruno, was eventually to collapse in Western civilization because of the "debunking" or "dehistoricization" of the Hermetic Corpus by Casaubon. But surely we can, today, understand the reality of psychic and spirit phenomena better than did either the secular Humanist pedants of the Renaissance, the narrow dogmatic Protestants of the Reformation, or the Aristotelian Catholics of the 16th century. And we also understand two other facts which could "rehabilitate" the Hermetic tradition of the Renaissance and undo Casaubon's "debunking." Yates nowhere mentions either of these facts.

The first fact is that since the discovery of the Nag Hammadi library we have clear indications that there were indeed *pre-Christian* gnostic traditions, and some of them of the positive, or "world-affirming Egyptian type." Furthermore, we now know enough about the dating of both Old Testament and New Testament canonical books and other sacred literature to realize that, even where a document itself may indeed have been edited considerably later, there is no reason to degrade it by claiming that everything in it was bound to have been first composed later than originally believed. The earliest present masoretic text of the Old Testament, for example, is from the 9th century A.D. Put in these terms, Casaubon's refutation of the *Hermetic Corpus* no more proves that all of its contents were purely invented after Plato and Jesus than modern critical scholarship can prove that the entire content of the Pentateuch was invented after the 9th century A.D.! In fact, we have no legitimate reason to assume that the traditions, oral or written, used by Hellenistic or even post-Christian editors of the Hermetic Corpus and the Asclepius were not more ancient ones in their day, and indeed may have stemmed from pre-Christian, pre-Platonic, and even in some cases from theurgical pre-Mosaic Egyptian theurgical sources.

The second fact that should make a difference in our attitude toward the legitimacy of the claims made in the *Hermetic Corpus* itself—or by Ficino, Pico, Agrippa, or Bruno, et. al. to the effect that there was indeed a "pricus theologia" or Primordial Tradition—is that we can infer such a tradition on other grounds entirely, i.e., the data of contemporary, universal forms of psychic and spiritual experience. Our mere possession of literary documents of any age could not be the basis of such an assertion. Its true basis is our own knowledge of the universal forms of psychic and spiritual experience, and of the multidimensional cosmic paradigms that always arise out of such experience.

Thus, the deliberate destruction of belief in a Primordial Tradition by secular humanist pedants, Protestant fundamentalists, and Catholic Aristotelians of the 16th and 17th centuries may now be seen in a new and truer perspective: as the defeat of the ancient wisdom tradition, and an unmitigated tragedy for Western civilization. For it has ultimately consigned modern Western philosophy and science to the cul-de-sac of materialistic and rationalistic reductionism, split modern "science" from human "spiritual perception," and jettisoned the acceptance of the psychic area entirely, consigning it to a rubbish heap. Since then it has been the "missing link" between the sacred and the profane in Western civilization.

Yates points out that many Renaissance men believed themselves, as do contemporary scientists and scholars in parapsychology and paraphysics whose works I have surveyed, to be reviving or returning to an earlier Primordial Tradition or "golden age" of integral human sciences, the scope and purity of which had been lost:

> *"The word 'renaissance' means 'rebirth' and it is expressive of the way the movement was understood by the scholars and thinkers who created it. They believed themselves to be reviving, or returning, to earlier and better times, not abandoning the past for the future, but seeing the future as a child of the past. The view of time as a cyclic movement, from pure golden ages through successive worse ages of bronze and iron, encouraged the thought that the search for truth was of necessity a search for the early and the ancient, the purity of which had been lost or corrupted. (This) . . . is a concept with which we must familiarize ourselves if we are to understand how modern times began, how the attempted return to the past was actually an act of creation which led to the future."*[12]

The goal which the innovators of the so-called "Hermetic" influences in the Renaissance (cabala, magic, and alchemy) postulated was the return to an earlier, partly mythological and perhaps partly historical age in which now-lost psychic knowledge and a holistic, multidimensional cosmology linked science and religion.

> *"Thus the Renaissance movement was essentially a movement toward recovery of the past, toward the retrieving of knowledge which had been lost. This attitude is particularly true of the revival of what we vaguely call "the Hermetic" tradition in the Renaissance. It was an attempt to return to sources of knowledge believed to be even older than the civilizations of Greece and Rome.*
>
> *"These writers have certain characteristics in common; they are concerned with what are vaguely called "the occult sciences," with astrology, and alchemy, with . . . sympathetic magic . . . [they are] philosophical treatises which expound a kind of religious philosophy of nature.*
>
> *"This philosophy had various ingredients; it was partly a reflection of Greek philosophical teaching, mainly Platonic and Stoic . . . there was certainly some Jewish influence . . . and, according to the writers of the treatises themselves, Hermes Trismegistus was really an Egyptian priest who lived in most ancient times; the philosophy which he taught came out of the secret traditions current in Egyptian Temples."*[13]

The Renaissance was thus essentially an attempt to revive an ideal "philosophy of the ancient world," which some scholars perceived, after the recovery of the Latin and Greek classics, and especially of Platonic and Neo-Platonic writers, to contain a cosmology or world-view which offered a holistic and integrated alternative to the Aristotelian-

Scholastic option, which had been dominant in Europe since the 12th-13th centuries.

In 1460, the translation and publication of the *Corpus Hermeticum* by Marsilio Ficino spread the influence of a philosophy involving the principles of ancient Egyptian ritual magic believed to have been the sources of the Greek Neo-Platonic wisdom. Medieval Jewish Cabalistic or mystical elements, which were completely compatible with Egyptian "Hermeticism," continued to be integrated with it by devout Catholic pietists from Ficino through Pico della Mirandola (*On the Dignity of Man*, 1487) to Cornelius Agrippa (*De occulto philosophio*, 1533).[14] Thus, Egyptian, Persian, and Greek ritual magic were combined with the Jewish mysticism of the medieval Cabala to provide restless Christian thinkers with an approach to questions of the relationship of religion and science to divine revelation and the study of nature.

Frances Yates says that the Renaissance thus put magic on a new footing, raising it from its despised position in the Aristotelian-Scholastic system to one of dignity and religious authority, which was exemplified by Shakespeare's Prospero, a magus with divine powers employed with moral dignity in the service of the good.[15]

The third element which was to be integrated in new Renaissance approaches to "science" and religion was the revival of ancient and medieval alchemy and its transformation into a noble philosophical paradigm—in allegorical form—for the spiritual and moral transformation of man and the cosmos. From the specific aim of making gold, to the scientific problem of the transmutation of substances as a whole, alchemical thought at the hands of Paracelsus (1490-1541) became the compact expression of the Hermetic and Cabalist interpretations of nature.[16] Great Christian mystics saw in the Renaissance union of ancient ritual magic with Jewish Cabala, and in the new Paracelsian alchemy, the blueprint of a new tradition, a new model or paradigm of man and the cosmos which could break the hold of the dead hand of Aristotelian-Scholasticism over the European mind.

> "This was the tradition which broke down Aristotle in the name of a unified universe through which ran one law, the law of magic animism. This was the tradition which prepared the way for the 17th-century triumph [of new science]."[17]

Other seminal thinkers of the Renaissance, from Copernicus to Francis Bacon, Johannes Kepler, and later Isaac Newton, were heavily influenced by the magical world view of the Cabala and alchemy, which laid the foundations for what Yates has called the "Rosicrucian Enlightenment."

Yates uses the term "Rosicrucian" to describe that tradition in the Renaissance of the use of reason (actually Platonic intuitive reason) and the study of nature, a tradition which gave birth to the Enlightenment rather than to any particular modern societies or organizations known as "Rosicrucian." However, Yates notes that the later Enlightenment was unfortunately sidetracked by the materialist-rationalist skepticism, which was to strip all of the "Rosicrucian" cosmological world-views and psychic perspectives from earlier Renaissance studies in "science," and to denude the latter by conceptionally destroying its relationship to the human consciousness, to primary mystical and spiritual experience, and thus to "religion" in general.[18]

The writers of "Rosicrucian" science—like Paracelsus in Bohemia; John Dee and Robert Fludd in England; and Michael Maier in Germany— tried to reform religion, science, and education in Europe through reintroduction of integrative, holistic models of man and the cosmos. They held a multidimensional concept of nature which included the ideas of innate intelligence in matter, parallel universes, the several energy sheaths or "bodies" in man, animals, and plants, and the harmony of the spheres. The Rosicrucian writers stood for the mystical mathematics of Pythagoras, astrology-astronomy, alchemy-chemistry, and the various metaphysical principles of ritual magic as seen in human psychical experiences such as telepathy, clairvoyance, precognition, prophecy, psychokinesis, spirit-communication and the invocation of angels and saints. They also believed in the idea of a universal "Primordial technology" of the mind and spirit of man which affected the rudimentary elements of matter and nature itself. As Frances Yates has said:

> "The Rosicrucian Enlightenment included a vision of the necessity for reform of society, particularly of education, and for a third reformation of religion, embracing all sides of man's activity, and saw this as a necessary accompaniment of the new science. Rosicrucian thinkers were aware of the dangers of the new science, of its diabolical as well as angelic possibilities, and they saw that its arrival should be accompanied by a general reformation of the whole wide world."[19]

The astute reader will see that the conception of a scientific revolution being linked closely with a religious one—with both founded upon the rediscovery of a new/old paradigm for understanding nature based upon psychic perception and action—is one which I have been describing in contemporary terms throughout the present book. In the 15th, 16th, and 17th centuries this movement had, of necessity, to come into opposition with the dominant Aristotelian-scholastic philosophy of Catholic Europe:

> *"The union of religious with scientific vision took the form in the Rosicrucian movement of that strangely intense alchemical movement, in which alchemical modes of expression seemed best suited to the religious experience. Koyse saw this movement as a natural development out of the Animist and vitalist Renaissance philosophies, asking whether alchemy does not provide a symbolism more suited to living religious experience than do the scholastic-Aristotelian doctrines of matter and form.*
>
> *"Those who seek above all a regeneration of spiritual life are naturally drawn towards doctrines which lay the main stress on the idea of life and propose a vitalistic conception of the universe. And the symbolism of alchemy is as apt for translating (into symbolic form) the realities of the religious life, as that of matter and form. Perhaps more apt, because less used up, less intellectualized, more symbolic through its very nature."*[20]

In this vein, the Rosicrucian stories of the life of Christian Rosencreuz, and the miraculous discovery of his marvelous tomb, may be seen as an alchemical-spiritual allegory of the rediscovery of the Primordial Tradition, or the modern rediscovery of ancient spiritual and mystical intuitions and insights into nature, the mysteries of mind and matter, and the cosmos. This, when combined with the Christian Revelation, was expected to lead ultimately to the establishment of "a new heaven and a new earth," i.e., the radical reformation and advance ment of science, religion, education, and the entire social order of Renaissance-Enlightenment Europe and, thence, of the whole world.

> *"... The Fama Fraternitates thus seems to recount, through the allegory of the vault, the discovery of a new, or rather new/old, philosophy, primarily alchemical and related to medicine and healing, but also concerned with number geometry ... not only an advancement of learning, but above all an illumination of religious and spiritual nature. This new philosophy is about to be revealed to the world and will bring about a general reformation."*[21]

Indeed, the conception of an ancient universal intuition and cosmic scientific, psychic and spiritual understanding, once lost but now rediscovered, is clearly proclaimed in the Rosicrucian document, *The Fama Fraternitates:*

> *"Our philosophy also is not a new invention, but as Adam after his fall both received it, and as Moses and Solomon used it. Also she ought not much to be doubted of, or contradicted by other opinions, or meanings; but seeing the truth is peaceable, brief, and always like herself in all things, and especially accorded by Jesus in omni parte and all members. And as he (Jesus) is the true image of the Father, so is she (our philosophy) his Image.*
>
> *"... And wherein Plato, Aristotle, Pythagoras and others did hit the mark, and wherein Enoch, Abraham, Moses, Solomon did excel, but especially wherewith that wonderful Book the Bible agreeth."[22]*

In another major Rosicrucian work, the *Confessio Fraternitates*, we find the same idea even more forcefully stated:

> *"No other Philosophy we have than that which is the head and sum, the foundation and contents of all faculties, sciences, and arts.*
>
> *"... all shall find more wonderful secrets by us than hithertofore they did attain unto, and did know, or are able to believe or utter ...*
>
> *"... all that, which from the beginning of the world, Man's wisdom, either through God's revelation, or through the service of the angels and spirits, or through the sharpness and depth of understanding, or through long observation, use, and experience hath found out, invented, brought forth, corrected, and until now hath been propagated and transplanted."[23]*

Here and elsewhere in the *Fama* and the *Confessio*, therefore, we find that the holistic, esoteric wisdom being claimed is:

a) ancient,

b) universal—i.e., found among certain sages of all cultures,

c) intuitively derived from:
   (1) nature, and
   (2) divine revelation—action through God, angels, and spirits,

d) essential to a true, balanced, and profound understanding of
   (1) religion, especially Christianity
   (2) science and technology

e) positive, rather than negative, in its attitude toward both God and the world (hence not "gnostic" in a pejorative sense),

f) and essential for the true reformation of the arts, sciences, religion, education, government, and human society.

Furthermore, we see in the Rosicrucian declarations that the subject matter and methodology of the essential esoteric wisdom involves:

a) *psychic and spiritual, as well as physical aspects of reality,*

b) *the cultivation of a cosmology, metaphysics and theosophy, as well as science, technology and philosophy, in order to understand and use it,*

c) *the integration of physical, mental, psychic, and spiritual arts, or techniques of observation and action, including the instrumental uses of the mind and spirit for effecting man's higher purposes in the physical, social, and spiritual worlds, in healing and the spiritual evolution of consciousness through clairvoyance, clairaudence, clairsentience, precognition, prophecy, telekinesis, out-of-the-body projection, spirit communication, angelic invocations, ritual magic for higher purposes in the service of the good, etc. (i.e., all of those functions which we have called sciences and technologies of the future.)*

Now it is obvious that many persons today, including historians raised on a steady academic diet of modern philosophical rationalism and materialism, would pre-emptorily dismiss all of this as so much misguided superstition which the rationalistic forces in the later German and French "Enlightenment" were quite successfully able to weed out. However, those who are really knowledgeable in the history of modern psychical research and in experimental parapsychology and paraphysics, and the studies in consciousness which I have reviewed in Books I and II of Volume I of my earlier series (*Quest for the Primordial Tradition*, Washington D.C.: University Press of America), will not be able to assume this. To do so would be to take a simplistic and erroneous position concerning the genuine psychic insights and intuitions of the great seminal thinkers of the Renaissance.

In the 16th through the 18th centuries, nevertheless, the opposition to the recovery of such universal psychical and spiritual insights into nature was unfortunately insurmountable. The lack of comprehension of the psychic dimension and its out-of-hand rejection by the vested interests of (1) Aristotelian-scholastic-trained churchmen, and (2) the incipient rationalistic-materialistic reductionism of certain skeptics associated with the Renaissance, such as Andreas Libavius, led not only to the rejection of the study of the human psychic faculties, but also to the utter separation of the transcendent or spiritual dimension from the study of nature:

> "The Hermetic tradition grew in importance and influence throughout the sixteenth and seventeenth centuries, though it had severe opponents. Many feared its magic. To what extent the witch scares in this period were

intensified by hostility to Renaissance magic is a problem which has hardly yet been examined. Orthodox theologians were disturbed by its lack of doctrine precision. Orthodox philosophers in the Aristotelian tradition strongly disapproved of it. Another important class of critics were humanist scholars . . . "[24]

The study of "nature" was, after the later German and French phases of the Enlightenment, reduced to the physical observation of its materialistic and mechanistic properties alone. The "natural sciences" became, for the first time only, the analytical computation of mere physical observations and deductions. The earlier classical and pre-Aristotelian-scholastic medieval interest in the divine intelligence within nature—or immanence—was to be reduced to defective mechanistic and materialistic models. By the time German Protestant theology rejected this—following Immanuel Kant—it was too late to try to rescue God, human consciousness, or the transcendent for "science." This led, in turn, to their utter and radical separation, thus setting the stage for the development of a "secularism" in the new sciences and humanities which was (1) to completely divorce all subjective matters in the human consciousness from any relationship with a divine intelligence behind and in nature, and (2) to jettison completely the pursuit of metaphysics and the entire conception of legitimate spiritual sciences.

Thus, the victory of the incipient atheism, or implicit agnosticism in modern science, and its methodological assumption that it cannot consider, much less answer, any questions involving supposed "invisible or supernatural influences" in the life of man or the cosmos stems largely from the inability to recover the Primordial Tradition by the seminal thinkers of the Renaissance. Why did they fail? Some have suggested political causes. Frances Yates argues convincingly that the scattered forces of the "Rosicrucian Enlightenment" in Europe unfortunately pinned their hopes, after the death of the esoterically inclined Emperor Rudolph II, upon the new Elector Palatine, Frederick V, and his young wife, Princess Elizabeth, a daughter of King James I of England.[25] Frederick had been patron to many new "magical" scientific and technological ventures and innovations at Heidelberg castle, and a circle of persons encouraged his acceptance of the throne of Bohemia in 1620 in defiance of the powers of the Catholic Hapsburg emperor Ferdinand. Yates brings forth rather convincing historical evidence to claim that the subsequent fall of Frederick's "winter throne" in Bohemia in 1620 before the onslaught of imperial troops led to the discrediting and persecution of the "Rosicrucian" elements in Catholic Europe.[26]

Thus the furor of Jesuit attacks on the esotericism of the earlier Renaissance, combined with a growing Protestant dispensationalist fundamentalism restricting all "true miracles" to a past "Age of Revelation" in the Biblical period (and which catered to peasant fears of witchcraft and sorcery), and finally rationalistic-humanist scholars' attacks on "superstition" and their burning desire to reduce the new science only to the physically and logically observable, all brought about the ultimate triumph, further development and entrenchment of the skepticism, philosophical materialism, rationalism, and logical positivism that were to charactrerize the 19th-century "natural sciences" and their inevitable warfare with fundamentalist versions of religion.

If this historical analysis of Frances Yates is correct, then we can conclude that unfortunate historical circumstances prevented the recovery of the Primordial Tradition. The past three centuries have then marked the development of a "deformed science" and a "deformed technology" which may have to be aborted, or rather reformed and humanized back in the direction of inclusion of the psychic and spiritual dimension, which, as we have said elsewhere, provide the missing link between the sacred and the profane in modern Western civilization.[27]

xi. conclusion: the return of the primordial tradition, the cosmic christ, and the crisis of contemporary western civilization

We may conclude that a general reformation of human culture, the arts, sciences, religion and education, in the light of psychic and spiritual knowledge has been tried before and failed. Perhaps it is now time, once again, to attempt to bring forth "things old and new," to revive the quest for rediscovery of the Primordial Tradition and the Cosmic Christ.

Today we have clearly reached an impasse in Western civilization, a cul-de-sac in the secular arts and sciences, and in established forms of religion. Without regaining an understanding of mankinds' psychic and spiritual nature, and of the potential of "new sciences" and "new technologies" through its recovery and use in daily living, some would say that humanity does not have much hope for survival, much less evolution into the "new being" of "Cosmic Christhood," or the process of the "Christification of humanity" described by St. Paul and Teilhard de Chardin in the West, or by Sri Aurobindo in the East.

Until new paradigms and higher states of consciousness are attained by human beings for the doing of real science or religion, there can be no way ahead to such a goal. The present crustification of the secular arts, sciences, and established religious institutions, as well as the cultural and social organization of Western civilization, prevent the birth of the "new being" and the return of the Cosmic Christ. Children and adults are conditioned by the lockstep of a materialistic-rationalistic and mechanistic philosophy of life which reduces everything to its lowest common denominator. No room is left in the midst of things for transcendence, for consciousness, for God, or for the ultimacy of spirit over matter and mind. The present organization of scientific knowledge, technological action, and religious "legitimacy" must be revised, or crumble of its own weight, before there can be any true progress toward "recovery of the Primordial Tradition" of psychic insight and spiritual intuition. This is the only way ahead to the future of science and of religion, or to the future of humanity itself in " . . . a new heaven and new earth."

The birth-pangs of that disintegration are all about us now. The process of the crumbling of the "walls of the Roman Empire" has begun anew. The only question that remains is whether enough persons will accept the challenge of building the new "world-view" of a multidimensional cosmos and of man's place in an integrated, psychoenergetic and eventually psychospiritual universe.

There is evidence from the history of religion and culture, scientific studies in consciousness, life energies, experimental parapsychology and paraphysics, and from personal experience, for the existence of a Primordial Tradition of intuition, insight and creativity required to meet this challenge. But scholars and common people alike must find the hidden powers of the mind and spirit for communication with the world of spirit. Such knowledge and such skills will be necessary for any movement toward a reintegration and revitalization of human existence on our planet and the ending of the emotional schism between technology, science, and religion in the world of tomorrow.

The psychic and spiritual powers of man, and of nature, are real and not imaginary. Psychic "sciences" and "technologies" are thus essential to a true and balanced understanding of the arts, sciences, and religion in transcultural terms.

The discovery of true science and technology, and the rediscovery of the Primordial Tradition of true and universal elements of religion, cannot occur until humanity awakens and takes seriously the unused, long-hidden psychic and spiritual potential of its own being, and of the cosmos itself.

Conclusion

Rekindling the Flame
From the Primordial Wick

*i. the "primordial tradition," the "Cosmic Christ,"
and the roots of the major religious traditions
of the ancient world*

There is a "Primordial Tradition" of intuition and insight, derived from a common phenomenology of psychic and mystical experience, which may be found at the roots of most of the major religious traditions of the ancient world, including those of India, Egypt, Persia, Greece and Israel. There is a lost esoteric Christianity of the "Cosmic Christ" which was founded upon that Primordial Tradition of ancient spiritual intuition and psychic insight. The recovery of the latter is linked to recovery of the former.

Our recognition of the experiential roots of such a Primordial Tradition will depend upon our own acquisition of real—not imaginary—psychic and spiritual faculties of perception, and the development within ourselves of higher states and forms of consciousness.

Primary experience of the human psychic faculties and of real spirit phenomena can bestow upon the honest investigator the invaluable insight that much of the language, myth, symbol, parable, and metaphor of the sacred literature of the world's religions, including the Bible and the Primitive Christian Church, find their common point of origin in an "alternative reality tradition" deep within the human psyche and spirit.

Alternative forms of perception of reality, and alternative forms of communication and interaction with other living beings and with the world itself, develop within the human consciousness with psychical and mystical experience. These forms of perception, communication, and interaction are quite alien to the linear, logical-

241

analytical, and conceptual methodology of modern "science" as we understand it today. Such alternative forms of action are dependent upon universal operating principles that possess their own reason and logic of a higher order. There is a universal phenomenology of psychic and spiritual experience which cuts across cultural, ethnic and religious barriers and conditioning factors. This common phenomenology of psychic and spiritual experience is known, not only to the saints and mystics of all traditions, but also to ordinary people, through flashes of intuition, extrasensory perception, in post-mortem contacts with the dead, in the near-death experience, in out-of-the-body experience, and in moments of "peak experience" in which one senses a higher order of reality behind the phenomenal world, and a sublime, inexplicable sense of unity with all things.

The universal phenomenology of psychic, spiritual and mystical experience, together with the intuitions and insights derived from it, have given birth to both the language of religion in the great myths of the world religions, and to that magical world-view which the skeptical British "logical-positivist" A. J. Ayer has incomprehendingly described as meaningless "God-talk."

This same universal phenomenology of psychic, spiritual and mystical experience has given birth to the "myth," "magic," and "God-talk" of the Christian tradition. This properly includes all talk in the Bible and in the tradition of the Church about such otherwise incomprehensible things as immortality, the incarnation of God, the Resurrection of Christ, visions of angels and of heaven worlds, invocation of deceased saints, miraculous healings, the powers of the human mind and spirit in prayer, and the holy, mysterious divine action which supposedly transpires at the Eucharist and in the sacraments.

The original psychic, spiritual, and mystical experiences of the founders of the Christian tradition, described in the New Testament and in the lives of the saints, include revelatory visions and dreams, apparitions of angels and of dead or dying saints, spirits, precognitions of the future, prophecies, psychic or spiritual healings, marvelous supernormal events such as journies into heaven worlds, telepathy, clairvoyance, levitations, materializatioins, the "channelling" of "higher truths" or "revelations" from God, angels, or the superconscious Self, theophanies of "the Divine Light," and of the "Cosmic Christ."

Modern theologians, clergy, and laity of Catholic and Protestant churches in general have codified and "tamed" the original tales of such earlier supernormal experiences and spiritual insights by a process of intellectualization, ritualization, and/or socialization. Often once-great intuitions are reduced to an unrecognizable form on the organizational level, resulting in "fundamentalism," "institutionalism," or rationalistic and reductionistic "liberal theology." Breaking from those established modes of modern Western religious thought entirely, "modern science" has simply dismissed such ideas altogether as "scientifically untenable." The result is that "religion" in the West has become irrelevant to science, and to the rest of human society, in the modern secular world-view.

ii. *modern science and philosophy have departed from the "primordial tradition" of higher spiritual perception*

Since the so-called "Age of Reason" and "Enlightenment" in the West, scientists and philosophers, following the lead of Réné Descartes, have generally postulated a radical gulf between "mind" and "matter," limiting so-called "objective" measurements to the latter and reducing inner or "subjective" experience to an arbitrary status. The ancient conception that valid knowledge ("scientia") about realities beyond the range of physical observation could be gained by some through supernormal faculties is arbitrarily dismissed as "pre-scientific superstition."

Together, modern science and most of our contemporary, established religious traditions have now dismissed entirely the ideas that (1) real psychic and spiritual experiences constituted the origins of their founder's teachings, and (2) these experiential roots could be explored and systematically studied today because human psychic and spiritual faculties are real, and there are higher metaphysical laws and purposes of the universe by which they operate.

Because modern scientists, philosophers, and religionists have not understood the reality of such psychic and spiritual faculties and metaphysical principles, they have worked diligently for the past several centuries to minimize and denigrate the importance of the shamanistic, psychical, and visionary experiences in general. Consequently they have undermined the historical roots of religion, including Judaism and Christianity. They have also created a radical polarization between science and religion, between the subjective and objective, and between mind and matter.

iii.   the questions raised by psi claims
and mystical affirmations today

In the light of contemporary psiological claims it becomes quite reasonable that some scholars involved in the academic study of religions should begin to ask basic questions concerning the role that *real psychic phenomena* may have played in religious experience and in the formation of religious beliefs, practices and institutions.

Theologians and churchmen must be willing, once again, to ask such questions: "Is there an authentic Christian 'gnosis'?" "Is there a valid, esoteric side to Christianity which, although now dormant or suppressed, could accommodate itself to the widespread awareness of psychic and spirit phenomena today as a 'natural theology' of experience?" "Could knowledge of such valid esoteric elements in Christianity help us to understand better the origins of the Gospel and of the Church as an institution, and of the sacramental system of Christianity?" "If an authentic esoteric Christian gnosis of the "Cosmic Christ" once existed in the church and sacraments, what happened to it?" "Is it still visible to 'those who have eyes to see?' "

I feel that those psychical researchers who are willing to consider the full range of modern occult and ancient esoteric religious possibilities will be able to pursue a fruitful dialogue with religion. In my estimation it is "conventional science" which will be shifting soon, and it would be short-sighted of parapsychologists to restrict themselves to reductionist scientific concerns alone.

The various codifications of the myths, doctrines, and rituals or primitive religions arose in an attempt to stabilize, describe, and communicate primarily spiritual, psychic, and mystical experiences and reactions to what was taken to be divine action in the lives of the founders of the world's religious traditions. But the "authorized" successors and representatives of those founders—the administrators, theologians and philosophers of subsequent generations—have more frequently than not ceased to have such primary psychic and spiritual experiences themselves.

Therefore, it is essential to examine once again the phenomenological roots of authentic religion through a serious investigation of the universal modes of human psychic and spiritual experience. It is reasonable that both historians of religion and modern theologians, as well as social scientists, should seek to gain further insight into the origins and meaning of the myths, dogmas, rituals, doctrines, and ancient and modern religious traditions through contemporary studies in human consciousness, parapsychology, and paraphysics.

In our day we may witness the exploration and recovery of such ancient insights in the exciting claims of researchers in human consciousness, parapsychology, and paraphysics. We must not only be prepared to review this material with a careful, even-handed and open-minded academic approach, but we must also at times be prepared to personally enter into such experiences to gain those insights of firsthand experience which alone can provide the intuition, insight, and wisdom required to interpret this material meaningfully.

It is essential at this juncture in the spiritual evolution of the human species that we seriously consider what all of the great religious "psychic" and "spiritual" experiences in the history of the develop ment of our earth's cultures and civilizations could mean. Are there supersensory states of consciousness and faculties of perception and action, as nearly all of mankind's religions have claimed? Does the opening or development of these faculties have anything to do with the future of mankind and of its attempts to build a better civilization on earth, as great mystics like the Catholic theologian Teilhard de Chardin in the West and Sri Aurobindo in the East have claimed? Are there really such things as "spirits," "UFO beings" from other planets or dimensions, "angels," etc.? Are there really other "dimensions" of space and time, or "heaven worlds" corresponding to those described by great mystics and seers, whether Christian, Jewish, Moslem, Hindu, or Buddhist? What has this to do with the "Cosmic Christ"?

Are all of the now-widespread claims to primary psychic and mystical experiences, or otherworldly contacts, merely bizarre symptoms of the breakdown of rationality, as some "professional skeptics" have loudly proclaimed, or could they represent an important shift in global consciousness to a new world-view, a model of an "ideal god-man," and a multidimensional universe? These are the kinds of questions that each person will have to answer for himself or herself, through personal spiritual and psychic experience. For these are the kinds of questions that both the religions and the sciences of tomorrow will have to entertain, and finally, to answer.

iv.   awakened faculties of spiritual and psychical perception

Without awakened psychic perception and spiritual insight, man is necessarily dependent upon ideas about supposed metaphysical truths about "God" or "man" mediated to them from the experience of others through various sacred books, institutions and traditions. Unfortunately the editing of such books and the custody of such institutions and traditions have customarily been found in the hands of "lesser men" without the "live psychic and spiritual experience" of higher dimensions which had once given vision to the founders of the world's religions.

Often "lesser men" who consider themselves "guardians of God" have tried to play intellectual games and power trips with the myth and magic, and with the language and message of the founders. A process of socialization, politicization, and institutionalization usually ensures that the false secular gods of nationalism, ethnocentricity, and sectarian imperialism are substituted for the "living God" and for the angelic or daevic encounters with Spirit and Space of the founders. The result is that religion often becomes—instead of an elevating, awakening, and unifying force in the process of human spiritual evolution—another deadening and enslaving force in the downward materialistic pull of human inertia.

"Religion" can—and has—become for us a source of divisiveness, competitiveness, intolerance, fanaticism, and combativeness, rather than a universal spiritual and psychic science or technology for growth and the higher transformation of consciousness. Large numbers of people abandon such falsification of religion altogether, but unfortunately find nothing authentic to put in its place in their lives.

This is precisely why there is an urgent need today for primary experience of psychic and spirit phenomena—not only in the "new mind technologies" through psychic development programs, but also in the experience of spirit phenomena. All of these so-called paranormal phenomena can perform an awakening function. Potentially, they can do for us what Mircea Eliade says the "siddhis," or psychic-spiritual powers, do for the developing yogi on the path, i.e., "break down the profane sensibilities" and make way for a new and higher form of consciousness.

This higher form of consciousness recognizes the numinous realities behind the dominant "salvation myths" of ancient civilizations and the "God-talk" of religion in general. Personal psychic and mystical experience alone can blow the lid off of A. J. Ayer's "logical positivism" that asserts all such "God-talk" or human language about transcendent realities to be "nonsense."

And personal experience of telepathy, distant-viewing and precognition, spirit-communication, etc. can exorcise forever the ghosts of John Locke, David Hume, and Immanuel Kant, who asserted that it was impossible for human beings to "know" directly such realities in the nominal world. Not only is direct psychic and mystical experience the origin of all metaphysical assertion about the "soul," and "immortality," about our higher powers of perception and action, and about the existence of a "God" or Supreme Intelligence, but it is also the only way to prove the reality behind such ideas to anyone.

When an awakening to such experiences occurs in anyone's life, all argument ceases. One no longer needs the crutch of either religious or scientific "fundamentalisms." The Primordial Tradition begins to reveal itself directly to the awakened soul, and the pseudo-security of either religious or scientific doctrines gives way to a living contemplation of the realities of God, nature, and the transcendent worlds of our multidimensional cosmos.

It is through such an awakening to the reality of psychic and spiritual phenomena that both fundamentalist and institutionalist forms of 19th-century science and religion will eventually give way to new, more holistic paradigms and to more adequate methodologies for understanding the multidimensional nature of our psychoenergetic universe.

A careful study of contemporary psychic and spirit experience will eventually uncover the primordial origins of human religious belief in the survival of bodily death, and of the cosmic paradigm of an archetypical "divine-and-human person," or "Cosmic Christ" found in most of the mythical and metaphysical traditions of antiquity, but today we seem to have reached a point in the cultural history of Western civilization where both science and religion, in their establishment forms, have failed to grasp the significance of the whole psychic area as the *natural* link between the Sacred and the Profane.

v. the church, synagogue, mosque, and temple have often obscured the primal human vision of the primordial tradition and the Cosmic Christ

The Church, as well as synagogue, mosque, temple and all other forms of human religious organization, exist not as the exclusive repositories of the Primordial Tradition but rather as flawed vessels to channel their living flow into the hearts and minds of a sleeping humanity. Their only authentically divine commission is to midwife the birth of the "new being" from the old race, half-beast and half-angel, which has sown the seeds of chaos and destruction all over the face of our sorrowing Mother Earth.

But instead of transforming us into the "new race" whose hallmarks are the gifts and fruits of the Spirit, the established religious traditions of the world, including Judaism and Christianity, have all too often failed in their witness to the Light. Their would-be leaders have frequently joined in the demonic battle of personal and tribal ego, power, and world domination. Their "authoritative" interpretations and judgments of the "Law of God," the Gospel, or the limits of reality itself have often reflected their own myopia and unregenerate subconscious projections. And often they have led their people into the dumb worship of their own collective egos masked as "God," but in fact a tribal war-totem which would wreak havoc and extract vengeance from its enemies.

By contrast the lives of the true masters, saints, prophets, and Mystics still stand as a damning judgment upon such "wolves" in sheep's clothing. They reflect the unconditional love, compassion, and mercy of God, and the uncreated image of that "ideal human person" infused with the breath of divinity which has been the eternal model for all of the dying-and-rising god-men, martyrs, magi, adepts, rishis, yogis, mahasiddas, bodhisattvas, buddhas, avatars, and the "Cosmic Christ" or "Primordial god-man" of human spiritual aspirations.

That "divine-and-human ideal person" was described by the mystics of Hellenistic Greece as "The Anthropos," or "The Man." The Persians called it (because androgynous, and neither "him" nor "her") the "Gayomart," the immortal model-Man who always rises up from death, like the Greek phoenix. In the Indian Upanishads this primal divine person is called the "Purusha."

In ancient Egypt the Primal Man was "Osiris," the Sky God who came to Earth as Man to establish a righteous kingdom which was his by inheritance, but who was killed and dismembered by his wicked half-brother Set, who seized his throne and began a reign on earth of unrighteousness. Osiris is reassembled by Isis, (a figure for the divine Mother-Sister Creatrix principle on the earth plane), rises, and ascends into heaven, where he becomes "King of the World-to-Come." His faithful followers are "Osirified" in psychic and spiritual mystery rites and thus become "partakers with Him" of salvation.

It was the truth behind all of these mystic-statements concerning the "Way" or "Pattern" for humanity's salvation, or transformation into the "new being" through "dying and rising again," that had already become the possession of Jewish mystics in the Hellenistic era before the Christian era. The disciples of Jesus recognized him as "of God" precisely because he conformed—in the details of his life, death, and post-mortem appearances—to the "Primordial Tradition" about the "Primal Man." In the canonical Gospels, Jesus is depicted as referring to himself throughout as the "Son of Man" (Aramaic *Bar Nasha*, or Greek *Uios Anthropou*), e.g. "son of the Primal Man."

The whole point of the "Orthodox" or "Catholic" Christian message or "Kerygma" in the canonical New Testament—which has been missed in most institutional packaging of Christianity over the centuries—is the proclamation that by identifying by faith and sacrament (higher ritual magic) with Jesus as the historicized "blueprint" of the Ideal Man, or Divine-Human Person, the same process that was realized in his life-and-death can be realized in his disciples or followers.

That divine process has as its sole objective the bringing-to-birth in Everyman of the same Divine-Human Person, the "New Being" of St. Paul. Jesus is depicted in the canonical gospels as asking his disciples if they do not know that, as the psalms of David had proclaimed, "ye are gods." And he tells his followers that the great " . . . works that I do, you will do too, and greater." Paul reminds the readers of his epistle that Jesus was the "first fruits of a New Creation," the "pioneer" of the salvation-process of spiritual growth, living in witness to the Light and dying to the "old Man," a process which they too must enter upon.

All of the "Message," mythically and magically stated in a life full of psychical and mystical experience, was an enactment of the entire Primordial Tradition itself. Thus Jesus had real links to the theme of the mystery tradition of Egypt and Greece, particularly in the cults of Osiris, Orpheus, Dionysius, and Apollo. And his thematic links to elements in the lives and/or teachings of such figures as Zoroaster, Buddha, Pythagoras, Plato, and pre-Christian Egyptian Hermeticists and Jewish gnostics surely could not have been unknown to the Essenes, Theraputae, and Nazoreans of Palestine and Syria. These Jews had a center at Damascus where St. Paul spent some time working out his formula of the "Gospel" after his conversion by the blinding-light theophany.

It is very important that Christians today understand the universal sources from which the mosaic of Judeo-Christian revelation and inspiration were taken. Indeed the ancient Jews originated in Meso-potamia, passed through the civilization of Egypt, entered Canaan, were dominated by other nations including Persia, Greece and Rome. They absorbed, modified, and re-presented in new cultural forms of their own (in the Yahwist cult) many of the Primordial insights of pagan wisdom. Intuitive sources of ancient-sacral knowledge, such as prophecy, trance phenomena, oracular consultations ad other psy-chic experiences, were used by Israelite and pagan alike. A whole common typology of intuitive wisdom deriving from such sources may be found among mystical Jewish groups well before the Christian era. And then early Christian writers themselves borrowed profusely both the insights and the symbolic vocabulary of pagan myths and mysteries to interpret and present their own perceptions of Jesus, his teachings, and their message about him.

It is important for Christians and Jews to know such historical facts in order to overcome false conceptions of the exclusivity of truth, or of "God's Revelation." Christians and Jews have no corner on God, in this sense. For He must have first revealed His Wisdom to the pagans—symbolized by Melchezideck and Enoch—who, whether in Palestine, Babylon, or Egypt, first developed many of the foundational conceptions and practices which were later incorporated into Jewish and Christian forms of inspiration, revelation, and cultic practice.[1]

The real point is that humanity's doorway to transcendent experience is a universal one, not a tribal one reserved for those of one nation, race, or cult. The way to the sublime vision of the Uncreated Intelligence and Light, Love, Peace, and Joy in the Spirit of the One God in and behind our multidimensional universe is one for all peoples. Advanced understanding of both religion and of science will require a mature perception of such realities, and a synthesis between the facts of our material, historical, scientific, technological, and spiritual existence on this planet. The time for the childish luxury of individual, or cultic, exclusivity and superiority is over.

This statement should not be interpreted to mean that Judaism with its great, living Torah and the Prophets, or Christianity with its Gospel, were not and are not unique "revelations" of God to man. They were and are—when correctly understood—both unique and important historical syntheses of "divine revelations" through the spiritual intuitions and psychic insights of particular ancient peoples and their successors. As such they "collect" the eclectic wisdom of many ancient peoples, put their own particular brands on them, and breathe their own fire into them.

But the other great world religions have performed similar functions as the "synthesizers" of universal wisdom, of particular forms of universal human spiritual and psychic insight. That is precisely what has made them "world religions," rather than localized experiments in religious expression. And today we have an emerging global village culture which needs a new synthesis of universal wisdom, and universal forms of mystical and pyschical experience, by which to draw the diverse peoples of the earth together in harmony toward the same goal of "Christification," or self-realization.

vi. *new synthesis, new paradigms, a new cosmology, and new integrative models for the convergence of science and spirituality*

Never has there been a greater urgency for a "new synthesis," or resolution of our spiritual and material polarizations. Today it would appear to many that we have reached a crisis point in the history of human culture, if not in the evolution of the human species itself. We are in a cul-de-sac at the end of a long sequence of developments in the outer, material sciences and technologies. In the dominant philosophies and in the popular imagination in modern technological societies these have been served from the inner technologies of spiritual and subjective consciousness.

As we have hopefully seen in these pages, a positive way ahead lies in the reconvergency of material, mental, and spiritual technologies in the forgotten mid-ground of psychic and mystical experience, in which the creative and communicative faculties also have their roots. Humanity must develop within itself new cosmologies, new "maps of transcendent meaning" through a higher degree of spiritual awareness, psychical and intuitive-rational acumen, and technological expertise, and by employing presently unheard-of methodologies combining inner and outer technologies.

The aim in this process must be "self-transformation" into a "new being," as well as the transformation of the material earth itself. Even the content of such a grand vision of divine human potential as the "Cosmic Christ" will remain hidden until we develop intuitive-psychical "eyes to see," and "ears to hear," the awaiting secrets of the universe which are at once both scientific and spiritual. This can be done through new psychic faculties which will include both rational and spiritual forms of awareness, or states of consciousness. In such higher states of awareness man's latent intuitive and other psi faculties may be opened and unfolded, not only for practical uses, but primarily as a means, or a psychic media, for his own ethical and spiritual trans-formation.

vii.   overcoming today's radical polarizations in religion, science, and society

Radical polarizations between so-called objective and subjective, rational versus non- or extra-rational, and material versus mental or spiritual factors have brought us into a cul-de-sac, a major culture crisis in which man's subjective consciousness may forever be dismissed as irrelevant by those who care to do so for whatever reason, whether they are artists, engineers, or counter-culturists. As long as conventional mind-sets in modern culture continue to accept only rationalistic, conceptualist mind, these polarizations will remain. Both subjective consciousness and objective material technology will continue to go their separate ways to hell. The *sacred* will always remain apart from the *profane*. All religious talk about God, the human soul or the evolutionary purposes of human history will continue to be consigned to a cosmic scrap heap by the positivistic secular forces that actually dominate today's world.

Such forces govern the power centers of modern technocracy in Washington, Moscow, London, Paris, Peking, Detroit and Coventry. In the past, the engineers, i.e., those positivistic and empiricistic philosophers and theologians, whether at Oxford or Tubingen, who have been acting as their unwitting security guards by defending the epistemological status-quo, have not been contributing to the quest for a new way ahead. They are merely a static thesis which has produced an antithesis in those artists and counter-culturists who would jettison "logical reason" altogether, or in those idealists who would cut the inner world of ideas and illusions adrift of all empirical safeguards and invite us to a grand trip into autistic illusions.

The only way ahead is to give insight to the blind, i.e., to give spiritual sight, by awakening and unfolding the "subtle faculties" of spiritual and psychical perception, and developing the "higher consciousness" in the human race.

Such a process will not be without its perils. The awakening of psychic faculties, or of the "kundalini," or of mystical experience in general can have frightful results in those who reject it, those who are not ready, or those whose consciousness is incapable of handling the experience. As Aldous Huxley said, "uncontrolled psychism" is an atavistic, or retrograde step. Psychic and mystical experience must not get too far ahead of one's spiritual and ethical development. Reason and intuition must be balanced.

One tangible hope that a future convergence of presently divided planetary philosophies and sciences could occur may be found in the "new mind technologies," or modern psychic development programs, combined with primary experiences of the multidimensional worlds of spirit phenomena, and the recovery of some understanding of the psychic origins of the Western religious traditions through experience of basic psychospiritual technologies. I have described such technologies elsewhere as the Missing Link between the Sacred and the Profane in the modern world.

ix. a developed psychic awareness and increased spiritual and ethical sensitivity to recovery of the primordial tradition of the Cosmic Christ

To say that psychic awareness will lead mankind to a greater degree of sensitivity to God, neighbor and nature is, admittedly, an act of faith. But the experiences of many persons who have opened their own psychic faculties rather late in life, after years of questioning the existential grounds of reality, show that greater intuition and sensitivity does more often than not lead to just such a heightened susceptibility to universal religious, ethical and spiritual conversion experiences.

Sri Aurobindo, Pandit Gopi Krishna, Teilhard de Chardin, and a host of others, including Edgar Mitchell, Masters and Houstin, Jose Silva, Theosophists and some Spiritualists see just such a universal unfoldment of dormant psychic faculties as the next stage in human evolution on the way to the "omega point" of the "Cosmic Christ."

Human evolution, according to the Pauline-Teilhardian model, is now on the brink of a psychic mutation which has been prepared, both biologically and culturally, for some millenia within the developing consciousness of the race. According to Aurobindo, when this inner process surfaces, more and more persons will either be born with and/or culturally educated into the skilled use of intuitive channeling skills which heretofore were dormant and in the normative possession of but a few.

We have seen that various extant types of Eastern and Western religious perspectives remain radically divided over the role of psychic phenomena in human experience. But in the light of some Western Pauline-Teilhardian religious perspectives, and in the light of the modern parapsychological research which we have summarized in this study, the suggestion of Brazilian psychical researcher Pedro McGregor would make pre-eminent sense:

> " . . . if science were to apply its enormous knowledge of electronics, biochemistry and nuclear physics systematically to the discovery of the spiritual nature of man . . . it could well make a breakthrough in the understanding of our nature and our predicament equal in impact to the discovery of how to split the atom."[2]

McGregor has also seen another central point that we have been trying to make in this study. Any new religious mythology that emerges as a successful one in the pluralistic global village of tomorrow will have to be one which unites. Not only will it have to unite persons with presently divided frames of mind on questions of mind and technology; it will have to unite the arts and the sciences of today, and the full scope of the imagination expressed in mankind's ancient religious quest for the Primordial Tradition and the Cosmic Christ, with a vision of the sciences of the future:

> "Religion, to have any meaning today, must take into consideration such diversities as the energy of the quasars, the millions of billions of possible worlds in the Universe, and the whole complex range of scientific knowledge here on Earth, as well as the moral and spiritual values by which the Intelligent Principle works. In a future world inhabited by a

super-civilization, religion will have an expression and a form beyond our present understanding.''[3]

It is to the development of that "expression and form beyond our present understanding" that we must now turn our attention. And we must remember that no expression or form of religion—or science—which does not do justice to the universal reality of the psychic and spiritual nature of the human person will survive in that "new world order" which has already begun to manifest in the awakened, higher consciousness of numerous persons in our planetary global village.

Notes

Chapter 1

1. E. R. Dodds, *The Greeks & The Irrational*. Berkeley & Los Angeles: University of California Press, 1968.

2. Michael Sablom, MD., *Recollections of Death*. New York: Simon & Schuster, 1982; Kenneth Ring, Ph.D., *Life at Death*, New York: Coward, McCann, & Geohegan, 1980. For evidence of the transcultural nature of mystical experiences involving psi phenomena as their basis, leading to belief in immortality, see: Robert Crookall, Ph.D., *The Supreme Adventure: Analysis of Psychic Communications*. Cambridge, England: James Clarke & Co., 1974. Karlis Osis, Ph.D., & Erlandur Haraldsson, Ph.D., *At The Hour of Death*, New York: Avon Books, 1977. Stanislav Grof, M.D. & Christina Grof, *Beyond Death: The States of Consciousness*, New York: Thames & Hudson, 1980.

3. D. Scott Rogo, *Parapsychology Review* (January-February, 1978).

4. *Ibid.*

5. Marilyn Zwaig Rossner, Ph.D., "God's Guidance & Natural Forms of Psychic Communication," a lecture reprinted by the Spiritual Science Fellowship. Montreal: September, 1978.

6. Richard A. Kalish, Ph.D. and David K. Reynolds, Ph.D., "Phenomenological Reality and Post-Death Contacts," *J.S.S.R.*, XII, No. 2, June, 1973.

7. Andrew Greeley, Ph.D., *Life Beyond Death*. Chicago: Thomas More Press, 1976, pp. 71-2.

8. Andrijah Puharich, M.D., "Introduction," *The Iceland Papers*. Amherst, WI.: Essentia Research Associates, 1979, p. 9 ff.

9. John Rossner, Ph.D., *From Ancient Religion to Future Science*. Washington, D.C.: University Press of America, 1979. Ch. VII.

10. *Ibid.*, Ch. VI.

11. The list of contemporary claims and hypotheses in the fields of parapsychology, paraphysics, life-energies research, and related areas of investigation in the paranormal found on pages 11-20 represent a summary of the contents of two of my previous books as follows:
    (1) *From Ancient Magic to Future Technology*, and
    (2) *From Ancient Religion to Future Science*.
    Together these two books—published by University Press of America in 1979—formed a university textbook entitled *Toward A Parapsychology of Religion*. It was my purpose not to "prove" any of the many, sometimes extravagant, cumulative claims made in these emerging fields of study, but rather to examine them for the "new paradigms" which they suggest. These happen to resemble some of the most ancient religous and metaphysical models of reality on the planet.

12. Pedro McGregor, *Jesus of the Spirits*. New York: Stein & Day, 1967, p. 237.

13. *Ibid.*, p. 238.

14. Irving Hexham and Karlo Poewe, *Understanding Cults & New Religions*. Grand Rapids, MI: Wm. B. Eerdmans Publishing Co., 1987, Chapter 5: "The Primal Core," pp. 60-72. (Hexham and Poewe found " . . . a significant role that primal experiences and fragments of the new mythology play in the lives . . . of individuals either before they join their new religion (as is most often the case) or after they join it," p. 62, *supra*.)
    See also David Hay and Ann Morisy, "Reports of Ecstatic Paranormal or Religious Experience in Great Britain and the United States: A Comparison of Trends," *Journal for the Scientific Study of Religion*, 1/7:255-65 (Hay and Morisy conducted a nationwide survey of the British population. It was found that 45% of those who had such primary mystical and psychical experiences had no contact with churches or organized religions).

Chapter 2

1. For background on the reconvergence of paradigms from ancient religions and metaphysical philosophies with insights from contemporary psychic discoveries, consult my earlier books, *From Ancient Magic to Future Technology* and *From Ancient Religion to Future Science*, ibid.

2. The particular summary of the "sheaths" ("shariras") and "bodies" ("koshas") included here is my own attempt to combine and simplify the ancient Indian yogic, Egyptian and Greek metaphysical descriptions which provided the basis for a widespread "primordial anthropology" in the Hellenistic world.

3. Jn. 14:10-12.

4. J. Shoneberg Setzer, Ph.D., "Making the Mystics Make Sense," *Quarterly Journal of the Spiritual Frontiers Fellowship*, V. (Autumn, 1973) pp. 226-247; VI (Winter, 1974), pp. 21-40; VI (Spring, 1974), pp. 80-88.

5. *Ibid.*

Chapter 3

1. Reported in *Time*, May 17, 1980.

2. Courtesy of Reginald W. Bibby, University of Lethbridge, "Project Canada 80: A Second Look at Deviance, Diversity, & Devotion in Canada" (a report prepared by Reginald W. Bibby for the United Church of Canada, 1980). Also R. Bibby, "Religionless Christianity: A Profile of Religion in the Canadian 80's," Social Indicators Research 13 (1983): pp. 1-16.

3. *Ibid.*

4. *Time*, May 17, 1980.

5. S. G. Lee, "Spirit Possession among the Zulu," in *Spirit Mediumship and Society in Africa*, ed. J. Beattie and J. Middleton. New York: Africana, 1969, pp. 128-55.

6. Stark & Brambridge, *The Future of Religion: Secularization, Revival, & Cult Formation*. Berkeley and Los Angeles: University of California Press, 1985, pp. 325 ff. See also Sir Alistair Hardy, *The Spiritual Nature of Man*, Oxford: Clarendon Press, 1979.

7. Mircea Eliade, *Shamanism*. Princeton, NJ: Princeton University Press, Bollingen Series LXXVI, 1964. Translated from the French by W. R. Trask.

8. Ernesto de Martino, *The World of Magic*. New York: Pyramid Communications, 1972. Translated from Italian by Paul Saye White.

9. Huston Smith, *Forgotten Truth: The Primordial Tradition*. New York: Harper & Row, 1976.

10. John Rossner, *The Psychic Roots of Ancient Wisdom & Primitive Christian Gnosis*, Lanham, MD: The University Press of America, 1983.

11. Willis W. Harmon, *An Incomplete Guide to the Future*. New York, London: W. W. Norton & Company, 1976, pp. 95-6.

12. *Ibid.*, p. 96.

13. G. Stanley Whitby, "On Deuteronomic Prohibitions" in *Life, Death, & Psychical Research*, ed. by J. Pearce-Higgins & G. Stanley Whitby. London, Rider Press, 1973.

14. Matthew 17:1; Mark 9:2; Luke 9:28 ff.

15. I Corinthians 12:28-30; 14:26-33.

16. Ignatius of Antioch, cited by James F. Malcolm, *Psychic Influences in World Religions*: Stansted, Essex: The Spiritualist National Union, (no date), p. 89.

17. St. Jerome, *"Epistle to Pope Damasus"*, in Preface to *The Latin Vulgate Version of the New Testament*.

18. Geoffrey Ashe, *Miracles*. London: Abacus Books, 1978, p. 158.

19. *Ibid.*

20. Hiroshi Motoyama, Ph.D., "Self-Training for Psychic Development," *Research for Religion & Parapsychology*. Vol. 7, No. 2 (December, 1981, preface). Tokyo: International Association for Religion & Parapsychology.

Chapter 4

1. Ernst Benz, "Christianity," *Encyclopaedia Britannica*, Vol. 4, Macropaedia, p. 530.

2. Jacob Needleman, *Lost Christianity*. New York: Bantam Books, 1980.

3. Elaine Pagels, *The Gnostic Gospels*. New York: Random House, 1980 and James M. Robinson, *The Nag Hammadi Library*. New York: Harper & Row, 1981.

4. Pagels, *op. cit.*, pp. xiii-xxxv; pp. 3-27, passim.

5. *Ibid.* pp. 28-47, passim.

6. *Ibid.*

7. *Ibid.*

8. *Ibid.*, pp. 48-69, passim.

9. *Ibid.* pp. 3-27, passim.

10. *Ibid.*

11. *Ibid.*

12. James M. Robinson, *op. cit.*, pp. 3-4.

13. Geddes MacGregor, *Gnosis: A Renaissance in Christian Thought*. Wheaton, IL: Quest Books, 1979, p. 78.

14. *Ibid.*, p. 79.

15. *Ibid.*, p. 79.

16. *Ibid.*, p. 81.

17. *Ibid.*, p. 82.

18. *Ibid.*, pp. 82-83.

19. *Ibid.*

20. *Ibid.*, p. 84.

21. Rudolf Bultmann, "Die Bedentung der neuerschlossenen mandaischen und manichaischen." Quellen, ZNW, 24, (1925), pp.

100-146. Cited, translated, and paraphrased in English by Edwin M. Yamauchi, *Pre-Christian Gnosticism*. Grand Rapids: Eerdmans, 1973, pp. 29-30.

22. E. Kasemann, *Leib und Leib Christi* (1933), cited by E. Yamauchi, *op. cit.*, p. 47.

23. Bultmann, *op. cit.*

24. Henry Corbin, *The Man of Light in Iranian Sufism*. London: Shambhala, 1978.

25. *Ibid.*, p. 15.

26. *Ibid.*, p. 16.

27. *Ibid.* p. 42.

28. Robert Ellwood, Jr., *Religious & Spiritual Groups in Modern America*. Englewood Cliffs: Prentice Hall, 1973, pp. 42-83. Jacob Needleman, *The New Religions*. New York: Pocket Books, 1972.

Chapter 5

1. Rudolf Bultmann, *Gnosis*, translated by J. R. Coates. London: Adam & Charles Black, 1952, p. 1.

2. *Ibid.*

3. *Ibid.*

4. *Ibid.*

5. Hans Jonas, *The Gnostic Religion*. Boston: Beacon Press, 1963.

6. Dame Frances Yates, *Giordano Bruno & the Hermetic Tradition of the Renaissance*. Chicago: University of Chicago Press, 1964, pp. 20-38.

7. *Ibid.*

8. Frederick H. Borsch, *The Christian & Gnostic Son of Man*. London: SCM Press, Studies in Biblical Theology, Second Series, 14, 1970, p. 113.

9. *Ibid.*, pp. 57-58.

10. Morton Kelsey, *God, Dreams, & Revelations*. Minneapolis: Augsburg Publishing House, 1968, pp. 103-153.

11. James M. Robinson, ed. *The Nag Hammadi Library*. New York: Harper & Row, 1981, p. 1.

12. John Meyendorff, *Byzantine Theology*. New York: Fordham University Press, 1978.

13. Dom Bede Griffith, *Return to the Centre*. London: Collins Fontana, 1978, pp. 98-112.

14. David G. Bromley & Anson D. Shupe, Jr., *Strange Gods: The Great American Cult Scare*. Boston: Beacon Press, 1981.

Chapter 6

1. For a comprehensive background on these three major types of myth, consult the excellent and extensive article on "Myth" in the *Encyclopaedia Britannica*, Macropaedia, 1974 edition.

2. Kersey Graves, *The World's Sixteen Crucified Saviors: Christianity before Christ*. New York: 1875. Chapters XVI and XXXII.

3. J. M. Robertson, *Pagan Christs*. New Hyde Park, NY: University Books, 1967 (Reprinted from 1903). See also Kenningdale Cook, *The Fathers of Jesus*. Vols. I & II. London: Kegan, Paul, & Trench, 1886.

4. W. E. Butler, *The Myth of the Magus*. Cambridge, England: Cambridge University Press, 1979. Chapter I, "The Ritual Hero," pp. 1-11.

5. *Ibid.*

6. Paramahansa Yogananda, *Autobiography of a Yogi*. Los Angeles: Self-Realization Fellowship, 1972.

7. Sir Wallace Budge, *Egyptian Magic*. New York: Dover Books, 1971 (London: 1901).

8. *Ibid.*

9. Morton Smith, *Jesus The Magician*. San Francisco: Harper & Row, 1978, p. 122.

10. J. M. Robertson, *Christianity & Mythology*.

11. Hugh Schonefield, *The Essenes*.

12. J. M. Robertson, *op. cit.*

Chapter 7

1. For a more extensive delineation of this theme, i.e. of viewing the Christian doctrine of the Incarnation as the "historicization of an Archetype," see Mircea Eliade, *A History of Religious Ideas*, Vol. 2, Chapters 22, 26, 27, 28, 29, & 30.

2. For clarification of the difference between "world-denying" and "world-affirming" varieties of gnosticism, see my book *The Psychic Roots of Ancient Wisdom & Primitive Christian Gnosis*, pp. 117-120.

3. See Dame Frances Yates, *The Rosicrucian Enlightenment*, London: Palladin, 1972, and *Giordano Bruno & The Hermetic Tradition*, London: Routledge & Kegan Paul, 1964.

Chapter 8

1. Oscar Cullman, "The Immortality of the Soul or Resurrection of the Dead" (Ingersoll Lecture for 1955), in *Immortality & Resurrection—Death in the Western World: Two Conflicting Currents of Thought*, ed. by Krister Stendhal, New York: Macmillan & Co., 1968.

2. Harry Wolfson, "Immortality & Resurrection in the Philosophy of the Church Fathers," in *Immortality & Resurrection, supra*.

3. *Greek-English Lexicon*, Liddell & Scott, New York: American Book Co., p. 55.

4. Sri Aurobindo, *The Mind of Light*, section entitled "The Divine Body," pp. 52-57.

5. Geddes MacGregor, *Gnosis: A Renaissance in Christian Humanism*. Wheaton, IL: Theosophical Publishing House, 1979, Ch. VII, "The Perils of De-Gnosticizing Jesus," pp. 73-93.

6. Robert Crookall, Ph.D., *The Supreme Adventure*. Cambridge, England: James Clark & Co., 1961.

7. *Ibid.*, p. 134.

8. John Denham Parsons, *The Nature and Purpose of the Universe*. London: T. Fisher Unwin, 1906, p. 147.

9. Lucian, translated by Avitus, published by Baronius in Annals. Eccles. A.D. 415, No. 7-16. Cited by Edward Gibbon, *Decline & Fall of the Roman Empire*, Vol. II, p. 67, note 77.

10. E. Gibbon, *Ibid.*

11. Eusebius, *Eccles. Hist.*, Trans. by J. E. L. Oultem, ed. by H. J. Lawlor, London: Wm. Hinemann, Ltd., 1958. Book VI, V.

12. Henry Corbin, *The Man of Light in Iranian Sufism*, op. cit., p. 73, 78, & 80 ff.

13. For a commentary on the relevance of the ancient Persian concept of the "Kaiomart" to the "Son of Man" or "Bar Nasha" concepts, see Kenningdale Cooke, *The Fathers of Jesus*, Vol. I, pp. 71 ff.

14. For insights into modern Hindu perspectives on Jesus' claims to Divinity see:
    Swami Vishnu Devananda, *Meditation & Mantra*, New York: Om Lotus Publishing Co., 1981, pp. 122 ff.
    Dom Bede Griffith, *The Marriage of East & West*. London: Collins Fontana Books, 1983, p. 14 ff.

15. For a discussion of the classical Indian conception of the meaning of the phrase "I am Sat, Chit, Ananda," see Swami Sivananda, *Bliss Divine*, Rishikesh, N. India: The Divine Life Society (no date).

16. Henry Corbin, *op. cit.*

17. Henry Corbin, *op. cit.*, "The Man of Light and His Guide," pp. 13-37.

18. Acts: 9:1-22.

19. I Tim. 1:12; Rom. 8:9-39.

20. Acts: 12-28.

Chapter 9

1. G. van der Leeuw, *Religion in Essence & Manifestation*, trans. J. E. Turner. New York, 1963, Vols. I & II. See p. 9, note 1, this essay.

2. Aubrey R. Johnson, *The One and the Many in the Israelite Concept of God*. Cardiff, 1942. See esp. pp. 8, 17-26 ff.
———*The Vitality of the Individual in the Thought of Ancient Israel*. Cardiff, 1949. See esp. p. 39 ff.
J. Pedersen, *Israel: Its Life and Culture*, trans. A. Miller. London, 1926, Vols. I & II, pp. 162-170, esp. pp. 46-63.
H. Wheeler Robinson, "The Hebrew Conception of Corporate Personality" in *Werden und Wesen, Beihefte. Zur Zeitschrift fur die Alttestamentliche Wissenschaft 66*. Berlin, 1936.
———"Hebrew Pscyhology," in *The People and the Book*, ed. A. S. Peake. Oxford, 1925, pp. 353-382.
Russell Shedd, *Man in Community*. A study of St. Paul's application of Old Testament and early Jewish Conceptions of Human Solidarity. London, 1958, pp. 1-89 passim.
Max Thurian, *The Eucharistic Memorial*; Part II, the New Testament. London, 1960. See esp. pp. 18-19.

3. J. A. T. Robinson, *The Body*. London, 1952. See esp. pp. 58-72.
Russell Shedd, *op. cit.*, pp. 93-199.
Max Thurian, *The Eucharistic Memorial*, Part II, The New Testament. London, 1961. See esp. pp. 5-33.

4. This concept is referred to as "psychic extension of personality." For its Biblical documentation see pp. 12-21 of this essay. For its non-Biblical documentation, consult G. van der Leeuw, *op. cit.*, on the general subject of "External Soul" in Babylonian, Egyptian, Jewish, Graeco-Roman, and Germanic concepts of psychic extension beyond the body, Vol. I, pp. 141-142, 289-298, and on the subjects of "Angels," pp. 141-146, "the Name," pp. 147-158.

For examples of extension in material objects and places, see "Things and Power," pp. 37-42, and "Sacred Stones and Trees," pp. 52-58, and "Sacred Space," Vol. II, pp. 393-402. See also "The Sacred Word," Vol. II, pp. 403-407 and the "Word of Consecration," Vol. II, pp. 408-412.

5. This concept is "corporate personality," for its Biblical documentation see pp. 22-26 of this essay. For its non-Biblical documentation see van der Leeuw, *ibid.*, Vol. I, "Sacred Community," pp. 242-273, and "Souls in the Plural," pp. 282-285.

6. This concept is "realistic representation." For its Biblical documentation see pp. 27-30 this essay. For its non-Biblical documentation see van der Leeuw, *ibid.* Vol. I, on the "representation" of the "King," pp. 214-215, of "Medicine Man and Priest," pp. 216-221 of the "Speaker,"pp. 222-226, of the "Preacher," pp. 228-229.

7. For the Biblical documentation of "cultic anamnesis" see Thurian, *op. cit.*, Part I. For its non-Biblical documentation see Dom Odo Casel, *The Mystery of Christian Worship* (London, 1962), Part I, Chapter 3, "The Ancient World and Christian Mysteries," pp. 50-62, esp. pp. 53-54 and Part II, Chapter I, "The Meaning of Mystery," pp. 97-165, passim. See also *Myth and Reality*, Mircea Eliade, trans. by W. R. Trask (New York, 1963), esp. Chapter V, "Time Can be Overcome," pp. 75-91 and Chapter VII, "Mythologies of Memory and Forgetting," pp. 114-138.

8. It should be noted that James Barr, in *The Semantics of Biblical Language* (London, 1961), and *Biblical Words for Time* (London, 1964) argues against the existence of much of the semantic evidence for the uniqueness of Hebrew versus Greek and other versions of thought found in the Old Testament by Biblical theologians, esp. Kittel, Pedersen, and Boman. In the first place, we should note that Barr's work is largely a positivistically conceived exercise in linguistic analysis which is generally unsympathetic to an understanding of Biblical psychic phenomena. Secondly, the existence of the primitive conceptions which we are discussing here does not imply at all their limitation to the Hebrew mind in antiquity, as many of the Biblical theologians seem to imply. Lastly, the evidence for these concepts does not rest solely upon linguistic evidence. As H. W. Robinson has said in *The Hebrew Conception, op. cit.*, (p. 51) the primitive solidarity

concepts are documented primarily by an anthropological and archaeological evidence and only partially and secondarily are they reflected, if at all, by semantics. Barr's objections, therefore, do not affect the topic under investigation here.

9.   Dom Odo Casel has made an extensive study of extra-Biblical instances of the operation of this concept in *The Mystery of Christian Worship*, ed. by Burkhard Neunheuser OSB, (London, 1962). See esp. Part I, Chapter 3: "The Ancient World and Christian Mysteries," pp. 50-53, and Part II, Chapter 1, "The Meaning of Mystery," pp. 97-141.

10. Casel, *ibid.*, pp. 53-54. " . . . in holy words and rites of present and future the reality is there once more." "The celebrant community is united in the deepest fashion with the lord they worship. There is no deeper oneness than suffering and action shared."

11. *Ibid.*, p. 53.

12. Max Thurian, *op. cit.*, has not referred to any of the extra-Biblical or non-Hebraic examples of "cultic anamnesis" in his study of it in the Israelite and Christian usage; but it is obvious that there is a common and universal primitive solidarity concept operative in pagan and Biblical sources. Compare the usage of this concept in Israelite and Christian worship, as summarized on pp. 55-59, of this essay, with Casel's statement of it as found in the general practice of antiquity.

13. M. Thurian, Part I, *op. cit.*, pp. 57-62.

14. Ex. 28:29 ff. quoted by Thurian, *ibid.*, pp. 57-58.

15. Ex. 12:14.

16. M. T. Thurian, *op. cit.*, p. 19

17. M. Thurian, *ibid.*, p. 19.

18. Gal. 6:16, Rom. 9: 6-8. See Shedd, *op. cit.*, pp. 126-150, and also E. Best, *One Body in Christ*, pp. 1-33, pp. 184-202. Note that Best recognizes the principle of "corporate personality" in the New Testament but, unlike Shedd, gives it a non-realistic interpretation, calling it "metaphor." The consequences of such a non-realistic interpretation as Best would like to supply may be seen

in the minority report of the dissenting Methodists in the Anglican-Methodist conversations in England, which by implication denies that the process of Christ's incarnation is in any sense continued or fulfilled in and through the Church as His "Body." The theory that New Testament terms for the Church are "metaphors" in the modern sense thus leads to a failure of "ontological nerve" in some contemporary Protestant thought on the nature of the Church. This position could only exist in a culture which has lost all conception of the natural modes of psychic action and instrumentality that were common to the whole ancient world.

19. Cor. 16:15, 10:17, 12:37, Rom. 12:4-5, Eph. 5:23, 30, 32 of Shell *op. cit.*, pp. 157-165, and J. A. T. Robinson, *op. cit.*, p. 11 ff. The term "Body" is not found in the Old Testament, but is taken by St. Paul from Stoic writings as an equivalent of the Hebrew expressions of solidarity found in Greek philosophical language.

20. John 15:1-11, Gal. 6:10, Eph. 2:19, 2 Cor. 11:2, Rom. 7:4-6, 12-17. See Minear, Paul: *Images for the Church in the New Testament* (Philadelphia, 1960), pp. 42-44, 54-55, 165-172, 173-220.

21. John 3:3, 1 Cor. 12:13, Gal. 3:27, Rom. 6:3-4. Shedd, *op. cit.*, pp. 185-188.

22. John 1:10, Mt. 8:16.

23. Acts 4:12, 3:16, Mt. 18:20, Eph. 1:21.

24. Gal. 4:06. See Johnston, George, "Spirit" *Theological Word Book of the Bible*, ed. by Alan Richardson. London, 1950.

25. John 14:26, 16:13, cf. Acts 1:02.

26. Mt. 10:5-9, Lk. 9:16-17, cf. Acts 14:3, 3:6-8.

27. Mt. 9:20, 14:36, Acts 5:15.

28. Acts 10:34-48.

29. John 13:20.

30. Mt. 25:40.

31. 1 Cor. 15:45, 2 Cor. 4:5, Col. 3:9-11, 2 Cor. 5:17 cf. pp. 43-54, this essay and Shedd, *op. cit.*, pp. 165-173.

32. Heb. 2:9-11, 2 Cor. 1:5-7.

33. 1 Cor. 15:20-22.

34. 1 Cor. 15:23-24.

35. 2 Tim. 2:10-12.

36. Heb. 2:17.

37. M. Thurian, *op. cit.*, Part II.

38. *Ibid.*

39. 1 Cor. 10:16 and Gal. 3:27 cf. Shedd, *op. cit.*, p. 189.

40. Thurian, *op. cit.*

41. H. Bergson, *Matter and Memory*, trans. by N. M. Paul & W. S. Palmer. Harper & Row, New York, 1959, pp. 125-127. Some Biblical scholars have seen such a similarity between Bergson's conception of "time" and that found in the primitive Israelite thinking. See Nathan Soderblom, *The Living God*. London, 1933, pp. 310 ff. Also Thorlief Boman, *Hebrew Thought Compared with Greek*, trans. Jules Moreau. London, 1960, p. 22 n. 1., and pp. 126-127, 129.

42. Marcel Proust, "The Swan's Way" in *The World of Psychology*, Vol. I., ed. trans. C. B. Levitas. New York, 1963,p. 151: "The past is hidden somewhere outside the realm, beyond the reach of intellect, in some material object, in the sensation which that material object will give us, which we do not suspect." Readers should note that this is exactly the psychic art known as "psychometry" in modern parapsychological terms.

43. Rom. 6:03, Gal. 3:27, and Shedd, *Ibid.*, pp. 185-188. See also Lionel Thornton's *The Common Life in the Body of Christ* (London, 1944), for a study of the fulfillment of the Old Testament solidarity concepts in the New Testament.

44. Mother C. Putnam, "The Image as Sacramental," in *Sacrament and Image*, ed. by A. M. Allchin, Fellowship of St. Alban and St. Sergius. London, 1967.

45. O. Casel, *op. cit.*, pp. 50-61.

46. John Rossner, *Toward a Parapsychology of Religion*, Washington, DC: University Press of America, 1979.

47. Plato, *The Republic*, Book VI, 510 B - 511 E; The Thaetetus, passim.

48. Werner Jaeger, *Early Christianity and Greek Paideia*. London: Oxford University Press, 1961, pp. 46-47.

49. Sister Innocentia Richards, Ph.D., *Discernment of Spirits*. Collegeville, MN: Liturgical Press, 1970, "The Old Testament," pp. 17-26; "The New Testament," pp. 30-54; and "The Patristic Period," pp. 55-60.

50. John Rossner, "Orthodoxy and the Future of Western Christianity," in *St. Vladimir's Theological Review*, Vol. 4, No. 3 (1970), 10 ff.

51. Arthur Koestler, *The Roots of Coincidence*, pp. 50-81.

52. Professor E. R. Dodds' vision of the relevance of such parapsychological studies for an understanding of the origins of ancient religious and classical Greek metaphysical ideas would seem to me to be a particularly relevant one.

53. E. R. Dodds, *op. cit.*, pp. 135-178; John Rossner, *Toward a Parapsychology of Religion*, Part I, Chapter IV, and Part II, Chapter VIII.

Chapter 10

1. Andrija Puharich, "Introduction," *The Iceland Papers*. Amherst, WI: Essentia Research Associates, 1979, pp. 7-8.

2. Colin Wilson, *The Occult: A History*. New York: Random House, 1971, pp. 458-553.

3. Lord Alfred Russell Wallace, *Miracles & Modern Spiritualism*. London: Spiritualist Press, 1955, and Harold Saxon Burr, *The Fields of Life*. New York: Ballantine Books, 1972.

4. Puharich, *op. cit.*, p. 9 ff.

7. *Ibid.*, pp. 12-14.

8. *Ibid.*, p. 14.

9. Dame Frances Yates, *The Rosicrucian Enlightenment*, London: Palladin, 1972, p. 11.

10. *Ibid.*, p. 11.

11. *Ibid.*, pp. 11-12; p. 268 ff.

12. *Ibid.*, p. 12.

13. *Ibid.*, pp. 12-13.

14. *Ibid.*, p. 15.

15. *Ibid.*, p. 16.

16. *Ibid.*, pp. 16-17.

17. *Ibid.*, p. 18.

18. *Ibid.*, pp. 54; 124-125; 266 ff.

19. *Ibid.*, pp. 277-278.

20. *Ibid.*, pp. 268-269; see also pp. 274 ff.

21. *Ibid.*, p. 75.

22. *Ibid.*, p. 295.

23. *Ibid.*, pp. 297-298.

24. *Ibid.*, p. 17.

25. *Ibid.*, pp. 56-57; 88-89.

26. *Ibid.*, pp. 41 ff; 43-57; 274 ff.

27. See Dom Bede Griffith on the presently deformed or "truncated" condition of modern science vis-à-vis what he calls the "eternal religion" or "sanatana dharma" in his *Return to the Centre*. London: Collins Fontana Books, pp. 94-112. See also the contemporary Iranian (Sufi) scholar Seyyed Hossein Nasr on this subject in his *Knowledge & the Sacred*: The Gifford Lectures for 1981. New York: Crossroad, 1981, "The Rediscovery of the Sacred," pp. 93-129; and "Scientia Sacra," pp. 130-159.

Conclusion

1. Margaret Barker, *The Lost Prophet: The Book of Enoch and Its Influence on Christianity*. London: SPCK, 1988. This important and seminal book suggests that visionary experiences of an "Archetypical God-Man," during "Heavenly Journies" like those of Enoch, Daniel, Ezekiel, Isaiah II, the Merkebah Mystics, St. Paul, and St. John the Divine gave birth to the primary conviction of the primitive Christian tradition that there is a "Second Power in Heaven," e.g., a pre-existent, "Cosmic Christ." It was this pre-existent "Cosmic Christ" or "Son of Man" which Jesus identified with himself, and which in fact served as the basis of subsequent orthodox Christian claims for the Divinity of Jesus as the "Incarnation of the Logos," or "Second Person of the Trinity."

2. Pedro McGregor, *Jesus of the Spirits*, p. 237. But really, we should say: "far greater in impact . . . " etc.

3. *Ibid.*, p. 238.

STAY IN TOUCH

On the following pages you will find listed, with their current prices, some of the books and tapes now available on related subjects. Your book dealer stocks most of these, and will stock new titles in the Llewellyn series as they become available. We urge your patronage.

However, to obtain our full catalog, to keep informed of new titles as they are released and to benefit from informative articles and helpful news, you are invited to write for our bi-monthly news magazine/catalog. A sample copy is free, and it will continue coming to you at no cost as long as you are an active mail customer. Or you may keep it coming for a full year with a donation of just $2.00 in U.S.A. ($7.00 for Canada & Mexico, $20.00 overseas, first class mail). Many bookstores also have *The Llewellyn New Times* available to their customers. Ask for it.

Stay in touch! In *The Llewellyn New Times'* pages you will find news and reviews of new books, tapes and services, announcements of meetings and seminars, articles helpful to our readers, news of authors, advertising of products and services, special money-making opportunities, and much more.

The Llewellyn New Times
P.O. Box 64383-Dept. 685, St. Paul, MN 55164-0383, U.S.A.

• • •

TO ORDER BOOKS AND TAPES

If your book dealer does not have the books and tapes described on the following pages readily available, you may order them direct from the publisher by sending full price in U.S. funds, plus $1.00 for handling and 50¢ each book or item for postage within the United States; outside U.S.A. surface mail add $1.50 per item postage and $1.00 per order for handling. Outside U.S.A. air mail add $7.00 per item postage and $1.00 per order for handling. MN residents add 6% sales tax.

FOR GROUP STUDY AND PURCHASE

Because there is a great deal of interest in group discussion and study of the subject matter of this book, we feel that we should encourage the adoption and use of this particular book by such groups by offering a special "quantity" price to group leaders or "agents."

Our Special Quantity Price for a minimum order of five copies of *In Search of the Primordial Tradition and the Cosmic Christ* is $38.85 Cash-With-Order. This price includes postage and handling within the United States. Minnesota residents must add 6% sales tax. For additional quantities, please order in multiples of five. For Canadian and foreign orders, add postage and handling charges as above. Credit Card (VISA, MasterCard, American Express) orders are accepted. Charge card orders only may be phoned free ($15.00 minimum order) within the U.S.A. by dialing 1-800-THE MOON (in Canada call: 1-800-FOR-SELF). Customer Service calls dial 1-612-291-1970. Mail orders to:

LLEWELLYN PUBLICATIONS
P.O. Box 64383-Dept. 685 / St. Paul, MN 55164-0383, U.S.A.

THE NATURE AND USE OF RITUAL
by Peter Roche de Coppens, Ph.D.
The New Age is not a time or place, but a *new state of consciousness*. To bring about this new consciousness, we need a viable source of revelation and teaching that gets to the heart of our Being and Reality: a way of living and seeing that leads to a gradual, organic and holistic (or 'holy') transformation of the present consciousness and being.

The basic aim of this book is to render explicit the essence of this process of *bio-psycho-spiritual* transformation in terms of our own indigenous Spiritual Tradition, which we can find in the very basic Christian Prayers and Documents.

Perhaps at no time in history has the need for new consciousness been greater — if indeed we are to survive and fulfill our destiny and the Divine potential that is seeded within each person.

At no time has the opportunity been greater, for access to the highest esoteric knowledge, the most refined spiritual technology, is now available to bring about the transformation of consciousness on a massive scale—only if each of us accepts this goal as our personal responsibility.
0-87542-675-1, 252 pgs., 5¼ x 8, illus., softcover **$9.95**

THE INVISIBLE TEMPLE
by Peter Roche de Coppens, Ph.D.
The Invisible Temple is not a building or location. It is not a particular congregation of people. It is wherever there is a focal point for spiritual energy. It is located where that energy is generated, amplified and transformed for whatever purpose is needed. In other words, The Invisible Temple exists for us when we become a spiritual light generator.

This book shows how you can generate, transform and amplify spiritual energy. Filled with illustrations and exercises, this book gives occult techniques for spiritual attainment. It can easily be used by Christians, Jews, Pagans and any others on a spiritual path. The structure of the book is also Qabalistic, and the symbols and rituals were actually drawn from a Qabalistic Tradition.
0-87542-676-X, 300 pgs., illus, 5¼x8, softcover **$9.95**

WHEELS OF LIFE: A User's Guide to the Chakra System
by Anodea Judith
This is an instruction manual for owning and operating the inner gears that run the machinery of our lives. Written in a practical, down-to-earth style, this fully-illustrated book will take the reader on a journey through aspects of consciousness, from the bodily instincts of survival to the processing of deep thoughts.

Discover this ancient metaphysical system under the new light of popular Western metaphors—quantum physics, elemental magick, Kabalah, physical exercises, poetic meditations, and visionary art. Learn how to open these centers in yourself, and see how the chakras shed light on the present world crises we face today. And learn what you can do about it!

This book will be a vital resource for: Magicians, Witches, Pagans, Mystics, Yoga Practitioners, Martial Arts people, Psychologists, Medical people, and all those who are concerned with holistic growth techniques.

The modern picture of the Chakras was introduced to the West largely in the context of Hatha and Kundalini Yoga and through the Theosophical writings of Leadbeater and Besant. But the Chakra system is *equally* innate to Western Magick: all psychic development, spiritual growth, and practical attainment is fully dependent upon the opening of the Chakras!
0-87542-320-5, 544 pages, 6 x 9, illus., softcover   **$12.95**

CHAKRA THERAPY
by Keith Sherwood
Keith Sherwood presents another excellent how-to book on healing. His previous book, *The Art of Spiritual Healing,* has helped many people learn how to heal themselves and others.

Chakra Therapy follows in the same direction: Understand yourself, know how your body and mind function and learn how to overcome negative programming so that you can become a free, healthy, self-fulfilled human being.

This book fills in the missing pieces of the human anatomy system left out by orthodox psychological models. It serves as a superb workbook. Within its pages are exercises and techniques designed to increase your level of energy, to transmute unhealthy frequencies of energy into healthy ones, to bring you back into balance and harmony with yourself, your loved ones and the multidimensional world you live in. Finally, it will help bring you back into union with the universal field of energy and consciousness.

Chakra Therapy will teach you how to heal yourself by healing your energy system because it is actually energy in its myriad forms which determines a person's physical health, emotional health, mental health and level of consciousness.
0-87542-721-9, 270 pgs., 5¼ x 8, illus., softcover   **$7.95**

METAPHYSICS: THE SCIENCE OF LIFE
by Anthony J. Fisichella

There are thousands of books and articles on "metaphysical" subjects, such as the meaning of life, the nature of God, the teachings of various religions, reincarnation, life after death, the various disciplines such as astrology, numerology, tarot, ESP research, healing, and many others. Is there a "golden thread of wisdom" which encompasses a broad-based understanding of the essential truths of the various teachings? Is there a primer where one can learn the fundamental concepts, the common denominator present in most spiritual teachings?

There is now, in Tony Fisichella's *Metaphysics: The Science of Life*. For the first time, here is one book which ties together the ancient and modern teachings about human life—which answers the basic questions that most thinking people ask: who am I, where did I come from, what am I here for, where am I going? Here is a book which can change your way of thinking, which can provide the reference you need to help solve practical problems, to find the direction you seek, to understand the teachings of great religions in their true context. Here is a book which can truly change your life.
0-87542-229-2, 300 pgs., illus., softcover **$9.95**

THE INNER WORLD OF FITNESS
by Melita Denning

Because the artificialities and the daily hassles of routine living tend to turn our attention from the real values, *The Inner World of Fitness* leads us back by means of those natural factors in life which remain to us: air, water, sunlight, the food we eat, the world of nature, meditations, sexual love and the power of our wishes—so that through these things we can re-link ourselves in awareness to the great non-material forces of life and of being which underline them.

The unity and interaction of inner and outer, keeping body and psyche open to the great currents of life and of the natural forces, is seen as the essential secret of *youthfulness* and hence of radiant fitness. Regardless of our physical age, so long as we are within the flow of these great currents, we have the vital quality of youthfulness: but if we begin to close off or turn away from those contacts, in the same measure we begin to lose youthfulness. Also included is a metaphysical examination of AIDS.

This book will help you to experience the total energy of abundant health.
0-87542-165-2, 240 pgs., 5¼ x 8, illus., softcover **$7.95**

GATEWAY TO THE ASTRAL WORLDS
By Denning & Phillips
If you have had difficulty projecting in past attempts, this is the kit for you! It contains *The Llewellyn Practical Guide to Astral Projection* book, with the clearest and most explicit instructions on how to project out of the body; the Llewellyn Deep Mind Tape for Astral Projection, featuring instructions, exercises, and special sounds that will help you prepare to project; a meditation card for inducing the altered state of consciousness necessary; a magical crystal; a magical oil and a special instruction booklet.

No single item can help everyone to project but this kit is so complete that your chances are considerably enhanced by its use. Astral projection is possible for everyone, as well as being a completely safe way to explore a fascinating array of new planes of reality and a previously unknown facet of your unconscious mind. For the ultimate vacation, take a trip on the astral plane!
0-87542-199-7, book, tape, booklet, oil, crystal $19.95

THE LLEWELLYN PRACTICAL GUIDE
TO CREATIVE VISUALIZATION
by Denning & Phillips
All things you will ever want must have their start in your mind. The average person uses very little of the full creative power that is his, potentially. It's like the power locked in the atom—it's all there, but you have to learn to release it and apply it constructively.

IF YOU CAN SEE IT . . . in your Mind's Eye . . . you will have it! It's true: you can have whatever you want—but there are "laws" to mental creation that must be followed. The power of the mind is not limited to, nor limited by, the material world—Creative Visualization enables Man to reach beyond, into the invisible world of Astral and Spiritual Forces.

Some people apply this innate power without actually knowing what they are doing, and achieve great success and happiness; most people, however, use this same power, again unknowingly, incorrectly, and experience bad luck, failure, or at best unfulfilled life.
This book changes that. Through an easy series of step-by-step, progressive exercises, your mind is applied to bring desire into realization! Wealth, power, success, happiness . . . even psychic powers . . . even what we call magickal power and spiritual attainment . . . all can be yours. You can easily develop this completely natural power, and correctly apply it, for your immediate and practical benefit. Illustrated with unique, "puts-you-into-the-picture" visualization aids.

0-87542-183-0, 304 pgs., 5¼ x 8, illus., softcover $7.95

THE LLEWELLYN PRACTICAL GUIDE TO THE DEVELOPMENT OF PSYCHIC POWERS
by Denning & Phillips

You may not realize it, but . . . you already have the ability to use ESP, astral vision and clairvoyance, divination, dowsing, prophecy, communications with spirits, mental telepathy, etc. It's simply a matter of knowing what to do, and then to exercise (as with any talent) and develop them.

Written by two of the most knowledgeable experts in the world of Magick today, this book is a complete course—teaching you, step-by-step, how to develop these powers that actually have been yours since birth. Using the techniques they teach, you will soon be able to move objects at a distance, see into the future, know the thoughts and feelings of another person, find lost objects, locate water and even people using your own no-longer latent talents.

Psychic powers are as much a natural ability as any other talent. You'll learn to play with those new skills, work with groups of friends to accomplish things you never would have believed possible before reading this book. The text shows you how to make the equipment you can use, the exercises you can do—many of them at any time, anywhere—and how to use your abilities to change your life and the lives of those close to you. Many of the exercises are presented in forms that can be adapted as games for pleasure and fun, as well as development.

0-87542-191-1, 244 pgs., 5¼ x 8, illus., softcover   **$7.95**

PSYCHIC POWER
by Charles Cosimano

Although popular in many parts of the world, *radionics* machines have had little application in America, until now! Using the easy, step-by-step instructions, and for less than a $10.00 investment, you can build a machine which will increase your psychic powers, allow you to read other people's minds, influence their thoughts, communicate with their dreams and be more successful when you do divinations such as working with tarot cards or pendulums.

For thousands of years, people have looked for an easy, simple and sure way to increase their psychic abilities. Now, the science of psionics allows you to do just that! This book is practical, fun and an excellent source for those wishing to achieve results with etheric energies.

0-87542-097-4, 224 pgs., illus., mass market.   **$3.95**